KOREA AND
THE POLITICS OF IMPERIALISM
1876–1910

THE CENTER FOR JAPANESE AND KOREAN STUDIES of the
University of California is a unit of the
Institute of International Studies. It is the unifying organization
for faculty members and students interested in Japan and Korea,
bringing together scholars from many disciplines.
The Center's major aims are
the development and support of research and language study.
As part of this program the Center sponsors
a publication series of books concerned with Japan and Korea.
Manuscripts are considered from all campuses
of the University of California as well as
from any other individuals and institutions
doing research in these areas.

PUBLICATIONS OF THE CENTER FOR JAPANESE AND KOREAN STUDIES

Chong-Sik Lee
The Politics of Korean Nationalism. 1963

Sadako N. Ogata
Defiance in Manchuria:
The Making of Japanese Foreign Policy, 1931–1932. 1964

R. P. Dore
Education in Tokugawa Japan. 1964

James T. Araki
The Ballad-Drama of Medieval Japan. 1964

Masakazu Iwata
Okubo Toshimichi: The Bismarck of Japan. 1964

Frank O. Miller
Minobe Tatsukichi: Interpreter of Constitutionalism in Japan. 1965

Michael Cooper, S.J.
They Came to Japan:
An Anthology of European Reports on Japan, 1543–1640. 1965

George Devos and Hiroshi Wagatsuma
Japan's Invisible Race. 1966

Ryutaro Komiya, ed.
Translated from the Japanese by Robert S. Ozaki
Postwar Economic Growth in Japan. 1966

Robert A. Scalapino
The Japanese Communist Movement, 1920–1966. 1967

Soon Sung Cho
Korea in World Politics, 1940–1950:
An Evaluation of American Responsibility. 1967

Kozo Yamamura
Economic Policy in Postwar Japan:
Growth versus Economic Democracy. 1967

C. I. EUGENE KIM | HAN-KYO KIM

KOREA AND THE POLITICS OF IMPERIALISM 1876-1910

1967
Berkeley and Los Angeles
UNIVERSITY OF CALIFORNIA PRESS

University of California Press
Berkeley and Los Angeles, California
Cambridge University Press
London, England
Copyright © 1968, by
The Regents of the University of California
Library of Congress Catalog Card Number: 68-12037
Printed in the United States of America

PREFACE

Decades after China and Japan had been opened by the West, Korea remained closed to outsiders. The peninsular nation lived a tradition-bound life unaware that drastic reforms were essential to cope with the gathering storm of international power politics. While the Japanese were willing to endure two major wars and decades of diplomatic struggle to gain the annexation of Korea, Koreans lacked the unity of purpose and power to frustrate their more aggressive neighbors.

This study begins with the first treaties Korea signed with Japan in 1876 and with the West soon thereafter and ends with the complete subjugation of the Korean nation to the Japanese emperor in 1910. During these years of internal intrigue and external manipulation — with China, Russia, Japan, and various Western nations all taking part — Korean society and government went through numerous upheavals, with which they were unable to contend. The study undertakes to describe and analyze these circumstances leading up to annexation and the Japanese establishment of a military dictatorship over this geopolitically strategic peninsular nation.

This story is worth the telling as a historical drama, but this is not the sole motive of the authors. In the past Korea's case has been unpublicized in the United States due to lack of scholarly interest. And yet, the lessons of history exemplified in Korea's efforts to safeguard national independence are still relevant in this second half of the twentieth century, when national groups in many areas of the world are struggling for genuine independence and for modernization of their political, economic, and social systems.

Furthermore, Korea's unsuccessful attempt to maintain independence is pertinent also to post-World War II efforts to establish political rapprochement between Korea and Japan. After 35 years of Japanese rule, Korea was liberated in 1945. There followed three years of military occupation by the United States in the southern half of the peninsula and by the Soviet Union in the north. The Republic of Korea in the south was established in 1948, and beginning in 1952, intermittent negotiations were held between Korea and Japan for the sake of "normalizing" official relations and settling many thorny issues resulting from the long Japanese rule. In 1965 a series of agreements was at last signed. But many problems remain, because the dealings between the two neighbors are deeply and emotionally affected by an unpleasant history of coercion and violence that began, in modern times, during the period under discussion here.

A joint work of this nature was difficult to accomplish. Without exhaustive research and an objective outlook, it could not have been done. The authors have made use of materials in English, Korean, Chinese, and Japanese. Of particular use in the research were the Japanese archive materials in Korea and Japan. It was also through the meeting of minds that both authors have endured many inconveniences in particular to their families, who have not only braved living in the foreign environment of the United States but also displayed understanding toward the scholarly tasks of American college professors. We are therefore most thankful to them.

For useful and critical comments on the manuscript during the various stages of preparation, we are indebted to many scholars and friends — particularly to professors Nobutaka Ike, Claude A. Buss, Kurt Steiner, and Philip W. Buck of Stanford University; Earl H. Pritchard of the University of Arizona; Donald Lach of the University of Chicago; Harold M. Vinacke of the University of Cincinnati; Hilary Conroy and Chong-sik Lee of the University of Pennsylvania; and Hugh Kang and Peter H. Lee of the University of Hawaii.

We also owe our gratitude to Mr. K. P. Yang of the Library of Congress; the staff members of the Far Eastern Library of the University of Chicago and of the Hoover Institution of Stanford University; Dr. Chong-myong Kim of the Japan Institute of International Affairs, Tokyo; the members of the Committee for the Compilation of National History, Seoul, Korea; and the colleagues of the authors at the University of Cincinnati and Western Michigan University, particularly professors Dieter Dux, Andrew C. Nahm, and Milton Greenberg. Mrs. Shirley Swenson and Miss Baiba Liliensteins helped us with typing and editorial work.

The glossary of oriental words beginning on p. 251 includes the proper names and terms used in the text with their corresponding Chinese characters. For the translation of these and other words of Chinese, Japanese, and Korean origin, the following systems are used: the Wade-Giles system for Chinese, the modified Hepburn system for Japanese, and the McCune-Reischauer system for Korean.

Portions of this manuscript have been published in the *Proceedings of the American Philosophical Society* (January 1962) and in the *Pacific Historical Review* (November 1962) and they have been included here with some modifications. We are thankful for the editors of these journals for their permission to reprint.

C. I. EUGENE KIM
HAN-KYO KIM

CONTENTS

PART I

THE BREAKDOWN OF
NATIONAL SECLUSION

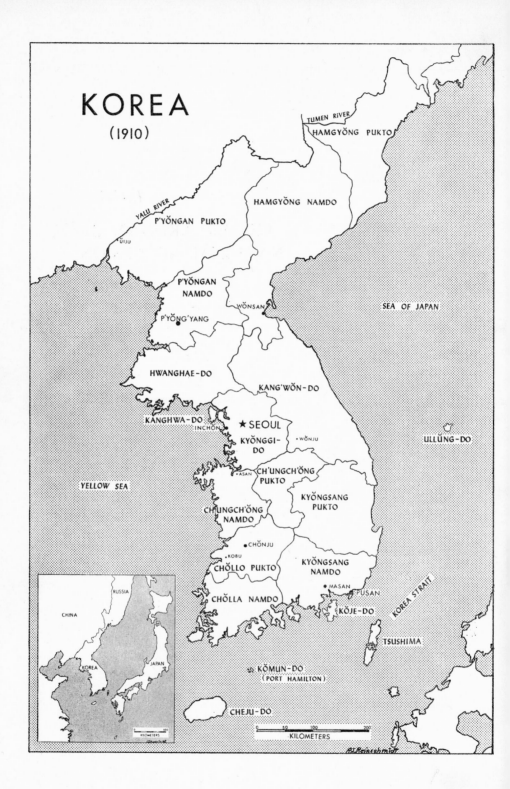

KOREA
(1910)

TUMEN RIVER

HAMGYŎNG PUKTO

YALU RIVER

HAMGYŎNG NAMDO

P'YŎNGAN PUKTO

ŬIJU

P'YŎNGAN
NAMDO

WŎNSAN

SEA OF JAPAN

P'YŎNG'YANG

HWANGHAE-DO

KANG'WŎN-DO

KANGHWA-DO

SEOUL

INCHŎN

WŎNJU

ULLŬNG-DO

KYŎNGGI-
DO

CH'UNGCH'ŎNG
PUKTO

ASAN

YELLOW SEA

KYŎNGSANG
PUKTO

CH'UNGCH'ŎNG
NAMDO

CHŎNJU

KOBU

KYŎNGSANG
NAMDO

CHŎLLO PUKTO

MASAN

CHŎLLA NAMDO

PUSAN

KOREA STRAIT

KŎJE-DO

TSUSHIMA

KŎMUN-DO
(PORT HAMILTON)

CHEJU-DO

CHINA

RUSSIA

KOREA

JAPAN

KILOMETERS

0   50   100   200

KILOMETERS

R.J.Reineshmidt

1.

Seclusion as a Way of Life

As the last quarter of the nineteenth century began, Korea was under the rule of the Yi dynasty (1392–1910). The political institutions of the dynasty modeled after those of China were in decay after centuries of debilitating factional strife and corrupt practices. The social structure was rigidly hierarchical and authoritarian. The basically agrarian economy, with little manufacturing and with localized small-scale commercial activities, perpetuated the misery of the peasantry and others in the lower classes. Neo-Confucianism provided the ideological basis for the ruling class and bestowed the mantle of legitimacy on the repressive rule of its practitioners. Korea's geography and its history of repeated foreign invasions — two major ones in the sixteenth and the seventeenth centuries — prompted a policy of national seclusion that isolated the peninsula from the rest of the world more effectively than similar policies of China or Japan. Korea as a nation was indeed a hermit.

The government of the Yi dynasty was in theory an absolute monarchy. Both the land and the people belonged to the king, and the law was what he willed it to be. All civil and military appointments down to the lowest level of administrative organization were supposedly made with his sanction from among those who passed competitive civil-service examinations based on the Chinese classics or military arts. Laws and precedents existed that tended to circumscribe the prerogatives of the king, but it was unthinkable that such restraints would be imposed if the monarch chose to ignore them. Traditional Korea, like China and other Asian countries, was never able to develop the Western concepts of rights and duties, and the government was typically that of men rather than law.

The central government in Seoul consisted of a Council of State, the highest policy-making organ, and six administrative departments (Civil Affairs, Revenue, Ceremonies, War, Punishments, and Works). An office of censors was a special agency to oversee and report on the behavior and loyalty of all the officials.

The country was divided into eight administrative provinces which were subdivided into smaller units of local government. Local officials were vested with judicial and administrative powers subject to various controls by the central government. Key officials at the provincial and the county levels were appointed by the central government for fixed and relatively short terms (only 360 days for a provincial governor), and no native son was assigned to the place of his origin. Close surveillance was maintained especially by the censorate in Seoul over all the local officials. The central control of local affairs, however, was tempered by the system of employing local residents as administrative and clerical assistants at various levels of local government.

From the beginning of the Yi dynasty, civil control of the military establishment had been strictly observed. Military officials had to yield precedence to their counterparts of equal rank in the civil branch, and no military commander was given the highest court rank. Very often, the Department of War was headed by a scholar-official. The professional military enjoyed prominence only during periods of emergency, and even then they were often subject to civilian leadership at the highest level. The military units in the capital consisted of the royal guards. In the provinces, the governor was *ex officio* the commander of the military forces, although he was often assisted by professional military officers who exercised the command authorities more directly over the provincial military and naval units.

Both the civil and the military officials were drawn from the aristocratic class called *yangban* (literally, "the two divisions," referring to the civil and the military branches of the officialdom), which bore a striking resemblance to the scholar-gentry class of

China. The *yangban* class, a small minority of the total population, had exclusive access to government positions, considered itself the sole repository of Confucian learning, owned lands cultivated by tenants, and enjoyed the prestige and the privileges of the highest social class in the nation. At the beginning of the Yi dynasty, the *yangban* included members of the royal clan distantly related to the royal family, persons who had rendered signal service to the country and the monarch, those who had acquired a high reputation for their learning, or individuals who were honored for filial piety. The title of *yangban*, once obtained, was hereditary; and it was lost only when the head of the family was charged with treason, or when a *yangban* voluntarily descended from his high status by engaging in any commoner's occupation, or when he married a widow or a slave. The title of the father extended to all his legitimate sons; and since by the system of adoption few families died out, there was a natural increase in the aggregate number of the *yangban* class.

In the course of the Yi dynasty, this class became divided into the "Seoul *yangban*" and the "local *yangban*," the latter being those who had settled in various parts of the country (especially in certain central and southern provinces) usually after having incurred royal disfavor. Some aspiring commoners occasionally succeeded in acquiring the "local *yangban*" status by marriage or by money, particularly in periods of official corruption. Other ambitious commoners entered Confucian academies and acquired the status of *yusaeng* (literally, "the Confucian scholars"), a satellite class of *yangban* with a partially overlapping membership. Often a *yusaeng* of non-*yangban* origin obtained an entry into officialdom, thereby elevating himself and his family to the *yangban* status. The *yangban* and the *yusaeng* classes together comprised the ruling stratum of the land, but their combined number at the end of the Yi dynasty was only about 3 percent of the total population. (See Appendix, Tables I–III.)

Many members of the *yangban* class were landlords. The Yi dynasty rewarded those who had rendered service to the royal family or to the government by gifts of land. The right to the land was hereditary and tax-exempt. At times of heavy land taxation or crop failure, the tax-free holdings of the *yangban* landlords increased through voluntary or involuntary transfer of the right to the land previously held by less privileged individuals.

The ruling class monopolized the triennial competitive examinations conducted by the government for the recruitment of civil officials and military officers. For those who failed to qualify for official positions, in many cases after repeated attempts, the only profession left for them without loss of their noble status was teaching. From all other occupations they were debarred by their rank, resulting in a host of idle, unproductive drones, "jealously clinging to all the ancient privileges of their rank, but content to extort their livelihood and the wherewithal for their pleasure from a peasantry that was always sunk in grinding poverty." [1]

The geographical distribution of the ruling class favored the southern provinces of Ch'ungch'ŏng and Kyŏngsang, according to a survey made in 1910.[2] (See Appendix, Table II.) The same survey, however, also showed proportionately high percentages of "unemployed" members of the ruling class, i.e. ex-officials and unsuccessful office-seekers, in these southern provinces. A similar finding could be drawn from biographical data on 72 prominent members of the ruling class who were granted the titles of nobility by the Japanese government after the Japanese annexation of Korea in 1910. Among those whose birthplaces were given, only 18 were from places other than the capital, while 23 were from Seoul.[3] On the basis of these limited findings, it appears that (1) a proportionately large number of high officials were recruited from Seoul and its vicinity, (2) the southern provinces had a higher concentration of the ruling class but were relatively underrepresented in the higher ranks of officialdom, and (3) the northern and the eastern provinces had comparatively fewer ruling class families and high officials. The unevenness in the geographical distribution of the ruling class and especially of the top wielders of power in the ruling class has a significant bearing on

[1] Joseph H. Longford, *The Story of Korea* (New York: C. Scribner's Sons, 1911), p. 34.

[2] Japan, Ministry of Foreign Affairs, *Nihon Teikoku Tōkei Nenkan* [Japanese Statistical Yearbook] (Tokyo, 1910), p. 947.

[3] Chosŏn Ch'ulp'an Hyŏp'hoe, *Chosŏn Sinsa Pogam* [Mirror of Korean Gentlemen] (Keijō, 1912).

the understanding of the political and social structure of the country and on the later analysis of the Korean resistance movement against Japan.

Rigidly separated from the ruling class was the rest of the population, which was in turn divided into three major classes, *chungin* (literally, "middle-men"), *sangmin* ("commoners"), and slaves. The *chungin* class, which was numerically small and politically insignificant, consisted of the descendants of the noble families of the preceding Koryŏ dynasty and included the practitioners of various skilled professions such as medicine, painting, mathematics, and astronomy.

The *sangmin* class was numerically the largest and was divided into various subgroups that included the farmers, who constituted about 85 percent of the entire population in 1910. Geographically, the proportion of the farming population was slightly higher in the northern provinces than in the south. Besides the farmers, the *sangmin* class included merchants, artisans, fishermen, and various other occupational groups which were numerically insignificant. (See Appendix, Table III.) Furthermore, as most of the farmers were largely self-sufficient, the products of the other occupational groups were primarily destined for the consumption of the small economically unproductive elements in the country.

There was no manufacturing class as such, and only one percent of the total population was engaged in primitive handicraft work. Most of the consumer goods, such as cotton, silk, linen, grass cloth, sandals, mats, and willow and wooden wares, were produced by women on the farms who raised or gathered the raw materials. Sometimes the men also made these articles during their leisure time. Also the carpenter, the blacksmith, the geomancer, or the stone mason of the average hamlet was "always one of the farmers who [added] to his stock in hand skill along these lines." [4]

The merchants and others, such as miners, innkeepers, gamblers and fortune tellers, who constituted a small minority, could be regarded as distinctive subclasses of *sangmin*. The merchants were the second largest occupational group next to the agricul-

[4] "He is a farmer," *Korean Repository*, V (1898), 229–234.

tural workers, even though they constituted only about 6 percent
of the population. Most of them were traveling salesmen carrying
goods on their backs or on pack horses from one fair to another
on prescribed days. Korea was lacking in shops and wealthy merchants, and the petty merchants who had a monopoly over interior
commerce were strongly organized by provinces and districts into
hierarchical groups that had such functionaries as chiefs, sub-
chiefs, censors, and inspectors.[5] Their organization was the so-
called guild of peddlers and hucksters, low in social prestige but
powerful enough to pretend that even the government could not
dare to interfere with their internal affairs. Actually, as the merchants traveled widely through the country, they became useful
government agents as "spies, detectives, messengers, and in time
of need, soldiers." [6] The peddlers' guilds had, on the whole, only
limited political significance, partly because their members were
widely dispersed geographically. When they did play a political
role, it was usually in connivance with the party in power rather
than in defiance of it.[7]

The lowest subclass of the *sangmin* was *ch'ŏnmin* or those
having such "vile callings" as musical and acrobatic entertainers, sorceresses, butchers, tanners, and the Buddhist monks;
the last named subgroup was the object of anti-Buddhist persecution by the government during the Yi dynasty. There was yet
another category of "vile callings" that encompassed the professional female entertainers known as *kisaeng*, the menial servants
in the palace or in various government offices, postal station
attendants, jail keepers, and lowly clerical workers in government
offices and military establishments at the national and local levels.
The last named group of public servants were collectively known
as *ajŏn*; despite their humble status, they often wielded considerable political influence, especially at the local level, as the link
between the populace and the government as it was represented

[5] Ch'oe Ho-jin, *Kindai Chōsen Keizaishi* [Modern Economic History of
Korea] (Tokyo, 1942), pp. 15 ff.

[6] William Elliot Griffis, *Corea, the Hermit Nation* (New York: C.
Scribner's Sons, 1907), p. 243.

[7] Keijō Teikoku Daigaku Hōbun Gakkai (ed.), *Chōsen Keizai no
Kenkyu* [Korean Economic Research], I (Tokyo, 1929), pp. 10–11.

by the centrally appointed *yangban* officials, who possessed but little knowledge of local affairs.[8]

The lowest social class below the *sangmin* was the slave. "Public slaves" were the criminals and some of their descendants who were assigned to certain government offices, while "private slaves" were sold and bought as servants at private homes for lifetime or for a fixed period of time. Their number during the Yi dynasty was not very large and the status was in many cases hereditary.[9]

In short, traditional Korea was a highly stratified society with little mobility, in which the numerically small *yangban* class ruled over the status-bound commoners, the majority of whom were farmers. The farm lands, the single most important source of wealth, were also the main source of government revenue. The farmers paid a land tax which in 1905 and 1906 provided as much as 65.1 and 69.6 percent, respectively, of the total government revenues. In addition they were required to supply labor for public works. An individual farm was small on the average (about 2.5 acres in 1913), and about three out of four farmers were either tenants or owned only a part of the land they cultivated.[10]

In rural villages, most of the families were related by blood; but each family, consisting of about four persons, maintained its own separate housing. This clannish or "sibbish" characteristic of many of these villages and their consanguineous solidarity have been among the most important factors in the behavior pattern of the rural populace.[11] These characteristics were more noticeable in the more secluded mountainous areas than in fishing villages or villages in the plain area. Clan solidarity was considered a self-protective device by the villagers who thought that the government was more against than for them. To them, the gov-

[8] Japan, Chōsen Chūsatsu Kempei Shireibu, *Chōsen Shakai Kō* [Analysis of Korean Society] (Keijō, 1912), pp. 37–40.

[9] *Ibid.*, pp. 41–42.

[10] Japan, Chōsen Sōtokufu, *Chōsen no Kosaku Kanshū* [Korean Tenant Farming Practices] (Keijō, 1929), pp. 22–23, 28.

[11] Yi Man-gap, *Han'guk Nongch'on ui Sahoe Kujo* [The Social Structure of the Korean Village] (Seoul, 1960), pp. 10–11. See also Shannon McCune, *Korea's Heritage* (Tokyo & Rutland, Vt.: C. E. Tuttle Co., 1956), p. 73.

ernment of the land-owning *yangban* officials was an exploiter and a suppressor that collected heavy taxes, demanded unquestioning obedience, and gave little in return.

In these villages, especially in smaller ones, the leaders were chosen by popular consent with official approval. They guided the conduct of village affairs and "usually acted as a cushion between the village and the official government." [12] They were the informal leaders or the local elite without ruling class status.

Autonomy in village life was further promoted by the existence of village guild associations — a phenomenon which was "unique and unexampled either in Japan or China." [13] These guild associations provided the informal organizational basis of local self-government. The following description illustrates the pervasiveness of guild associations in the village:

> There are many economic, social and mutual benefit societies in Korea. It is fair to say that the Korean people have a genius for organization. In a list of societies whose constitutions and records are in hand, the following varieties are noted: Family and clan societies, neighborhood and brotherhood guilds, societies for providing aid at weddings, funerals, in sickness and in controversies. Others have for their object the conduct of periodic feasts or picnics. There are many lottery organizations whose functions are limited to membership, craft guilds, merchants' companies and monopolistic guilds, labor organizations of villagers to guard the forests, to establish and conduct community schools and to help poor boys prepare for the government examinations.[14]

In this discussion of the Korean village, mention should be made also of provincialism or local loyalty which conditioned the attitude of the rural people. Tied to the native soil, they naturally identified themselves with the local community; the central government in Seoul or even the provincial government was remote and "alien."

Yet, the farmers were on the whole obedient, patient, and po-

[12] Shannon McCune, p. 43.

[13] Japan, Chōsen Sōtokufu, *Chōsen no Shūraku* [Korean Villages] (Keijō, 1933), I, 490.

[14] "The Village Guilds of Old Korea," *Transactions of the Korea Branch of the Royal Asiatic Society of Great Britain and Ireland*, IV (1913), Part II, p. 13.

litically inert even in the face of legal or illegal exactions imposed upon them.[15] Therefore, the fact that there were increasingly frequent rural uprisings as the nineteenth century wore on — over 20 instances reported in 1862 alone — was an even more ominous indication of the gravity of popular discontent.[16]

Away from the rumbles of these rural disturbances, the government in Seoul continued to indulge in vicious factional struggles which had pitted groups of high officials and Confucian scholars against one another since the last years of the fifteenth century. Although these factions endeavored to attack each other in the name of Confucian orthodoxy, the struggle was essentially a contest for political domination. In the mid-sixteenth century, the two rival factions were named as "the men of the east" and "the men of the west." Later each of them divided into subfactions creating an intricate web of alliances and counteralliances. At each occasion of royal succession or selection of the royal consort, there was a flareup of new intrigues and sanguinary attacks; the emergence of a new faction in power invariably involved a wholesale purge and sometimes physical elimination of opposition factions. Other problems of the government and the nation appeared to have been subordinated to the requirement of this life-or-death struggle within the ruling class. The national crisis created by the Japanese invasion of Korea in the 1590s failed to put an end to the factional feud. The military conquest of Korea by the Manchu forces in the 1620s and the 1630s was equally without effect in this regard.[17] Engulfed in chronic partisan strife, the government was unable to govern, the centripetal system of bureaucracy lost its efficiency and impartiality, and official "squeeze" and other corrupt practices of officials with uncertain tenure became rampant.

Factional rivalry colored official Korean reaction to the entry of Christianity into the peninsula. The first Korean convert to the Western religion was baptized in Peking and returned home in 1784; the new faith rapidly spread among "the men of the

[15] *Korean Repository*, V (1898), 454–457.

[16] Ch'oe Ho-jin, p. 322.

[17] Hatada Takashi, *Chōsenshi* [Korean History] (Tokyo, 1951), pp. 125–35.

south," the faction to which the first Korean Christian belonged. When the first wave of anti-Christian suppression hit the nascent Christian community in 1801, the target was as much the "south" faction as the "wicked" religion of the West.

Trading ships and warships from the West followed the Christian evangelists to Korea in the ensuing decades. British, French, and Russian ships reconnoitered the Korean coasts seeking trade, beginning with the voyage of the H.M.S. *Providence* in 1797 around the southern coast of Korea to the Wŏnsan area on the east coast. Reports of "strange-looking" ships came to Seoul in 1816, 1832, and thereafter with increasing frequency.[18]

These disturbing developments and the news of Chinese capitulation to British arms in 1842 and the success of the American naval squadron in opening Japan in 1854 failed to eradicate or ameliorate the intensity of the internal feud within the Korean ruling class. The ruling faction was firm in its resolve to fend off Western advances and was equally determined to continue the pattern of partisan conflict at home.

For centuries the cardinal principle in the conduct of foreign relations was embodied in the phrase *sadae kyorin*; *sadae* (literally, "serving the big") referred to relations with China and *kyorin* (literally, "friendly dealings with the neighbor") to those with Japan. Confucian culture viewed international relations as an extension of interpersonal relations within a family. The inequality of status based on the distinction between a superior and an inferior was as natural in international relations as it was in interpersonal relations. A nation's behavior toward another had to reflect its status relative to that of the other. On the one hand, Korea owed loyalty and obedience to China, the "elder brother nation"; on the other, she treated Japan in a friendly manner as her equal. The most important outward manifestation of this principle was the ceremonial and periodic exchange of official envoys among the three countries in accordance with rigid rules

[18] Charles Dallet, *Histoire de l'église de Corée* (Paris: Victor Palmé, 1874), I, 109 ff; Melvin Frederick Nelson, *Korea and the Old Orders in Eastern Asia* (Baton Rouge: Louisiana State University Press, 1945), p. 110. See also Yi Nŭng-hwa, *Chosŏn Kidokgyo kŭp Waegyosa* [History of Christianity and Foreign Relations of Korea] (Seoul, 1925), pp. 70, 130–134.

of protocol. Very limited trade relations were maintained by means of the exchange of official "gifts," barter exchanges under official supervision by licensed merchants at two border towns between Korea and China, and the periodic visits of merchants from the Japanese island of Tsushima to the Korean port of Pusan to obtain food grains and other necessities for the islanders. Except for these transactions, the Korean borders and coasts were sealed to any traffic of men and goods.[19]

Korea's geographical location, its relative military weakness throughout most of its history, and the foreign invasion of the past justified the bare minimum of dealing with its immediate neighbors. Korea appeased China with a show of respect for the "Celestial Empire," and pacified Japan with limited trade benefits. As for the rest of the world, Korea had had no contact in the past and did not see any need for establishing any relations in the mid-nineteenth century. Korea hoped to be left alone, but it was a vain hope.

In 1866 a French squadron of seven warships and 600 men invaded the Korean island of Kanghwa not too far from Seoul and demanded satisfaction for the execution of several French missionaries who had earlier entered the forbidden land in disguise. The expedition failed to accomplish any of its objectives and withdrew. In 1871 a similar expedition of five American warships — protesting destruction of an American trading ship, the *General Sherman*, in an inland river of northwestern Korea — was equally unsuccessful, despite more elaborate diplomatic and military preliminaries.[20]

In these years of foreign invasion the Korean government was under the leadership of the father of the reigning monarch. The

[19] Nelson, chap. 6; George M. McCune, "Exchange of Envoys Between Korea and Japan During the Tokugawa Period," *Far Eastern Quarterly*, V (May 1946), 308–325. See also Japan, Ministry of Foreign Affairs, *Nihon Gaikō Bunsho* [Japanese Diplomatic Documents], VI, 169–170; and I, 666–671. The last named hereafter referred to as *NGB*.

[20] Griffis, pp. 403–419; Dallet, II, 570–588; U.S. Dept. of State, *Papers Relating to the Foreign Relations of the United States*, 1867, Pt. I, pp. 414–417, 428, 544–547; *ibid.*, 1870–71, pp. 139–140; Charles O. Paullin, *Diplomatic Negotiations of American Naval Officers, 1778–1883* (Baltimore· The Johns Hopkins Press, 1912), pp. 284–292.

king (named Yi Hyŏng but referred to as King Kojong before 1897 and as Emperor Kojong thereafter) was a mere twelve-year-old boy when he ascended the throne in 1864 as an adopted son of the preceding sovereign. His real father, who had been a relatively little-known prince of royal blood, became the regent, assuming the title of *Taewŏn'gun* ("Prince of the Great Court"). Using his prerogatives as regent to the fullest extent, the *Taewŏn'gun* at first instituted a drastic shakeup in the government in order to crush the old ruling faction that had virtually usurped the sovereign power of the kings earlier in the century. He attempted a few reforms, including the abolishment of the privileged and tax-exempt Confucian academies known as *sŏwŏn*. The *sŏwŏn* was the center of Confucian learning but was also a potential antigovernment institution because its membership usually included influential local *yangban* or *yusaeng* scholars whose ambitions for official careers had been frustrated one way or another. These academies, largely concentrated in the southern provinces, also had historical or personal ties with one or the other faction in the capital.

The *Taewŏn'gun* with his "strong personality and imperial will" was too highhanded and tactless in his domestic reforms to be successful, but he was even more obstinate in his refusal to adopt more realistic policies toward other countries. It was his myopic chauvinism that resulted, directly or indirectly, in the death of the French missionaries and the *Sherman* incident which invited the foreign invasions. It was also the regent who rejected overtures of the new Meiji government of Japan in the early 1870s to revise the old relations in accordance with Western practices.

Neither his domestic nor his foreign policies, however, were to have lasting effect. Soon after the regent's subjugation of the old court faction, a new faction headed by his daughter-in-law, Queen Min, was created. The Min family had been an obscure *yangban* family when one of its members was chosen by the regent to become the royal consort. The young queen, an ambitious woman possessing considerable political acumen, caused many of her blood relatives to be appointed to key posts in the government. When the king came of age in 1874, the queen influenced the king's decision to assume the full measure of royal responsibility, forcing the *Taewŏn'gun* into semiretirement. Emerging as the most powerful faction in the court, the Mins adopted a new and more conciliatory outlook toward Japan, either out of their genuine conviction of need for modification of the traditional policy or, more likely, in the hope of discrediting the *Taewŏn'gun's* antiforeign policy.

It is clear at this point that Korean contacts with other countries were sporadic and generally resisted by the Koreans. Power struggles within the government monopolized the attention of the *yangban* classes and aggravated the suspicion and distrust of the rest of the populace. Expediency and narrow partisan interests dictated the course of foreign involvement.

2.

First Treaties with
Japan and the West

In 1876 the Meiji government of Japan, after several years of unsuccessful attempts to establish official relations with Korea, sent a formidable military expedition to Korea commanded by Lieutenant-General Kuroda Kiyotaka. His objective was to conclude a treaty of friendship and commerce with Korea. For this purpose, Kuroda was to play the role of an aggrieved party demanding satisfaction for an alleged Korean attack in 1875 against the Japanese warship *Unyō*. The Japanese man-of-war had intentionally violated the territorial waters of Korea at a strategic location near the mouth of the Han River and had drawn fire from the shore batteries. The treaty was to revive the diplomatic intercourse between the two nations that had been severed by the Korean regent in 1868, when the newly established government of Japan attempted to introduce into the traditional pattern of formal communications innovations that were more in line with Western practices. The question at stake was not merely a matter of protocols and technicalities; it involved the far more important issue of the viability of the traditional system of international relations in northeast Asia under drastically changed circumstances.[1]

[1] Melvin Frederick Nelson, *Korea and the Old Orders in Eastern Asia*, chaps. 1 and 6. As for the *Unyō* incident, a Japanese writer declared recently that it had resulted from a deliberate Japanese attempt to intimidate the Korean government with a show of naval strength. Japanese provoca-

Kuroda's mission, if successful, was bound to bring about a basic modification in this China-centered international system and in Korea's status vis-à-vis the "Celestial Court." It was not surprising, therefore, that the Japanese government dispatched to China, almost simultaneously with its decision to send the Kuroda expedition, an able Western-trained diplomat to obtain China's acquiescence in the new status in the Sino-Korean relations. More specifically, Japan desired that China should relinquish its suzerainty over Korea.

The Sino-Japanese conversations were inconclusive at best. Li Hung-chang, the governor-general of Chihli Province and the de facto foreign minister of China, rebuffed the Japanese demand with the ready explanation that Korea, although independent in all matters relating to her government and religion (*chŏnggyo chaju*), was subordinate to China. However, in the face of Japan's seeming willingness to risk a war with Korea, if necessary, to obtain a treaty, Li felt compelled to advise Korea to consider the Japanese demands in a friendly manner. This was the maximum concession Li would make. In return the Japanese envoy decided to leave the matter for the time being without pressing for a clearcut renunciation of suzerainty by China.

Coalescence of these three factors — Japanese determination, Chinese counsel, and a change in the Korean government (as the *Taewŏn'gun* yielded to the greater strength of the Mins)— helped to produce a treaty of amity, friendship, commerce, and navigation signed at Kanghwa city by Sin Hŏn for Korea and by General Kuroda for Japan on February 26, 1876. The treaty was modeled after the Western treaties with Japan and China and provided for the exchange of diplomatic emissaries, opening of two ports besides Pusan, and granting of extraterritorial rights for Japanese citizens in Korea. In other words, Japan imposed "unequal" terms on Korea that were similar in nature to the provisions of the "unequal" treaties which the Western powers had extracted from Japan only a dozen or more years before. Furthermore, the most significant statement, in the light of future devel-

tion is therefore responsible for the incident. See Yamabe Kentarō, *Nikkan Heigō Shōshi* [A Brief History of the Merger of Japan and Korea] (Tokyo, 1966) pp. 22–27.

opments, was contained in Article I which read: "Corea being an independent State enjoys the same Sovereign rights as does Japan."[2] The Chinese government apparently chose to interpret the term *chaju* as meaning "autonomy" or "autonomous" rather than "independence" or "independent," for, when the full text of the treaty in Chinese was reported to Peking by the Korean government, neither the Tsungli Yamen, the foreign office of China, nor Li Hung-chang raised any objection.[3]

The period immediately after the signing of the Kanghwa Treaty witnessed a sharp increase in Korean-Japanese contacts. Official envoys were sent and received, and by the end of 1880, a permanent Japanese diplomatic mission was established in Seoul. Detailed agreements about trade and commerce were negotiated and signed, and the volume of trade increased rapidly. A group of promising young Koreans was sent to Japan in 1881 to study various aspects of a modern society; some of these students, upon their return from Japan, became the leaders of a movement for modernization and reform. However, a reaction to these innovations and changes soon set in. Within Korea, Confucian traditionalists submitted memorials that denounced "the wicked learning" from abroad. An abortive putsch directed against the king and the Mins was uncovered in 1881, and it was generally believed that the *Taewŏn'gun* was the leading spirit behind the conspiracy.[4] In China, Li Hung-chang viewed with alarm the steady growth of Japanese influence in Korea. He had long held that the greatest danger to Korea and eventually to China would come from Japan. As countermeasures, Li proposed to Korea that (1) it should build up its military strength and (2) should conclude treaties with the Western powers "in order to check the poison with an antidote."[5] Of the Western powers which had

[2] Quoted from the English rendition of China, Imperial Maritime Customs, *Treaties, Regulations, etc., Between Corea and Other Powers: 1876–1889* (Shanghai: Statistical Department of the Inspectorate General of Customs, 1891), p. 1.

[3] T. F. Tsiang, "Sino-Japanese Diplomatic Relations, 1870–1894," *Chinese Social and Political Science Review*, XVII (April 1933), 61.

[4] Kim Han Kyo, "The Opening of Korea" (unpublished master's dissertation, University of Chicago, 1957), pp. 19–29, 33–50.

[5] Li Hung-chang to Yi Yu-wŏn, August 29, 1879, in *NGB*, XVII, 370–

shown interest in establishing official relations with Korea, Li singled out the United States as the best partner to Korea's first treaty. In Li's estimate the United States had no territorial design and was the most reliable of the Western nations.[6]

An imperial edict of February 23, 1881, directed Li Hung-chang and the Chinese minister in Japan, Ho Ju-chang, to enlighten and guide Korea, thus relieving the tradition-bound Board of Rites in Peking of this responsibility. The edict symbolized a change in China's policy toward Korea and was calculated to pave the way for a Korean-American treaty. From this time onward until 1894 Li Hung-chang was directly in charge of China's Korea policy. The same edict explicitly disapproved Ho Ju-chang's proposal that China should either negotiate a treaty with the American envoy on behalf of Korea or else order Korea, by means of an imperial edict, to negotiate the treaty. China's intervention, instead, was to be confined to giving advice to Korea.[7]

In compliance with the edict, Li had the Customs Tao-t'ai at Tientsin transmit a message to the Korean government in which he expounded seven advantages which should be expected from the conclusion of a Korean-American treaty and urged the Koreans to dispatch a high official to China to negotiate it. The Korean official, however, was to carry an innocuous title of "officer in charge of students" — Korean students in China — in order to disguise his diplomatic assignment. Such devious tactics were adopted as a precaution against unwelcome intervention by "a neighboring country" — probably Japan.[8] Turning his attention to another aspect of the treaty-making project, Li di-

---

371. Yi, who at times occupied the premiership, was the Korean correspondent through whom Li Hung-chang communicated with the Korean government in a semiprivate manner.

[6] *Ibid.*

[7] *Ch'ing-chi wai-chiao shih-liao* [Diplomatic Source Materials of the End of the Ch'ing Dynasty], comp. Wang Yen-wei and ed. Wang Liang, 125 *ts'e* (Peking, 1932–1935), *Chuan* 25, pp. 1a–2a. Chuan hereafter abbreviated as *Ch.*

[8] Kim Yun-sik, *Unyangjip* [Collected Writings of Kim Yun-sik], ed. Hwang Pyŏng-uk, 8 vols. (1913?), *Kwŏn* 15, pp. 16a–16b. *Kwŏn* is the Korean equivalent to *chuan*. Kim Yun-sik (1831–1919) was a moderate and occupied many high posts in the Korean government in the 1880s and the 1890s.

rected two of his trusted subordinates, Ma Chien-chung and Cheng Tsao-ju, to prepare a draft treaty. This departure from the role of a benevolent adviser to that of a more active participant was justified, in Li's mind, because of Korea's inexperience in matters of diplomacy.[9]

In March 1881 the Korean government at last established a new office, *T'ongni Amun* — a name very similar to the Tsungli Yamen in China — to handle matters of foreign relations and defense. The prime minister was to be the president of the new office which was staffed by high-ranking officials of the kingdom. The move suggested the resolve of the king and the ruling Min faction to increase and widen Korea's contact with the outside world. However, as the ruling group became more favorably inclined toward discarding the tradition of isolation, the opposition from conservative quarters became increasingly vociferous. Memorials poured in denouncing the "wicked learning" and those Koreans who tolerated it.[10] The *Taewŏn'gun*, though nominally in semiretirement, was a source of inspiration for the antiforeign outburst. It was against this background of political turbulance that a 40-year-old son of the *Taewŏn'gun*, hence a halfbrother of the king, plotted the aforementioned court revolution to usurp the throne. The conspiracy failed to materialize and the would-be king and his supporters were arrested in September 1881 and later executed.

The manifestations of antiforeign and antigovernment opposition intimidated the Korean court and caused a delay in its response to Li Hung-chang's advice regarding the American-Korean treaty. It was not until the winter of 1881–82 that Kim Yun-sik was able to go to China at the head of a 70-odd-man mission that included 37 students who were to be trained at Chinese armories and machine shops. Kim had been a prefect in Chŏlla province before his appointment as the "officer in charge of the students." Kim was not a member of the Min faction, but he was an advocate of opening the door to learning from the outside world.[11] Soon after his arrival at Tientsin, Kim sent a

[9] *Ch'ing-chi wai-chiao shih-liao*, Ch. 25, pp. 5a–6b.

[10] For details on these memorials see Yi Nŭng-hwa, chap. 27.

[11] Sometime in late November or early December 1881, shortly before his departure for China, Kim submitted a memorial to the king setting forth

long memorandum to Li Hung-chang to explain the reasons for his delay and, more important, to request an edict from the Chinese court commanding Korea to send a plenipotentiary to negotiate a treaty with the American envoy. The imperial command was necessary, Kim argued, in order to overcome domestic opposition to the treaty; any further delay, in his estimation, would enhance the danger of a possible Japanese or Russian obstruction.[12]

This memorandum is highly revealing. It is evidence of how a political faction in Korea solicited Chinese intervention to overpower domestic opposition. It was neither the first nor the last time that the prestige and influence of China or of some other foreign power was sought by Korean political groups as help in partisan strife. With regard to the more immediate question of Korean-American negotiation, Kim's memorandum reveals that (1) Kim was not, or he did not consider himself as having been, authorized to act as plenipotentiary; and (2) Kim assumed that a Korean plenipotentiary would conduct the actual negotiations, little suspecting how extensive the "assistance" of Li Hung-chang was to be in the forthcoming negotiations.

Li Hung-chang rejected Kim's proposal for an imperial edict not only because there was no precedent, but because it would also give undue advantage to the American negotiator by informing him that his counterpart would be under a binding order to conclude a treaty. Li advised Kim to remain at Tientsin.

The American negotiator was to be Commodore Robert W. Shufeldt, U.S.N. Shufeldt had visited Korea twice previously (in 1867 and 1880) in unsuccessful attempts to establish a diplomatic channel of communication with the government in Seoul. Despite these failures, he was determined to be a Commodore Matthew Perry in opening Korea. Shufeldt returned to the Far East in the summer of 1881 and sought Li's friendly intercession. The American officer was now to be rewarded for his long wait.

On March 25, 1882, the formal negotiations began between Li Hung-chang and Shufeldt. Kim Yun-sik was not present at

his views on the foreign and domestic issues facing Korea. He emphasized the danger from a continued policy of national isolation, see Kim Yun-sik, *Kwŏn* 9, pp. 2a-4a.

[12] *Ibid., Kwŏn* 12, pp. 25b–29a.

this first session, nor was he to be at any subsequent meeting. Following the preliminary remarks, Shufeldt presented the American draft of a treaty. It contained ten articles and was apparently modeled upon the American treaties with Japan and China. The main provisions were the establishment of diplomatic relations on the basis of equality and reciprocity, relief for the shipwrecked, the right of American nationals to reside and trade at the open ports, extraterritoriality, tariff rates on exports and imports not exceeding 10 per cent *ad valorem*, and a most-favored-nation clause. Besides these stipulations that were more or less common in the treaties which Western nations concluded with Asian countries in the nineteenth century, Shufeldt's draft also included a ban on opium trade. It, however, contained "no reference to China's claim to suzerainty over Korea, on the inclusion of which, it was well known, the viceroy was determined to insist."[13]

In contrast the Chinese draft which Li handed to Shufeldt in return, referring to it as a "Korean" draft,[14] contained, at the beginning of Article I, an explicit statement that "Korea is a vassal state of China, but has always enjoyed autonomy in both its internal and external affairs."[15] China's claim to suzerainty was also implied in an unusual ratification procedure stipulated at the end of the draft treaty; Korea was to forward a copy of the signed treaty to the Board of Rites in Peking.[16]

[13] Charles O. Paullin, "The Opening of Korea," *Political Science Quarterly*, XXV (1910), 489.

[14] It was the draft that had been prepared by Ma Chien-chung and Tseng Tsao-ju. The Korean government accepted it as Korea's own draft and forwarded it to Tientsin when Kim Yun-sik came to China. See Li Hung-chang, *Li Wen-chung-kung ch'uan-chi* [The Collected Writings of Li Hung-chang], ed. Wu Ju-lin (Nanking, 1908), *Memorials, Ch.* 43, p. 34b. Hereafter cited as *Li's Memorials*. Li's other writings in this 100 *t'se* collection will be cited as *Li's Communications* to the Tsungli Yamen, *Li's Telegrams*, etc. See also T. F. Tsiang, "Sino-Japanese Diplomatic Relations, 1870–1894," p. 68.

[15] Quoted from T. C. Lin, "Li Hung-chang: His Korean Policies, 1870–1885," *Chinese Social and Political Science Review*, XIX (1935–36), 223.

[16] For the full text of the Chinese draft see *Li's Communications, Ch.* 13, pp. 10a–12b. An English translation appears in Okudaira Takehiko, *Chōsen Kaikoku Kōshō Shimatsu* [Negotiations on the Opening of Korea from Beginning to End] (Tokyo, 1935), pp. 103–108.

The most important difference between the Chinese and the American drafts related to the question of Korea's status vis-à-vis China. Li focused his remarks at the March 25 meeting on this issue and expressed his resolve that "the mistake" of the Kanghwa Treaty of 1876 between Japan and Korea should be avoided. Shufeldt maintained that the question of Chinese suzerainty had no bearing upon the right of the United States to deal with Korea, a nation which was self-governing in domestic and foreign affairs. Shufeldt did not attempt to deny or challenge the Chinese claim of suzerain rights; he rather argued that a statement to that effect had no place in a Korean-American treaty. Shufeldt also expressed his opposition to the last sentence of the disputed Article I which, by providing for mutual assistance or mediation, seemed to commit the United States to the role of protector, conjointly with China, of Korea.

Unable to resolve the knotty issue of China's suzerainty claim, the negotiating parties finally worked out a compromise. Pending further instructions from Washington, the contested statement of Chinese suzerainty was deleted from the provisional text for the time being. Should Washington approve its inclusion in the treaty, it was to be restored as Article I. Should Washington withhold approval, it would remain deleted, but Shufeldt would forward to the American president a formal communication from the Korean king acknowledging Korea's inferior status vis-à-vis China. This compromise enabled the two representatives to conclude the negotiations by affixing their signatures on the provisional treaty on April 19. After waiting for several more days for Washington's response, which never came, Shufeldt decided on his own to go to Korea to consummate the project.[17]

Meanwhile, Li Hung-chang prepared the stage for the final act. Soon after the April 19 meeting, the provisional treaty text was dispatched to Korea by a special courier aboard a Chinese warship. Accompanying the document was a letter from Li addressed to the Korean prime minister, Yi Ch'ae-ŭng, that described in detail the Tientsin proceedings and informed the

[17] It is not clear why a response was never made by Washington. See Paullin, "The Opening of Korea," p. 493; *Li's Memorials*, Ch. 43, pp. 35a–36b.

Koreans of an impending visit of Shufeldt to Korea. Li also com-
mended the provisional articles for Korean acceptance and added
that a separate communication acknowledging Chinese suzerainty should be issued by the Korean king in case a statement
to that effect could not be included in the treaty itself.[18] Li's letter
contained little that had not been known to the Korean government. Kim Yun-sik, the Korean officer "in charge of students,"
had been busy as an intermediary between Tientsin and Seoul.
Although he was never present at any of the sessions, he was kept
well informed and was frequently consulted by Li.[19] Kim reportedly gave his full concurrence to the Chinese demand for
recognition of Chinese suzerainty in the treaty text. According to
Kim's own admission, he frequently had to act on his own discretion in the absence of specific instructions from Seoul. This was
most probably due to a deliberate decision of the Korean king
and the ruling Min faction to assume as little responsibility as
possible for the momentous — and largely unpopular — decision
to open Korea's doors to a Western nation. A letter Li received
from Yi Ch'ae-ŭng only three days prior to the last Li-Shufeldt
session at Tientsin reiterated the Korean inclination to "look up
to and place sole reliance upon" the Chinese viceroy.[20]

Li Hung-chang was more than willing to comply. In order to
impress the Koreans with China's initiative in the Korean-American treaty negotiation and to counter any agitation against the
treaty, Li ordered a squadron of three Chinese warships under
the command of Admiral Ting Ju-ch'ang to Chemulpo (Inch'ŏn).
Ma Chien-chung also went to Korea to handle political problems.
On the day following the departure of the Chinese squadron, the
U.S.S. *Swatara* left Chefoo for Korea with Shufeldt on board.
The signing ceremony took place on May 22 with Ma and Admiral Ting in attendance. It was followed by a reception on board

[18] For the text of Li's letter to Yi see *Li's Communications*, *Ch*. 13,
pp. 33a–34b.

[19] Kim devoted 80 to 90 percent of his official activities to matters related to the treaty negotiation, paying only scant attention to his nominal
function as the leader of the student group; see Kim Yun-sik, *Kwŏn* 15,
p. 16b.

[20] For the text of Yi's letter to Li see *Li's Communications*, *Ch*. 13,
pp. 32b–33a.

a Chinese warship. Sometime afterward, but prior to Shufeldt's departure from Korea on May 24, the Korean statement of dependency was delivered to Shufeldt for transmission to the president of the United States.

The Treaty of Amity and Commerce, known as the Chemulpo Treaty of 1882, was almost identical to the provisional treaty text signed by Li and Shufeldt. (The final text signed by the Koreans included, as a part of Article VIII, an additional ban on the export of grain.) As agreed upon in the Li-Shufeldt compromise, there was no explicit statement on the status of Korea vis-à-vis China in Article I. Instead, the first article merely stated that there was to be "perpetual peace and friendship" between the United States and Korea and should either party become subject to unjust or oppressive treatment by a third nation, the other party to this treaty was to exert its good offices for an amicable arrangement "thus showing their friendly feelings." [21]

The statement which the Korean king sent to the president of the United States declared that Korea was a state dependent upon China, although it was self-governing in matters of internal government and foreign intercourse. Korea and the United States should treat each other on equal terms, the statement continued, and the duties that devolved upon Korea as a nation dependent on China were not the concern of the United States.[22] It was dated May 15, 1882, or seven days before the signing of the treaty. Ma deliberately had it antedate the treaty in an effort to create a legal effect comparable to an equivalent statement in the treaty itself.

To a contemporary Western observer, it might have been difficult to reconcile the two documents that Shufeldt brought back from Korea. The treaty contained nothing that could have implied that Korea was anything but a fully independent nation. The letter from the Korean king, however, acknowledged that China was suzerain over Korea. This apparent incongruity was a reflection of the basic disparity between the Western politico-legal concept of sovereignty and the "Confucian familism" which

[21] Henry Chung (comp.), *Treaties and Conventions Between Corea and Other Powers* (New York: H. S. Nichols, 1919), pp. 197–204.

[22] For a competent textual analysis based on three different English translations of the Korean statement, see Nelson, pp. 145–49.

characterized the Sino-Korean relationship. Theoretically, the former permitted no room for the kind of status that Korea occupied vis-à-vis China. Paradoxical as it may sound, Korea was independent, and yet it was dependent on China in the manner of a younger brother who relies on an elder brother for leadership and occasional assistance.[23] At the Tientsin meetings, Li Hung-chang had attempted unsuccessfully to obtain a formal recognition of this familial relationship by the United States. The Li-Shufeldt compromise formula did not signify any genuine progress in bridging the gap between the Chinese and American views on this issue; it was, rather, a cover-up that further obfuscated the area of basic disagreement. Each party, therefore, was left free to read its own interpretation into these documents.

The United States chose to regard the Treaty of Chemulpo as an evidence of Korea's sovereign independence. In March 1883 Secretary of State Frelinghuysen flatly stated that "as far as we are concerned Corea is an independent sovereign power . . . ; in her relations to China we have no desire to interfere unless action should be taken prejudicial to the rights of the United States." In this lengthy memorandum addressed to the first American minister to Korea, Frelinghuysen took note of Article II of the treaty of the exchange of *diplomatic* representatives and that part of the preamble that listed the names of two *Korean* plenipotentiaries appointed by the *Korean* king to negotiate the treaty.[24] "It will be seen," Frelinghuysen declared, "from these extracts as well as from the tenor of the treaty that the negotiations were conducted as between two independent and sovereign nations." The secretary minimized the dominant roles played by Li Hung-chang and Ma Chien-chung by saying that "the Chinese officials were familiar with its terms [terms of the Treaty of

[23] In 1887, the president of the Korean Foreign Office told the American minister to Korea, Hugh A. Dinsmore, that "Korea is truly an independent kingdom and China is only our elder brother and because we are weak and a small country we ask China to advise and assist us." See Payson J. Treat, "China and Korea, 1885–1894," *Political Science Quarterly*, XLIX (1934), 535.

[24] After his arrival in Chemulpo for the signing of the treaty, Shufeldt was introduced by Ma to two Korean representatives, Sin Hŏn and Kim Hong-jip. But their contacts with Shufeldt were minimal.

Chemulpo] and in a friendly manner aided the representative of this [the United States] government." Frelinghuysen did take account of the letter from the Korean king, but contrary to what Li Hung-chang had hoped, the puzzling content of the letter did not deter him from concluding that Korea was independent.[25] Indeed, little congnizance was taken of the anomalous Korean missive which did not fit into Western diplomatic practices.[26] Following the ratification of the treaty by President Arthur, Frelinghuysen appointed, in February 1883, General Lucius H. Foote as envoy extraordinary and minister plenipotentiary to Korea. Foote's rank equaled those held by the American representatives in China and Japan.

Thus viewed, the Li-Shufeldt compromise appears to have been an unilateral capitulation on Li's part. To quote from a respected scholar of American diplomatic history, the treaty was "one of the great mistakes of his [Li's] career," while the Korean letter to the president of the United States was "worthless." [27] Similar but more impassioned criticisms were voiced within Chinese official circles not too long after the signing of the American-Korean treaty. Li, however, refused to admit the alleged shortcomings of his handiwork. In response to a critic, Li wrote in January 1884 that the Korean letter would, in case of a future attack on Korea by any foreign power or in the event of Korean insubordination to China, justify Chinese intervention. The omission of an explicit statement of Chinese suzerainty over Korea from the treaty text was inevitable, Li argued, because the Westerners would feel that such a statement was injurious to their own dignity. In short Li's self-defense lay in his contention that it was the best treaty obtainable and that the letter from the Korean king had the legal effect of justifying any future intervention by China

[25] Frelinghuysen to L. H. Foote, March 17, 1883, George M. McCune and John A. Harrison (eds.), *Korean-American Relations: Documents Pertaining to the Far Eastern Diplomacy of the United States.* Vol. I, *The Initial Period, 1883–86* (Berkeley and Los Angeles; University of California Press, 1951), p. 25.

[26] Nelson, p. 149.

[27] Tyler Dennett, *Americans in Eastern Asia* (New York: Barnes and Noble, Inc., 1941), pp. 460–461.

in Korean affairs.[28] Whether Li's own interpretation was acceptable or not to the United States and subsequently to other Western
nations, China did intervene in Korea, from July 1882 onward,
in a manner unwitnessed since the first half of the seventeenth
century. Li's active policy toward Korea held the peninsular kingdom within the Chinese orbit until China was forcibly ejected
from Korea in 1894. Thus, China's internal weakness, particularly in the military sphere, and not Li's handling of the Korean-
American treaty of 1882, is responsible for the end of Chinese
influence in Korea.

As for Korea, the Chemulpo Treaty symbolized a success for
the anti-isolation policy of its leadership. Whatever selfish, ulterior
motives the king and the ruling Min faction might have had, they
had battled since the mid-1870s to terminate Korea's hermit
status. By letting China take the lead and carry the main burden
of negotiation, the Korean leaders paid the least possible price of
political commitment and maximized their defense against attacks
from the powerful isolationist groups at home. They had shown
no sign of reluctance in acknowledging Korea's dependent status
in the royal communication sent to the United States. When antiforeign disturbances broke out in Seoul in the wake of a soldiers'
mutiny in July 1882, the Korean government, through its agents
in China, gave reassurance to the American minister in Peking,
John R. Young, that it would carry out the treaty provisions, and
expressed its hope that the United States would ratify the treaty
and send a diplomatic representative to Seoul.[29] To the relief of
these Koreans, the United States not only ratified the treaty but
also promptly dispatched Minister Foote to Korea. On May 19,
1883, the instruments of ratification were exchanged at the
Korean capital.

With the coming into force of the Chemulpo Treaty, Korean
history entered a new era. After the United States other Western

[28] See Li's refutation of charges made by *Tao-t'ai* Shao of Shanghai in
Li's Communications, Ch. 15, pp. 19a–20a.

[29] The text of this undated communication from "Chao and Chin" [Cho
Yŏng-ha and Kim Hong-jip] and received by Young sometime before October 2, 1882 appears in Tyler Dennett, "American Choices in the Far East in
1882," *American Historical Review*, XXX (1924), 92, n. 16.

nations followed suit. Introduction of multiple foreign influences made the already bitter partisan strife within Korea more somber and complex. Korea took a few halting steps toward modernization without much success. Overshadowing such internal developments loomed an international power struggle that left its marks on the peninsula. As Tyler Dennett states with a touch of dramatics, the Chemulpo Treaty "set Korea adrift on an ocean of intrigue which it was quite helpless to control." [30]

Shufeldt's diplomatic endeavor attracted close attention from other nations interested in Korea. Japan was not particularly pleased to see the Chinese intercession open the way for a Korean-American treaty. Tokyo's reaction to the Shufeldt treaty was a matter of some concern for Washington, and conflicting estimates were given by American diplomatic agents.[31] It is possible that the entry of the United States into the Korean scene as a potential rival especially in commerce might have given the Japanese a cause for anxious watchfulness. On the other hand, Shufeldt's steadfast rejection of Chinese suzerainty over Korea was a vicarious victory for Japan which had for some years championed the cause of Korean independence. On the whole, it appears safe to say that Japan did not view the Shufeldt treaty with resentment. Some Western diplomats in China, on the other hand, showed more utilitarian interests in Shufeldt's negotiations. Britain, France, and Germany hastened to negotiate with Ma Chien-chung, and within less than a month and a half, Korea made treaties with these leading Western nations.

Diplomatically speaking, Korea had now emerged from her

[30] Dennett, *Americans in Eastern Asia*, pp. 461–462.

[31] The American minister in Peking, John R. Young, suspected that Japanese "susceptibilities had been wounded by the American Convention with Corea." But the Japanese foreign minister, Inoue Kaoru, assured the American minister in Tokyo, John A. Bingham, that Japan viewed the ratification by the United States of the Chemulpo Treaty with great satisfaction. Shufeldt thought that Japan would have liked to manipulate his negotiation in such a way that Japan would receive the credit for the treaty. For details on these three views, see Payson J. Treat, *Diplomatic Relations Between the United States and Japan, 1853–1895*, 2 vols. (Stanford: Stanford University Press, 1932), II, 163, 176; Dennett, *Americans in Eastern Asia*, pp. 467–468.

seclusion. Though the changes signified by these treaties were profound, the ending of the stage-by-stage, drawn-out process of opening was almost anticlimactic. The negotiation sessions at Chemulpo were, on the whole, devoid of substantive issues. Examination of the available sources indicate that the Korean delegates, Sin Hŏn, Cho Yŏng-ha, and Kim Hong-jip, played no vital role. Instead, the Koreans merely confirmed what had already been decided between the Western plenipotentiaries and Li Hung-chang and Ma Chien-chung. At the time of the 1876 Kanghwa Treaty with Japan, the Korean government acted more freely on its own. Ironic as it may seem, Korea's entry into the modern world community of sovereign nations was an occasion that signified and, as the later developments were to testify, heralded increasing foreign (Chinese) enroachment upon Korea's self-government. An explicit statement of the Chinese policy in this regard was contained in a communication that Ma Chien-chung addressed to the Korean king. He cautioned the king to conclude treaties with foreign powers in the future only after applying to Li Hung-chang for "a [Chinese] agent to manage the treaty affairs." [32]

In negotiations for treaties between Korea and the Western nations other than the United States, Li granted the Koreans freedom to decide on their own concerning any reduction in Korea's tariff rates. His primary concern was the recognition of China's suzerain claims over Korea, and not the question of trade and commerce. Certainly Britain, for one, had no intention of rejecting China's claim of suzerainty over Korea. On the contrary, one can well agree with Dennett that Great Britain desired to have Korea remain under the shadow of China so that British interests would find a measure of protection against the southward movement of Russia.[33] In later years, Great Britain betrayed her willingness to recognize Chinese suzerainty in such studied actions as assignment of a consul-general, subordinate to the British minister in Peking, to serve as the British representative in Korea, or by conducting negotiations in 1885 and thereafter

[32] Griffis, *Corea, the Hermit Nation*, pp. 149–150.
[33] Dennett, *Americans in Eastern Asia*, pp. 472–473.

primarily with the *Chinese* government concerning forceful occupation and use of a *Korean* island group by the British navy.[34]

By 1893 Korea had concluded treaties with the United States, Great Britain, Italy, Russia, Germany, France, and Austria. With the exception of the Austrian treaty, the others were all accompanied by the dependency statement issued in the name of the Korean king and addressed to the appropriate chief of state of the Western nation concerned. The Austrian negotiator objected to such a statement; the compromise took the form of a similar statement issued by the Korean government, instead of the king, and addressed to the Austrian government.[35]

In summary, the first treaties Korea made with the nations of the West were "unequal" and were similar to those Japan and China had made by 1860 or thereabouts and provided for the following: (1) establishment of diplomatic and trade relationships; (2) establishment of treaty ports and foreign settlements therein; (3) extraterritorial rights; (4) treaty tariff system; and (5) most-favored-nation clause. However, there were certain peculiarities attending the Korean treaties. First, the initial and primary impetus for Korea's opening came from two Asian neighbors of Korea — Japan and China. The events leading to the signing of the Shufeldt treaty already showed that these two nations helped open Korea for reasons that were antithetical to each other. Japan represented the force of change and innovation, while Chinese influence was on the side of maintaining the status quo. For a little over a decade following the Shufeldt treaty, the two conflicting forces were in competition, thus adding a new dimension to the endemic factional strife within Korea. Second, Korea's opening was not immediately attributable to any suc-

[34] Harold J. Noble, "The United States and Sino-Korean Relations, 1885–87," *Pacific Historical Review*, II (1933), 295–296. Noble contrasts the rank of the British representative in Korea with that of other nations. The German consul reported directly to Berlin; France stationed a commissioner. Japan, Russia and the United States maintained legations in Seoul.

[35] Yüan Shih-k'ai, Chinese Resident in Korea in 1885–94 suspected that the Koreans themselves persuaded the Austrian envoy to advance this proposal, see *Li's Communications*, Ch. 20, pp. 28a–29a; *Li's Telegrams*, Ch. 14, pp. 7b–8a.

cessful Western military exploit as was the case with China or Japan. And yet it was not the result of a voluntary decision made by sufficiently powerful and enlightened Koreans. Consequently, there was neither an overwhelming shock nor adequate self-generated awareness that would have impelled the Koreans to adopt measures of modernization. Third, as has been stated earlier, the treaties did not settle the legal status of Korea to the satisfaction of the parties concerned. Japan and the United States were foremost in upholding Korean independence, while China and, to a lesser extent, Great Britain acted on the assumption that the traditional suzerain-dependency tie between China and Korea had not been altered in any way.[36] Caught between the two mutually exclusive influences, Korea's position was fraught with danger and temptation. International rivalry over the ambivalent status of Korea invited China's vigorous assertion of actual as well as nominal suzerain control over the peninsula.

[36] For further discussion see Nelson, chap. VIII, particularly pp. 149–151, 161–163. Nelson's theme is that the West — primarily the United States — ignored the real position Korea occupied in the "Far Eastern order," while China's lack of knowledge of the Western system helped create this confusion. On the other hand, Treat writes, on the basis of the official American interpretation, that, "when treaties with the United States, Great Britain and Germany soon followed, all with Li Hung-chang's active approval, it is evident that China lost *any right* which she might have claimed to interfere in the affairs of Korea" (italics in the original). See Paysen J. Treat, "China and Korea, 1885–1894," *Political Science Quarterly*, XLIX (1934), 512.

3.

Political Disturbances
After the Opening

Within a few months after the conclusion of the Shufeldt treaty, an incident erupted in Korea that highlighted the peculiar nature of the treaties Korea had concluded — the Soldiers' Mutiny of the Year of Im-o, or 1882. A group of soldiers mutinied in Seoul and attacked high-ranking Min officials and the Japanese on July 23. In a matter of a few days, the Min regime was overthrown and the *Taewŏn'gun* made a sudden comeback from his forced semiretirement. This incident symbolized the life-and-death struggle between two political factions, the one headed by the queen and the other by her father-in-law. The mutiny was not, however, confined to the domestic political arena. It invited armed interventions from China and Japan and showed Korea's complete impotence in the face of outside force.

The immediate causes for the mutiny were corruption and graft in the higher echelons of the military establishment. According to one estimate, there were nearly ten thousand soldiers in the Seoul area in 1882.[1] Beginning in February 1882, they were organized into two guards each headed by a general of the first rank. In addition to the regular guards, there was a "Special Skill Force" of about three hundred men that had been undergoing, since 1881, modern training under a Japanese army lieutenant. The Special Skill Force was separated from the regular hierarchy of

[1] Tabohashi Kiyoshi, *Kindai Nissen Kankei no Kenkyū* [A Study of the Japanese-Korean Relationship in Recent Times] 2 vols. (Keijo, 1940), I, 770–771.

military command and received special care and favor from the
Korean king who intended that it should grow into the nucleus of
a modern army. Toward this elite corps, the soldiers in the regular
guards, who were poorly fed and clothed, felt envy and hostility.[2]
Discrimination was salt poured into the open wound of discontent
which these mistreated soldiers had long felt toward their government. A relatively minor incident in early July 1882 — riotous
behavior by a few soldiers against an official in charge of distrib-
uting rice rations — quickly led to a large-scale mutiny. On
July 23 the angry mutineers raided the home of the president of
the Board of War — a prominent member of the Min faction.
Homes of several other high officials were similarly looted and
razed. The wrath of the soldiers was also directed against the Special Skill Force, whose barracks were destroyed, and the Japanese
drill master, who met an untimely death at the hands of the rioters.
As evening approached, the mutineers staged a mass attack
against the Japanese legation in a seemingly spontaneous outburst
of pent-up animosity against the foreigners.[3]

Although Japanese Minister Hanabusa had been warned of
such an eventuality earlier in the day by a high Korean official,
no effective defense was prepared against angry mob assault.
Hanabusa appealed for Korean assistance, but none was forthcoming. Hanabusa was forced to lead 28 Japanese, including
about a dozen armed police guards, out of the riot-torn capital.
Marching through the night they reached Inch'ŏn (Chemulpo)
on the afternoon of July 24. The prefect of Inch'ŏn first gave
a hospitable reception to the small group of exhausted Japanese.
During the night, however, Hanabusa's group was attacked by
the Korean soldiers of Inch'ŏn garrison. Hanabusa was now convinced that the disturbance was not a simple riot of a few mutineers in Seoul but a political coup aimed at overthrowing the
Min regime, which implied a possible return to the policy of national seclusion. The situation appeared extremely serious and
Hanabusa decided to return to Japan. The Japanese refugees
seized a small Korean junk and set out to sea.[4]

[2] *Ibid.*; *NGB*, XV, 153.
[3] Tabohashi, I, 773.
[4] See Hanabusa's own account of the "riot in Seoul" in *NGB*, XV, 217–

In Seoul, the second day of mutiny witnessed the transformation of the riot into a political revolution. A group of the rioters was received by the *Taewŏn'gun*, who reportedly exhorted them to bring down the Min regime and expel the Japanese.[5] Perhaps emboldened by the interview with the ex-regent, the mob surged into the royal palace where two high officials, including the president of the Board of War, were hacked to death in the very presence of the king. In search of the queen, the rioters roamed vainly through the innermost sanctuary of the palace.[6] Meanwhile a reign of terror descended upon the entire city; Yi Ch'ae-ŭng, the prime minister and a brother of the *Taewŏn'gun*, was murdered for his "crime" of collaboration with the Min faction.

The king, whose own life was in no way safe, was at last compelled to ask his father to come to the palace; and the appearance of the *Taewŏn'gun*, escorted by two hundred mutineers, put an immediate end to the wild melee. Thereupon, the king entrusted to the ex-regent "all the small and large matters of the government," and the ex-regent instituted counterreforms. He nullified the unpopular changes in the military establishment, abolished recently created offices such as the *T'ongni Amun*, and replaced Min officials with the followers of the ex-regent, including the appointment of his eldest son to command an army guard in Seoul. At the same time, the court announced the passing of the queen, and nationwide preparations for a funeral were undertaken — a funeral for the queen who was very much alive at a hideout in a small village in Ch'ungch'ŏng province.[7]

The news of the mutiny in Seoul did not reach the outside world until the harassed Japanese minister arrived at Nagasaki on July 29 aboard the British surveying ship, the *Flying Fish*, that

221. He listed 18 Japanese casualties: four dead, nine missing (later, confirmed to have been killed), and five wounded.

[5] Tabohashi, I, 773.

[6] The queen slipped out of the palace disguised as a commoner and made her way to safety, carried on the back of a faithful palace guard who was later promoted to a generalship.

[7] Professor Yi Sŏn-gŭn suggests that the announcement of the queen's death might have been a deliberate attempt to calm the fiercely anti-queen rioters. See Yi Sŏn-gŭn, *Chosŏn Ch'oegŭn Chŏngch'isa* [Political History of Korea in Modern Times] (Seoul, 1950), pp. 55–60.

had rescued the Japanese party in the open sea off Inch'ŏn. In Tokyo a cabinet meeting was held. Some advocated a hard line of action that might lead to a punitive expedition. However, advocates of a more moderate approach, including the foreign minister, Inoue Kaoru, prevailed. A small military force was to be sent to Korea, but only for the purpose of affording protection to the Japanese envoy and other Japanese nationals. Inoue took pains to disavow any aggressive intent on the part of Japan in his notes of August 3 sent to the Western and Chinese envoys in Tokyo. Soon afterward he traveled to Shimonoseki to confer with and give instructions to Hanabusa. Hanabusa was to return to Seoul with a military escort consisting of four men-of-war and one infantry battalion to negotiate a diplomatic settlement.

The Japanese demands called for an official apology, indemnities, punishment of the anti-Japanese assailants, and the right to station Japanese troops in Seoul as legation guards. Japan also considered (but did not insist on) demanding the cession of either Kŏje island near Masan or Ullŭng Island (Dagelet Island) in the Sea of Japan some 80 miles southeast of Korea. In making these demands, Hanabusa was not to take any forceful action but "to retreat to Inch'ŏn and await further instructions." [8] On August 12, Hanabusa landed at Inch'ŏn and, despite protests from the *Taewŏn'gun* government, led the Japanese troops into Seoul on the 16th.[9] This was the first time since the mid-seventeenth century that foreign troops entered the Korean capital.

Dispatch of the Japanese force to Korea elicited a similar response from China. An imperial edict of August 8 authorized the sending of Chinese naval and land forces to Korea. The Chinese forces were to restore peace in Korea, the edict declared, as further evidence of China's "benevolence" toward a dependent nation. The presence of the Chinese forces would also serve to restrain the Japanese from carrying out any imperialistic schemes

[8] *NGB*, XV, 226–229; Tabohashi, I, 790–798.

[9] Hanabusa was encouraged to carry out his original plan of introducing the Japanese soldiers into the Korean capital by Cho Yŏng-ha of the Min faction. Cho had been known as an advocate of friendly relations between Japan and Korea as far back as 1874. See *NGB*, XV, 204; Tabohashi, I, 803–804.

against Korea.[10] (Kim Yun-sik, the officer in charge of students, and Ŏ Yun-jung, an official who had been sent to Tientsin to draw up a Sino-Korean trade convention, blamed the *Taewŏn'gun* faction for the mutiny and expressed their fear that Japan might seize the opportunity to interfere in the internal affairs of Korea.)[11]

The Chinese minister in Tokyo notified the Japanese government of China's decision and justified the troop movement as an effort to mediate between Japan and Korea. The Japanese politely refused to recognize the need for Chinese troops in Korea, but the Chinese troops did arrive in Seoul. Furthermore, when Hanabusa presented the Japanese demands to the Korean king, he was incensed to learn that the Korean prime minister, who was appointed as a plenipotentiary, could not attend to matters of diplomacy because of his preoccupation with responsibility for the queen's funeral. Ma Chien-chung, Li's agent in Korea, counseled Hanabusa not to rupture relationships between Japan and Korea and to be more patient. Ma, acting largely on his own, also sought the forcible removal of the antiforeign *Taewŏn'gun*.

The father of the Korean king must have appeared *persona non grata* to the Chinese on at least three counts. First, he attempted to overthrow the rule of the Min faction that had been faithfully following the Chinese guidelines on matters of foreign relations. Second, he created a situation which invited the Japanese troops to Korea, thus precipitating the danger of a military conflict between Japan on the one hand and Korea and China on the other. Maintenance of China's traditional suzerain rights over Korea without risking a war with Japan had been the objective of the long and arduous efforts of Li Hung-chang for the opening of Korea to the West. The mutiny, coming so soon after the signing of the first treaties with the Western nations, threatened to ˙ undo much of Li's own diplomatic achievements. Third, the *Taewŏn-gun*-inspired disturbance threatened the foundation of a lawfully constituted government in a dependent nation. The third point appears to be the most formal and the least genuine reason

[10] For the text of the imperial edict see *Ch'ing-chi wai-chiao shih-liao*, Ch. 28, pp. 12b–13a.

[11] Tabohashi, I, 831–832.

for the decision to proceed against the *Taewŏn'gun*. It was this "formal" charge that Ma decided to use against the Korean regent. After judiciously waylaying the regent's bodyguards, Ma arrested and charged the *Taewŏn'gun* with disrespect to the emperor of China in usurping the power which the emperor had invested in the king of Korea. Because he was the father of the king, however, he would be leniently dealt with. One hundred picked Chinese soldiers under the personal command of Admiral Ting escorted the Korean captive to a waiting Chinese warship, and hence to Tientsin.[12]

The removal of the *Taewŏn'gun* had an immediate salutary effect on the suspended negotiations between Japan and Korea. Following the appointment of new Korean representatives who favored the opening of their country, a treaty was readily agreed upon.

According to this treaty, Korea was to pay an indemnity fixed at 500,000 yen — a heavy burden for the Korean treasury. Article V permitted Japan to station "some" soldiers as legation guards and Korea undertook the responsibility for the maintenance of their barracks. There was a vague promise of withdrawal of the armed guards "if the Japanese minister regards them unnecessary." The last article bound Korea to send a special envoy to Japan to express apologies. Also signed on this date were two amendments to the existing treaty of commerce and navigation providing for (1) extension of the "free walk" areas and the opening of Yanghwajin, a river port only a few miles southwest of Seoul, and (2) complete freedom of movement for Japanese officials in the interior of Korea. Besides these written agreements,

---

[12] *Ibid.*, 846–848. According to a Japanese source, the *Taewŏn-gun* managed to send a letter, before his departure for China, to his eldest son, Yi Chae-myŏn. In the letter, he implied that the journey to China was being undertaken on his own volition and spoke hopefully of his return "within ten or so days." He also vented his hostility against Japan and the Western nations but cautioned his son to be quiescent for the time being. For the text of this letter see *NGB*, XV, 281. The Chinese military authorities in Korea posted a public notice in Seoul announcing that the ex-regent had been ordered to China by the emperor to account for the recent disturbance. It assured the Koreans the punishment would not be severe. See *ibid.*, p. 425.

the Koreans agreed to destroy the stone monuments with anti-foreign slogans which the *Taewŏn'gun* had erected throughout the country soon after the French invasion of Kanghwa in 1866.[13]

While diplomatic negotiations proceeded at Inch'ŏn, the Chinese military authorities made surprise raids on houses in the eastern sector of the capital city and arrested over 170 persons. Ten of them were summarily executed and the rest were turned over to the Korean authorities for investigation and punishment.[14] This vigorous Chinese intervention without any pretense of subterfuge and carried out in the name of assistance rendered for the benefit of a dependent nation went significantly unchallenged by Japan. As for the Korean government, two high officials were dispatched to Peking to "thank" the Chinese throne.

A plea of clemency for the *Taewŏn'gun* was dutifully submitted by the Korean representative, but the Min faction was unequivocal in pointing the finger of accusation at the ex-regent as the true culprit in the July mutiny.[15] In spite of vigorous and persistent denials of involvement by the prisoner, the Chinese authorities became convinced of his complicity and determined that he was to be detained at Paoting for the rest of his life and be denied contact with the outside.[16]

The detention of the Korean ex-regent in China for an indefi-

[13] *NGB*, XV, 200–202. Professor Hilary Conroy suggests that these terms are comparable to those exacted from Japan by the Western nations after the Heusken murder, the Namamugi incident or the punitive expeditions to western Japan undertaken by the four Western powers. Hilary Conroy, *The Japanese Seizure of Korea: 1868–1910 — A Study of Realism and Idealism in International Relations* (Philadelphia: University of Pennsylvania Press, 1960), pp. 106–107.

[14] *Li's Memorials*, Ch. 44, pp. 6a–6b; Tabohashi, I, 851–852.

[15] One of the two Korean emissaries reportedly told Li that the plea for clemency was motivated by the "personal feelings" of the king. It seems probable that the queen and the Mins acquiesced in the royal wish in order to maintain Confucian respectability. A report prepared by the *Tao-t'ai* of Tientsin for Li concluded that the mutiny was started by the discontented soldiers but that the *Taewŏn'gun* utilized the upheaval for his own political comeback. See *Li's Memorials*, Ch. 44, pp. 15a–15b, 11b–12a.

[16] *Ibid.*, p. 13b. The details of the regulations governing the treatment of the *Taewŏn'gun* at Paoting appear in an unspecified document reproduced in *NGB*, XV, 280.

nite period of time sealed the fate of his followers in Korea — at least for the time being. The government in Seoul was once again in the hands of the Mins and their collaborators. In order to recapture the ground temporarily lost during the turmoil, decrees were issued in the name of the king promising rectification of "past mistakes" and granting a general amnesty for the rank-and-file participants in the mutiny. One of the decrees emphasized, in a didactic tone, the need to learn Western technology for the purpose of strengthening the national defense. The religion of the West, however, was still branded as being "wicked." [17]

So ended in failure the mutiny against the policy of opening and also against the ruling Min faction. The manner in which the status quo was restored set a portentous precedent for foreign armed intervention in Korea. Two hundred Japanese soldiers that had come as Hanabusa's escort remained in Seoul as legation guards. More impressive was the strength of the Chinese forces under General Wu Ch'ang-ch'ing that stayed on in Korea in order to keep the Japanese influence in check.[18]

Later in the year 1882, Li Hung-chang, ostensibly acting on a Korean request, sent the former German consul at Tientsin, Paul Georg von Moellendorff, to advise the Korean king on foreign affairs.[19] Chinese officers were also sent to reorganize and train the Korean troops when the Japanese-trained Special Skill Force was disbanded, at Korea's request. China also supplied modern

[17] The royal decrees, issued in September 1882, were drafted by Kim Yun-sik. The "past mistakes" included extravagant public works projects, changes in coinage, abolition of Confucian temples and *sŏwŏn* etc., thus putting the blame on the *Taewŏn'gun* under whose regency in the years prior to 1874 most of these "mistakes" had been committed. For the texts of the decrees see Kim Yun-sik, Kwŏn 9, pp. 31*b*–32*b*.

[18] Li stated in his memorial of November 15, 1882, that the purpose of the Chinese forces in Korea was to restrain Japan; see *Li's Memorials*, Ch. 45, p. 11*a*. Two years later Li added another justification for the Chinese troops in Korea, namely to prevent the Koreans from acquiring "extraordinary," in other words revolutionary, inclinations under the Japanese influence. See *Li's Communications*, Ch. 16, p. 10*a*.

[19] The text of a written communication from the Korean king to Li dated October 28, 1882, requesting the dispatch of an adviser on foreign affairs, appears in *Li's Memorials*, Ch. 45, p. 15*a*. However, the Korean request might have been solicited by the Chinese.

weapons to the army. Three thousand Chinese soldiers plus two thousand Korean soldiers under Chinese control assured a near-complete military control over Korea.

The terms of a new Sino-Korean trade agreement signed shortly after the mutiny gave further evidence of China's determination to assert her suzerain status with renewed vigor. It is doubtful that such drastic measures would have been undertaken without the opportunity afforded by the mutiny of 1882. Such developments must have been contrary to the original intentions of the chauvinistic *Taewŏn'gun* or his followers. Herein lay the irony — a tragic irony — that demonstrated, above all, the hopeless state of affairs in Korea and its inability as a nation to sail under its own steam in the troubled and strange waters of international politics. It was against this background that a group of young reformers entered the political scene.

During the years from 1882 to 1884, a small number of young officials in the government gradually united in their desire for national independence and domestic reform. They came to be known as the "party of independence" (*Tongnip Tang*) or as the "party of civilization" (*Kaehwa Tang*). Because of their pro-Japanese leaning, they were also called the "Japan party" (*Ch'inil Tang*). In terms of the political program they advocated, however, we shall refer to them as the "Progressives."

The leaders of the Progressive party came from respectable, *yangban* families which, however, lacked political power or wealth in the 1880s. By far the most active of these leaders was Kim Ok-kyun, who was in the ten-man study group the Korean government had sent to Japan in 1881.[20] After a brief return to Korea in 1882, Kim went back to Japan with the Korean mission of apology that was headed by Pak Yŏng-hyo and Sŏ Kwang-pŏm. Officially Kim's second sojourn in Japan was for the purpose of study and observation; actually his time was spent in negotiating a Japanese loan and in establishing close contact with Japa-

[20] See the background information on the Coup of 1884 written by George C. Foulk, the United States naval attaché in Seoul, which was enclosed with Minister Foote's dispatch dated December 17, 1884, to the secretary of state in McCune and Harrison, I, 103. This highly valuable report shall be hereafter referred to as "Foulk's Report on the Coup."

nese liberals, especially with Fukuzawa Yukichi. In December 1882, Kim helped Pak Yŏng-hyo obtain a 170,000 yen loan from the Japanese government. Fifty thousand yen of the borrowed fund was used to pay the first installment on Korea's indemnity obligation to Japan; the remainder, apparently, was appropriated by Pak and Kim for their own use, in part to defray the expenditures during their sojourn in Japan.

Kim endeavored to raise a larger additional loan from either a Japanese source or through a Western firm in Japan in return for certain economic concessions in Korea. He allegedly asked for three million yen, a staggering sum in those days, without having been properly authorized by his government to contract a foreign loan. How he intended to use the money if obtained is not very clear, although he must have been painfully aware of the need for such funds to launch any reform project, such as sending students abroad for study or even seeking converts among high government officials to the cause of reform.[21] Kim had better success in his attempt to cultivate the friendship of Fukuzawa Yukichi and his followers. In the early 1880s, especially after the July mutiny in Korea, the "liberals" in Japan took a keen interest in the Korean situation and urged a more clear-cut policy of support for Korean independence — independence unencumbered by Chinese control — upon the less enthusiastic government of Tokyo. What motivated these friends of Korea is explained by Professor Conroy in these words: "Japanese liberals involved themselves in the Korean problem partly out of sympathy for the nascent progressive movement in Korea and its Korean leaders and partly in the hope that by contributing to it they would contribute to the achievement of liberal goals in Japan."[22] Through his contact with Fukuzawa, the youthful Korean eagerly imbibed the heady wine of nationalism and liberal reformism. Kim Ok-kyun was made aware of the incompatibility of Korea's sovereign independence with the suzerain control that

[21] See Conroy, p. 139; Tabohashi, I, 911–914.

[22] Conroy, p. 133. Professor Conroy's study is based on an extensive examination of Japanese materials and skilfully dissects various strands of liberalism in Japan at this time. It differentiates the Keiō school group led by Fukuzawa from the Liberal party followers of Itagaki Taisuke or Gotō Shimpei. See *ibid.*, pp. 127 ff.

China asserted; Korea had to liberate itself from the Chinese shackles. This required the overthrow of the Min faction in the Korean government that took orders from the Chinese.[23] At the same time, Kim realized that the viability of Korean independence in the modern world was predicated upon a thorough overhaul of the old regime, and the development of modern Japan undoubtedly inspired him. The antiquated government structure would have to be built up, economic resources would have to be developed with the use of modern technology, and the educational system should be oriented to the study of Western teachings. In short, there must be reforms in every aspect of national life.

As the first step, Kim arranged for a group of 40-odd Korean students to study in Japan and also for a smaller group of Japanese to go to Korea to help introduce reforms. The Koreans arrived in Japan in July 1883 and enrolled at various technical schools. It was one of the Japanese who traveled to Korea under this arrangement, Inoue Kakugorō, who published the first newspaper in Korea, with the help of Kim Yun-sik who was then vice-president of the Foreign Office.

The official policy in Tokyo in 1882–83, however, remained noninterventionist. Takezoe Shinichirō, who was reputed to be popular in Chinese official circles, replaced Hanabusa as the Japanese representative in Korea, and the Japanese troops in Seoul were reduced early in 1883. In October 1882, Iwakura Tomomi, the most influential figure in the government, declared it unwise to cause a war with China over "insignificant" Korea.[24] To the Japanese government, the most pressing diplomatic issue was to obtain revisions of the "unequal" treaties with the Western nations. Therefore, any sign of rash bellicosity that might possibly prejudice the "respectability" of Japan in the eyes of the West was anathema. It would be erroneous, however, to conclude from this that Japan had decided to wash its hands of Korea altogether.

[23] Professor Tabohashi suggests that the real motive for the Progressive movement was ambition for power, pure and simple. This is plausible, but the question of motives remains a moot issue. See Tabohashi, I, 900.

[24] The text of Iwakura's memorandum on the Korean question, dated October 6, 1882, and addressed to Prime Minister Sanjō Sanetomi appears in *NGB*, XV, 253–254.

Ever since 1876 it had been the established policy of Japan to treat Korea as an independent nation. Moreover, in the final analysis, Korea was geographically and traditionally too close to Japan to be disregarded. These two conflicting considerations produced a compromise formula which, like so many compromises, was somewhat ambivalent and paradoxical. Briefly stated, the new guideline was to assist Korean independence and reform while maintaining friendly relations with China;[25] it was a policy that was easier stated than carried out.

When Kim Ok-kyun returned to Seoul in April 1884, he found a growing anti-Chinese sentiment coupled with rising interest in modern innovations. The billeting of Chinese troops near the royal palace, the policing of the capital by Chinese soldiers, and the overbearing aggressiveness of Chinese officials in Korea — all drew varying degrees of resentment. The military reverses China was suffering at the hands of the French in Indochina were regarded by the Koreans as the cause for withdrawal of half the Chinese troops from Korea in February 1884, and this apparent weakness of China made some anti-Chinese Koreans all the more restive and aggrieved at the continual Chinese domination.

There were other auspicious signs for the Progressives. In the course of 1883–84, Korea's contacts with the United States quickly increased and the king displayed much enthusiasm for strengthening American-Korean ties. In October 1883 he requested the services of an American adviser on foreign affairs and an American military instructor.[26] At this time, the first diplomatic mission from Korea was touring the United States, headed by Min Yŏng-ik, a nephew of the queen and one of the most powerful Min officials.

The return of the Korean mission from America gave a new stimulus to modernization and reform. The influential Min Yŏng-ik spoke of his intention "to use his utmost energy toward the development of his country." One of the immediate tangible results of the tour was the establishment of the so-called American

25 Tabohashi, I, 906–907.

26 The American government showed little interest in this request. See Foote to secretary of state, October 19, 1883, in McCune and Harrison, I, 53–54.

Farm in Korea on a large tract of land granted by the government and managed by a member of the diplomatic mission who had brought back seeds from America.[27] Ensign George C. Foulk, newly appointed as the American naval attaché in Seoul, received frequent requests for aid and advice from the king and the Progressive party leaders on a wide range of questions, including the hiring of agricultural directors, school teachers, and other foreigners.[28] While these moves were afoot, the Chinese drill instructors were removed and Moellendorff, the German adviser, who had come to Korea as a Chinese agent left the Korean foreign office, presumably to make room for the Americans who were expected to arrive.

It is important here to note again the position which the king occupied at this time. He was 32 years old in 1884 and showed a deep interest in things that were "new and strange." Theoretically, he was an absolute monarch whose fiat was the law of the nation. Since the 1882 mutiny, however, his prerogatives as ruler had been subject to restraints, sometimes crippling, that emanated from the Chinese authorities and also from the powerful Min faction. During the summer months of 1883, for instance, the king came out on the losing end in the controversy over public finance. The Chinese general Wu had proposed the issuance of a new debased coin and won the support of Min Yŏng-ik and Moellendorff. Kim Ok-kyun opposed the devaluation plan and proposed borrowing foreign funds. The king threw his support to Kim. The Wu-Min-Moellendorff plan prevailed and the new coin with lower metallic content poured out in early fall, causing inflation. The issue here is not the merit of the fiscal policy itself; the episode illustrated the relative impotence of the king despite his theoretical omnipotence. Under the circumstances, it would not have been surprising if the king developed hostility, or at least annoyance, toward the Chinese-Min coalition. This was

[27] Quotation and facts based on "Foulk's Report on the Coup," McCune and Harrison, I, 106–107.

[28] *Ibid.*, pp. 108–109. Foulk as well as Minister Foote were under orders not to give anything other than "personal suggestions" in matters affecting the internal development of Korea. See Frelinghuysen to Foote, September 18, 1883, in *ibid.*, p. 31.

probably the reason why, as Foulk observed with a touch of sarcasm, "all the work of the three progressive leaders was warmly aided by the King, who had ample opportunities of time at least for encouraging it, the actual machinery of his internal government being worked entirely by the Mins, and in which he had little or no power to act." [29]

The political situation in Korea in the summer of 1884 was thus characterized by a division between the Mins and the Progressives. Chinese support was behind the Mins, while the less-well-entrenched Progressives had the sympathy of the king, the collaboration of the Fukuzawa group, and the interested concern of the Japanese government on their side.

Near the end of October 1884, the two groups reached a point of irrevocable rupture in their relations. Foulk became convinced that "a crisis was near at hand and one which would probably result in bloodshedding and violence." [30] Just at this time, the Japanese Minister Takezoe returned from leave in Japan and, in his meeting with Kim Ok-kyun, alluded to the possibility of more active Japanese support for the Progressives. Fearing that the news of such a shift in Japan's policy would expose them to a full-scale purge by the Mins, the Progressives proposed to strike first, with Japanese assistance.[31] Inoue Kakugorō served as the liaison agent through whom Japanese volunteers and weapons were obtained. On November 25, Kim secured Takezoe's commitment for the use of Japanese legation guards in support of the coup. Thus, the stage was set for one of the most crucial events in the politics of the powers surrounding the peninsular kingdom.

Accusations have been made that the Chōshū clan, which was numerically in the minority within the Japanese oligarchy, deliberately provoked a disturbance in Korea in order to bolster its own political position within Japan. According to Fukuzawa

[29] "Foulk's Report on the Coup," McCune and Harrison, I, 106.

[30] *Ibid.*, p. 111.

[31] "Kim Ok-kyun's Dairy" appears in Itō Hirobumi (ed.) *Chōsen Kōshō Shiryō* (Materials on Negotiations with Korea), 3 vols. (Tokyo, 1936), I, 430–467. This was not a "diary" but a spiteful memo prepared by Kim after he settled down in Japan as a political refugee; it was intended as an exposé of Inoue Kaoru's complicity in the coup written for Japanese readers. It, therefore, must be used with caution.

Yukichi, Itō Hirobumi, counselor of state and future prime minister, and Inoue Kaoru, the foreign minister in 1884, instructed Takezoe, "a crazed and inept scholar," to incite the Korean Progressives. When the coup failed, the accusation continues, the two Chōshū statesmen took it upon themselves to negotiate the diplomatic settlement with Korea and China in order to cover up their complicity in the bloodshed.[32]

This charge, however, is directly at odds with the nonintervention policy to which the two statesmen subscribed as high members of the government. Moreover, as late as November 28, Itō instructed Takezoe to advise the Korean Progressives to use moderate methods.[33] The circumstances surrounding the accusation cast considerable doubt on its validity.[34]

Was Takezoe then personally responsible for abetting the Korean conspiracy? He spent the first ten months of 1884 in Japan, during which time he had conferences with Itō and Inoue Kaoru. Although there were some divergences in emphasis, the conferees reaffirmed the paradoxical policy of promoting Korean independence but "within the definite limits imposed by avoiding conflicts with China." "As for the Independence party, Takezoe could handle it in whatever way seemed best to him," since the Korean party was regarded as "a dubious factor, neither strong nor important." But a closer watch on these Koreans and their Japanese friends was to be maintained. The conferees were mindful of the recently uncovered conspiracy to start a revolution in Korea in which antigovernment Japanese liberals and even the French minister to Japan were involved.[35]

It would seem, then, that Takezoe was given a large degree of freedom in dealing with the Progressives, as long as he stayed within the bounds of the two basic objectives — promotion of Korean independence and avoidance of war with China. The first objective would be most logically implemented by assisting the Korean Progressives, the only native political force irrevocably

[32] "Fukuzawa Yukichi Memorandum," n.d., *Chōsen Kōshō Shiryō*, II, 59–62.

[33] *Ibid.*, I, 295.

[34] *Ibid.*, II, 51–57, 63–64; Conroy, p. 135.

[35] The quoted passages are taken from Conroy, pp. 143–144. Conroy bases his discussion on Tabohashi's work cited above.

in favor of independence from China. Implementation of the second objective would be influenced by Takezoe's estimate of what would provoke China to fight Japan.

In early 1884 the Chinese government was in a major political crisis; the unfavorable turn of the war with the French provided an opportunity for the anti-Prince Kung forces to oust the prince from Tsungli Yamen. His successor, Prince Shun, was relatively unknown and untried in the management of China's foreign policy. The Japanese foreign office was not unaware of this development. In view of the war burden and of the suspected new orientation in the Tsungli Yamen, it might have appeared to Takezoe that China would be less willing at this time than before to risk a war against Japan, even if Japan openly aided the anti-Chinese Progressives in Korea. Prior to October 1884, the Kim-Takezoe relationship had been anything but a cordial one.[36] At his meeting with Kim on October 31, however, Takezoe reportedly asked, "What will be your plans [that is, the plans of Kim's group] if a foreign power should give assistance for the reform of your country?"[37] When Kim and his friends asked Shimamura, Takezoe's chief aide, for armed assistance by Japanese troops, the Japanese official gave the enigmatic statement that "it would not be difficult . . . to expel the Chinese forces in Korea with the one company of Japanese legation guards."[38] Whether or not Takezoe or Shimamura were serious and meant what they seemed to have implied, these utterances were followed by a suddenly heightened revolutionary fervor among the Korean Progressives.

Within a fortnight following his return to Seoul, Takezoe seemingly became aware of and concerned about the looming specter of a coup. On November 12, he wrote a dispatch to Tokyo suggesting two alternative courses of Japanese policy in Korea. Plan

[36] "Kim's Diary," *Chōsen Kōshō Shiryō*, I, p. 917. Shimamura's contemptuous reference to Kim's "chronic ailment, namely impetuosity" in his dispatch to Tokyo as late as summer 1884 reflects the coolness of the treatment which the Japanese legation in Seoul gave Kim. See *NGB*, XVII, 382.

[37] "Kim's Diary," *Chōsen Kōshō Shiryō*, I, 434; Tabohashi, I, 928.

[38] See Shimamura's own account of his meeting with the Korean Progressives on November 4 in *Chōsen Kōshō Shiryō*, I, 272.

A called for open support of the "Japan party" and military actions to expel the Chinese forces from Korea. According to Plan *B*, Japan was to avoid a rupture of relations with China and "let things take their own natural course of development in Korea," while care should be taken to protect the Japan party from a major catastrophe. Even in case Plan *B* should be adopted, Takezoe proposed to "bite" at the China party from time to time in order to control its growth. He warned that if the China party should have its way unchecked, "the Japan party would be in mortal danger . . . and will surely resort to political assassination." [39] Itō favored the moderate Plan *B* and so instructed Takezoe on November 28; however, the instruction did not reach Takezoe until after the outbreak of the coup. [40]

To Summarize: (1) Although Itō Hirobumi and Inoue Kaoru did not deliberately aim to incite the coup, the ambiguous policy they adopted and relegated to Takezoe for implementation contributed greatly to the coup. (2) Takezoe's misjudgment and ineptitude directly involved him in the coup preparations from which he could not extricate himself; had it not been for his display of anti-Chinese bellicosity and his implied support for the Progressives, the fire of revolutionary enthusiasm might have remained under control. And (3) the Korean Progressives and the Fukuzawa liberals in Japan were ultimately and most immediately responsible for the coup.

The occasion chosen for the coup was a banquet on December 4, 1884, celebrating the opening of the first post office in Korea. Min Yŏng-ik was severely wounded by would-be assassins. Dynamite was exploded within the palace and shots were fired throughout the city to convince the king that he should seek Japanese protection. In deference to the wish of the queen, Kim also went through the motions of requesting help from the Chinese, but did not actually do so. The requested Japanese guard was supplied by Takezoe. The Mins and high government officials unfavorable to the coup were either murdered or denied access to the court.

[39] "Two Alternative Korean Policies" by Takezoe and addressed to Itō and Inoue Kaoru in *Chōsen Kōshō Shiryō*, I, 265–268.

[40] *Ibid.*, pp. 295–296.

On December 5 the coup leaders formally organized themselves into a new government, which interestingly included a
few *Taewŏn'gun* supporters. They hastily drafted and promulgated, in the name of the king, a series of reform decrees the
next day. Kim Ok-kyun was the chief architect of these decrees,
which called for a streamlining of government offices, a reform
in land taxes, and equal rights for all people. The most radical
changes of all, perhaps, were the cancellation of the grain seed
loans and the reforms in public finance, whereby a government
office — the Board of Revenues — was to have complete and exclusive control of governmental finance thus eliminating the self-
enriching practices of the royal household and powerful *yangban*
families.[41]

Meanwhile, preparations were afoot to unseat the Progressive
regime. At the suggestion of the Chinese, the anticoup Korean
officials submitted a formal request for Chinese aid. During the
afternoon of December 6, the Chinese General Wu sent a letter
to Minister Takezoe notifying the latter of his plan to move into
the palace "to protect the king and also to help defend your [the
Japanese] contingent." Wu disclaimed any hostile intention
against the Japanese.[42] Receiving no satisfactory response from
either Takezoe or the king, the Chinese troops of over one thousand men began to move into the royal palace by force. As the
Chinese soldiers marched through the palace gates, some Korean
guards switched sides and joined the Chinese columns. After a
brief but lively exchange of fire between the hopelessly outnum-
bered Japanese defenders and the Chinese attackers, the king
finally chose to go over and seek the protection of the Chinese.
Takezoe led his soldiers out of the palace grounds without further
incident, and Kim Ok-kyun and his Korean comrades went with
them.

By this time, the city teemed with anti-Japanese mob riots.
Japanese civilians were assaulted and even Western residents
feared for their lives. Takezoe and his soldiers retreated to
Inch'ŏn, leaving the burning legation building and many Japa-

[41] Tabohashi, I, 965–966. These reform decrees were annulled two days
after their promulgation.
[42] *Ibid.*, pp. 976–977.

nese civilians behind. The marriage of convenience between Takezoe and the Progressives was speedily dissolved, and the Progressive leaders barely managed to flee to Japan.[43]

The reconstituted government of the Min faction had the urgent problem of what to do about Takezoe. Some argued that his complicity in the coup was undeniable and that he should be held responsible for the armed clash on the palace grounds. Presumably the Chinese authorities in Korea supported this view. On the other hand, an amicable settlement with Takezoe was advocated by others including the king himself. The latter view was partly due to fear that the Japanese might attempt, with a larger military force, to avenge the humiliation of December 6. The divergence of views resulted in a strangely incongruous policy.

When Takezoe refused the Korean foreign office request of December 7 to return to Seoul, the Korean government decided upon direct negotiations with the Japanese government. On December 12, Sŏ Sang-u, vice-president of the Board of Rites, was delegated to go to Tokyo to demand, among other things, (1) the recall of Takezoe, (2) limitation of the number of Japanese legation guards to 50, and (3) extradition of the traitors, that is, the coup leaders who had fled to Japan.

The foreign office in Tokyo received the first news of the coup through the Chinese minister to Japan on December 11. The immediate reaction within the Japanese government was condemnation of Takezoe's precipitate actions that exceeded the authority entrusted to him. In the words of Itō Miyoji, a legal counselor and personal secretary to Itō Hirobumi, Takezoe's entry into the Korean palace was "against the treaty stipulations and also in defiance of the government order." It was "inexcusable." However, Itō Miyoji advised that the Japanese government had no alternative but to launch a diplomatic offensive by dispatching a special envoy with an impressive military escort to defend Takezoe's actions.[44] At the same time the Japanese foreign office hoped for a diplomatic settlement with China to avert any

[43] For further information on the developments during these three days, see *ibid.*, pp. 946–991. See also Yi Sŏn-gŭn, *Han'guksa* [Korean History], *Ch'oegŭnse P'yŏn* [Volume on Recent History] (Seoul, 1961), pp. 615–670.

[44] Tabohashi, I, 1015–1017.

unfortunate development arising from the armed clash in Seoul. The Chinese minister had voiced a similar wish.[45] In short, Japan decided to defend Takezoe vis-à-vis Korea while pursuing a policy of conciliation in dealing with China. The Tokyo government also ordered Takezoe to return to Seoul for fear that his absence from the Korean capital might further aggravate the tense situation.

The Chinese reaction to the Japanese moves was a cautious one. Li Hung-chang did not think Japan wanted a war at this time. Neither should China provoke hostilities with Japan. Li believed the way to check Japanese influence in Korea was by means of adroit diplomacy and not naked force.

Japan's special envoy to Korea was her foreign minister, Inoue Kaoru, who entered Seoul on January 2, 1885, escorted by two battalions of Japanese soldiers. Inoue ultimately became convinced that Takezoe was in fact guilty of having actively and improperly supported the coup.[46] As a way out of this dilemma, he chose not to discuss the question of Takezoe's responsibility. Instead, he confined himself to demanding satisfaction for the Korean mob violence against Japanese citizens and properties. Inoue communicated these one-sided conditions for negotiation to the Korean foreign office and hinted that Korea's refusal to accept Japan's demands would mean war. Five demands were presented to the Korean government: (1) a letter of apology from the Korean king, (2) payment of 110,000 yen to the families of Japanese victims, (3) punishment of those guilty of murder of a Japanese military attaché and of burning the Japanese legation building, (4) payment of 40,000 yen for a new legation building, and (5) payment for construction and maintenance of army barracks for one thousand Japanese soldiers.

Most of the Japanese demands were accepted, and the Protocol

[45] See the notes exchanged between Li and Yoshida on December 14, 1884, in *NGB*, XVII, 337–338.

[46] Tabohashi, I, 1019–1020. See Inoue's confidential instructions to Kondō, Japanese chargé in Seoul, dated January 31, 1885, in Kim Chŏngmyŏng (ed.), *Nikkan Gaikō Shiryō Shūsei* [Collection of Sources of Diplomatic Relations Between Japan and Korea], vol. 7 (Tokyo, 1963), pp. 328–331. Publication of this multivolume series started in 1962. It contains many documents that the *Nihon Gaikō Bunsho* series does not include.

of Seoul was signed on January 9, 1885.[47] The Korean government, which had made stinging denunciations of Takezoe immediately after the coup, yielded to the militant diplomacy of Inoue whose only concession to Korean sensitivity was to keep Takezoe, still the incumbent Japanese minister in Korea, completely out of these negotiations. Two days later, Inoue left Seoul, taking with him Takezoe and a battalion of his escort forces. Left behind in Korea was a new minister to replace the discredited Takezoe and one army battalion.

The Protocol of Seoul represented only a part of Japan's diplomatic objectives with regard to Korea. The armed clash in Seoul between Chinese and Japanese soldiers pointed to the necessity of a new understanding with China in order to avoid recurrence of similar incidents that might touch off a Sino-Japanese war. Jingoistic anti-Chinese sentiment within Japan was a cause of serious concern for the Japanese oligarchy and made it the more urgent that a political accord be reached with China.[48] On February 8, 1885, the Japanese cabinet decided to seek proper punishment of the Chinese commanders in Korea who were responsible for the Seoul incident and also to provide for mutual withdrawal of their troops from Korea. Itō Hirobumi was appointed an ambassador plenipotentiary to China; Japan hoped that the Chinese plenipotentiary would be Li Hung-chang.[49]

The impending Sino-Japanese negotiation threw the Korean

[47] For the text of the Protocol of Seoul, see *NGB*, XVIII, 348–349. A slight reduction in Korea's payment for the construction of a new Japanese legation building was the only substantive concession that Inoue accepted.

[48] In January 1885 there was a student demonstration in Tokyo favoring a warlike policy toward China. See Tabohashi, I, 1066–1067. An "imperial instruction" had to be issued to all prefectural governors throughout Japan to curb anti-Chinese political activities. See Conroy, pp. 169–170. A group of anti-oligarchy politicians in the "liberal" wing sent a memorandum to Itō Hirobumi advocating "intervention in Korea's internal affairs" and expressing their confidence that "our dozen or so warships and ten or twenty thousand soldiers will be more than enough to crush all of China's warships and soldiers" if war should break out due to Japan's more aggressive Korea policy. See *Chōsen Kōshō Shiryō*, II, 126–132.

[49] *NGB*, XVIII, 197. Itō was to be accompanied by General Saigō Tsugumichi, commander of the Formosan expedition of 1874. Saigō's appointment was a tactical move on the part of the oligarchy "to quiet the excitement on the part of the military men as well as the public." Quoted

court into a state of profound alarm. Unable to gauge the intentions of either Japan or China, the Koreans feared that a Sino-Japanese war might be fought on Korean soil. There were now 600 Japanese soldiers and nearly 2,000 Chinese soldiers stationed in the Seoul area. In early March 1885 the rumor of war gained so much currency in the Korean capital that some residents of Seoul sold their belongings and moved into the country. The Korean government, fearful that either Chinese or Japanese soldiers might, in a war, take the king under their custody, made a request to Sir Harry Parkes, the British minister to China, that British soldiers be sent to protect the king.[50] The Koreans could do little to influence the forthcoming conferences between the representatives of China and Japan.

The Japanese terms presented by Itō included: (1) withdrawal of both Chinese and Japanese troops from Korea, (2) punishment of the Chinese commanders responsible for the Seoul incident, (3) satisfaction for the Chinese attack on the Japanese residents in Seoul, and (4) effective measures to guarantee non-recurrence of a similar incident. Li Hung-chang, the Chinese plenipotentiary, vehemently defended the legality of the Chinese armed intervention in Korea; instead, he contended, the blame should rest with three individuals, the indecisive king, the seditious Kim Ok-kyun, and the impetuous Takezoe. Itō, on his part, defended Takezoe's action with equal vigor.[51]

Itō's obstinate insistence on forcing China to accept responsibility for the Seoul incident of the previous December at the risk of breaking up the negotiation went considerably beyond what his colleagues in Tokyo expected of him. Foreign minister Inoue had to cable Itō on April 9: "I fail to see why you should insist on the two points of punishment of [Chinese] commanders and of reparation. Try not to rupture the negotiation." [52] One suspects

from an English text telegram from Inoue Kaoru to Enomoto Takeaki, Japanese minister in Peking. See *ibid.*

[50] See the dispatches from Kondō Makuwa, Japanese chargé in Seoul, dated March 12, 1885, in *NGB*, XVIII, 206–210.

[51] For Li's version of the April 3 meeting, see *Li's Communications*, *Ch.* 16, pp. 18*a*–21*b*. For Itō's version, see *NGB*, XVIII, 229–237. The two accounts are substantially the same.

[52] *NGB*, XVIII, 262–263.

that Itō's unyielding posture was due to his desire to win a diplomatic "victory" as a substitute for a triumph on the battlefield which some of his countrymen were demanding vociferously. Moreover, he perhaps felt that he had to justify his coming to China by obtaining concessions other than those he had already expected China would willingly grant.

It was at the fourth official session convened on April 10 that Li, in an obvious move to delay the hour of decision, proposed to discuss the question of the mutual evacuation of Korea. Itō gave his willing consent and the danger of an early rupture in the negotiations was lifted. Both delegates disclaimed any design of a military occupation of Korea. Li made a feeble attempt to reserve the right to maintain a small number of Chinese military instructors in Korea but did not insist when Itō objected. The Japanese statesman appeared to be particularly earnest in his statement that Japan, being poor and weak, could not afford to annex another poor and weak nation like Korea. The April 10 meeting ended on a hopeful note, an accord on the withdrawal of both armies from Korea within four months after the conclusion of a treaty.[53]

When each delegation presented its own draft agreement at the next session held on April 12, the conference once again hit a sour note. The Chinese draft not only provided for Chinese military instructors in Korea but stipulated that China might in the future dispatch soldiers to Korea if requested by the Korean king at a time of internal disturbance.[54] Itō's objection to these exclusive rights for China led Li to attempt to distinguish between China's relationship with Korea and that of Japan; the former was based on the traditional tie between the suzerain nation and a dependent nation, while the latter arose out of recent treaties. There was as little possibility in 1885 as in 1876 that either side would make an explicit concession on the core question of Korea's independence. After the adjournment of the session, Li sent an urgent request to the Yamen for new instructions and warned the latter of a possible rupture of the Tientsin talks.[55]

[53] *Li's Communications*, Ch. 16, pp. 33b–37b; *NGB*, XVIII, 263–275.
[54] See *Li's Communications*, Ch. 16, pp. 38b–39a.
[55] *Ibid.*, pp. 37b–38b.

By the time Li met Itō at the sixth session on April 15, he had received new instructions which authorized him to modify the Chinese terms. Li was to offer, if necessary to save the conference, the following maximum concessions: (1) either China or Japan could dispatch troops to Korea, provided the other signatory party was notified; and (2) neither party should send military instructors to Korea. Li did make these offers on April 15 and Itō readily consented. With regard to the hitherto shelved questions of punishment of the Chinese commanders and of reparation payments, Li rejected Itō's suggestion to solicit the arbitrational service of the president of the United States. Instead, Li offered to send Itō an official communication promising the reprimand and punishment of those Chinese officers and soldiers who, upon further investigation, should be found guilty of wrongdoing. Itō regarded this proposal as a great concession on the part of China and accepted it with no hesitation.[56]

The Treaty of Tientsin signed on April 18 contained three articles. Article I stipulated that the Chinese and the Japanese troops now in Korea should be withdrawn within four months from the date of signing of the treaty in order to avert any future complication between the two nations. Article II dealt with the question of foreign military instructors in Korea. The training of Korean troops to safeguard public order and peace was to be encouraged, but neither Japan nor China were to send any instructors for this purpose. Instead, the Korean king should hire foreign instructors other than Chinese or Japanese. By Article III both signatories or either one of them could dispatch soldiers to Korea in case of future uprisings or other serious disturbances in Korea. In such an event, an advance official notification was to be given to the other party. The troops so dispatched were to be withdrawn completely upon settlement of the disturbance.[57]

At the time of the signing ceremony, Li handed Itō a memorandum that expressed his "extreme regret" over the December 6 clash between the Chinese and Japanese troops and promised to reprimand the Chinese commanders for the "carelessness" and

[56] *Ibid., Ch.* 17, pp. 2b–7a; *NGB,* XVIII, 290–315.
[57] For the text of the treaty, see *ibid.,* 309.

to punish those soldiers against whom concrete evidence of assault upon Japanese citizens was found.[58]

On April 19, the day after the signing of the treaty, as Itō departed from Tientsin for home, Li wrote a lengthy memorial setting forth the reasons for the concessions he had granted the Japanese. In the memorial, Li stressed the point that the long-run benefits for the tranquility of Korea by inducing the Japanese to withdraw their troops from Korea outweighed any short-run disadvantages that might accrue from the evacuation of Chinese troops. Moreover, Li asserted that the Chinese forces in Korea were never meant to be permanent garrison forces. If it should become necessary in the future, China could send back soldiers to defend Korea against either Japan or any Western nation. Concerning his promise of reprimand or punishment for Chinese military personnel, Li minimized the significance of his concession by comparing his role to that of a father who would find it necessary to reprimand his son for a brawl with a stranger.[59]

Judging strictly from the immediate gains or losses of diplomatic maneuvers, the Tientsin negotiations appeared to have been a Japanese victory.[60] Li did not obtain the punishment of Takezoe or any other responsible Japanese officials for the part they had played in an act of subversion in a country which China had been treating as a dependent nation. On the contrary, he implicitly admitted the possibility that the Chinese had misbehaved. On issues other than the withdrawal of troops, Li's concessions did not have the official blessings of the Yamen; Wu Ta-cheng, Li's own deputy, allegedly disapproved of Li's abandonment of China's exclusive claim to the right of armed intervention in Korea.[61] The treaty contained no reference to China's special status in Korea; on the contrary, Japan was given a status equal to that of China.

[58] *Li's Communications*, Ch. 17, pp. 8a–8b; NGB, XVIII, 309.

[59] *Li's Memorials*, Ch. 53, pp. 24a–27b.

[60] Such an interpretation has been expressed by Tsiang, "Sino-Japanese Diplomatic Relations, 1870–1894," *Chinese Social and Political Science Review*, XVII (1933) 87; Dennett, *Americans in Eastern Asia*, p. 480. A similar but much qualified interpretation appears in Nelson, p. 172.

[61] Although *Li's Collected Writings* does not contain reference to Wu's objection, Itō's version of the April 15 meeting specifically mentioned this point. See *NGB*, XVIII, 292.

These criticisms, however, seemingly failed to do justice to other perhaps more important considerations. Li's primary objective in the negotiations was the preservation of peace with Japan. The Franco-Chinese conflict and the possibility of a Franco-Japanese alliance against China could not be dismissed.[62] China had to avoid providing any *casus belli* to Japan. Li obtained his first objective. Secondly, Li had long considered Japan a potential aggressor in Korea. The presence of Japanese forces in Korea, however small, was most unwelcome, while the stationing of Chinese soldiers in Korea to counterbalance the Japanese was a burden, necessary as it was, for China. When Itō proposed mutual withdrawal, therefore, Li had cause to congratulate himself. For the sake of attaining these objectives, Li had to save Itō's face and the conference. Li's promise to reprimand or punish his own men was a cheap price and had little practical significance. The principle of equal reciprocity which Li accepted on the question of military instructors and of future armed intervention in Korea was by far the most serious concession in its future implications. Here, however, the history of the ensuing decade, which was characterized by an unprecedentedly high degree of Chinese control of Korean affairs, was to come to the defense of Li. Indeed, the Treaty of Tientsin, despite the Chinese concessions embodied in the text, marked the beginning of an abrupt decline of Japanese influence in Korea.

The conclusion of the Sino-Japanese negotiations completed the diplomatic process of clearing away the debris of the coup of 1884. The Japanese and the Chinese forces were evacuated by July 22, 1885, nearly a month before the date set for the completion of such a troop movement. The threat of war in Korea was lifted for the time being.

[62] At the time of Itō's arrival in China, the Franco-Chinese negotiations at Paris had reached a critical period. See Payson J. Treat, *Diplomatic Relations between the United States and Japan, 1853–1905*, II, 218. As for the rumored possibility of a Franco-Japanese alliance, the Japanese government denied it repeatedly, thus attesting to the currency of such speculation. See *ibid*. Conroy suggests that a diplomatic alliance between Japan and France would have been easy to arrange if Japan had been willing. See Conroy, p. 172.

PART II

CROSSCURRENTS OF FOREIGN INFLUENCE AND INTERNAL REFORM

4.

The Decade of Chinese Dominance, 1885-1894

Despite the Sino-Japanese agreement of 1885 and the subsequent removal of foreign troops, peace and harmony were not to prevail in Korea. The Mins feared the return of their foes — the Progressives and the *Taewŏn'gun* — reinforced by either Japanese or Chinese support. Chafing under the increasingly rigid control of China, the Korean court sought Russian influence to check China in 1885–1886. The results were nearly catastrophic.

In this period the cast of characters did not change, but their loyalties did. The central figure in the ill-fated appeal for Russian protection was the German adviser to the Korean government. Von Moellendorff had come to Korea as an agent of China, but before long he came to identify himself more with Korea than with China. He was tireless in his efforts to be accepted by the Koreans and to work for needed reforms. He attempted to institute a school for interpreters, to establish a mint, to develop mines and a few manufacturing plants, and also to improve silk and tobacco production.[1] When the December coup erupted, Moellendorff's sympathy lay with the Mins. The unreliable performance of the Korean soldiery during the coup and the possibility of a large-scale conflict between the Chinese and the Japanese troops apparently so impressed Moellendorff that he began to contemplate the advisability of military reforms under foreign tutelage. The needed foreign assistance, however, could hardly come from either China or Japan; not only were they parties to the explosive

[1] "Baron von Moellendorff," *The Korea Review*, I (1901), 245–252.

rivalry but also, in Moellendorff's estimate, China was herself backward and Japan could not be trusted.[2] The only other foreign power of any consequence in Korea, the United States, had been lacking in willingness.

It is, therefore, hardly surprising that Moellendorff proposed to the king, soon after the collapse of the coup, that an appeal be made for Russian assistance. The king, who had grown restive under the ever-increasing Chinese influence, was more than willing to approve Moellendorff's scheme for obtaining protection and military instructors for the Korean army. Not only did the king consent to this scheme, he also, on his own initiative, sent a secret mission to Vladivostok to present a similar request. Moellendorf contacted the Russian legation in Japan during the last days of 1884 and held a series of secret meetings with a Russian official in Seoul and Tokyo over the next several months.

Both missions appear to have been successful as far as Russian willingness to provide military instructors was concerned; but the president of the newly created Korean Foreign Office, Kim Yun-sik, categorically rejected the entire project, pointing out, among other things, the irregularity of these negotiations conducted without the knowledge of the government. Kim and several high officials whom he called upon for assistance submitted strongly worded memorials against the projected agreement. Kim also solicited support from the foreign representatives in Seoul, including the Chinese, Japanese, and American envoys. The king, faced with the strenuous opposition of his ministers and in fear of a forceful intervention by Japan and China, either separately or jointly, decided to reverse his stand and disapprove the Moellendorff project.

The entire blame for the abortive Russo-Korean agreement was placed upon the hapless Moellendorff. In a show of hurt innocence, Korea formally requested Moellendorff's recall. On November 25, 1885, Moellendorff left Seoul for Tientsin after a little over two eventful years of service as the first Westerner to advise the Korean government.[3]

[2] *Ibid.*, p. 252.

[3] Tabohashi, II, 3–17; *Li's Communications, Ch.* 17, pp. 33*b*, 53*b*–54*b*;

On the surface the matter was closed. However, the episode was neither forgotten nor completely forgiven by the Chinese. This only widened the breach between the Chinese and the Mins which had become obvious when China returned the *Taewŏn'gun* to Korea in the fall of 1885, despite strong objections from the queen and her followers.

Japan's attitude toward these developments in Korea was extremely circumspect. The Japanese foreign minister Inoue wrote to his consul at Tientsin: "Unlike three years ago many complications have recently arisen in Korea and we must not lightly intervene. Our policy toward that nation [Korea] is to avoid interference as much as possible and merely to watch the development of its national fortune with attention."[4] It appears beyond doubt that Inoue meant by the term "complications" the involvement of Korea in the British-Russian rivalry for stakes larger than the control of Korea.

In April 1885 four warships of the British China Station occupied a group of three Korean islets (known as Kŏmun-do or Port Hamilton) without any prior notification to Korea. The British action was directed against Russia and not Korea, but the Korean reaction to the arbitrary British action was a mixture of apprehension and indignation. Turning deaf ears to the British declaration that the occupation would be only temporary, the Korean government demanded an immediate evacuation. The Korean government feared that, if Britain were allowed to remain, Russia might also demand territory. However, China considered the temporary presence of the British a welcome check on possible Russian aggression and therefore refused to back the Korean demands for evacuation. Caught between Russia and Great Britain and receiving no active support from either Japan or China, the Korean protest languished. The British forces stayed on and were not withdrawn until 1887.[5] This refusal of the

---

Ch. 18, pp. 2*b*–3*b*; Foulk to secretary of state, July 5, 1885, in McCune and Harrison, I, 81–83. See also Kim Yun-sik, *Kwŏn* 12, 39*b*–40*a*.

[4] Quoted from *NGB*, XVIII, 390.

[5] See a series of British diplomatic documents *in* Great Britain, The Foreign Office, *British and Foreign State Papers*, LXXVIII, 44, 145, 148, 153–157. For Li Hung-chang's reaction, see his letters to the Yamen and

Chinese to grant Korea diplomatic support was another wedge between the ruling Min faction and China.

Disenchantment of the Korean government toward China, however, did not afford Japan any advantage; for the Min faction distrusted Japan. When the Progressives' coup collapsed in December 1884, the restored Min regime immediately demanded of Japan the extradition of the coup leaders. Again and again the request was made to no avail, and the Min regime continued to be haunted by the fear of invasion of Kim Ok-kyun and his comrades. To the Japanese government, the presence of the Korean exiles was an unwelcome source of embarrassment; however, Tokyo did not hand them over to the Korean government because of the sure knowledge that they would be executed.

Aside from these rebellious Koreans, moreover, there were Japanese adventurers who, in 1885, planned to undertake an armed expedition to Korea. The conspiracy was the work of a few members of the antigovernment Liberal party in Japan. The speedy and effective suppression of the conspiracy by the Japanese government and the absence of an organizational tie between the group and the Korean exiles were not sufficient to dispel the fear and suspicion of the Korean court that Kim Ok-kyun, with some form of Japanese support, might at any time attempt an invasion.[6]

The fear of a Japan-based invasion, however, did not induce Korea to invite and welcome China's "protection." The growing unpopularity of China among the Koreans was in no small measure due to the arrogance, impetuosity, and aggressiveness of the top Chinese official in Korea, Yüan Shih-k'ai. Yüan, the future president of the Chinese Republic, was a young (26 years old in 1885) protégé of Li Hung-chang and had served under General Wu in Korea in 1882. Returning to Korea in November 1885 as "the Commissioner stationed in Korea to Superintend Diplomatic and Commercial Affairs," Yüan became Li's ears and mouth in carrying out China's Korea policy. For the next nine years until 1894 he was virtually a Chinese viceroy in Korea, al-

to the Korean king written in May 1885 in *Li's Communications*, Ch. 17, pp. 9a–10a, 18b–19a, 11b–12a. The text of the first official Korean protest is reproduced in *ibid.*, pp. 20a–20b.

[6] Tabohashi, II, 135–164.

though he was usually referred to as "Resident." He showed no qualms in asserting Chinese authority in the peninsular kingdom even by means of extreme measures; and when in the summer of 1885 another Korean overture to Russia was uncovered, he proposed to Li that the Korean king be forcibly deposed. Although the monarch retained his throne, Yüan's daring and angry proposal symbolized the extraordinary position that China occupied in Korea.[7]

Suspecting that the king and his close court advisers had been the perpetrators of anti-Chinese intrigue, Yüan also pressured the Korean government to send a circular to all the foreign representatives cautioning the recipients to disregard any further communication from a Korean source that did not bear the seal of the Foreign Office. Yüan could depend on Kim Yun-sik, the president of the Korean Foreign Office and his reliable ally, to prevent any anti-Chinese act by the royal court in league with a foreign power.[8] When the Korean court decided in 1887 to establish legations in Japan, the United States, and Europe, China of course objected because maintenance of China's suzerainty over Korea required vigilant superintendence of Korea's dealings with other foreign powers. There is no question that the Korean government, in establishing legations abroad, was acting within its rights under the treaties it had concluded with foreign powers with China's approval.

In July 1887, Min Yŏng-jun, an influential member of the Min party, was appointed minister resident in Japan. Following Min Yŏng-jun's departure, the Korean government formally notified the Board of Rites and the Tsungli Yamen in Peking about what had taken place. Li Hung-chang, speaking for the Peking court, responded with a rebuke for Korea's failure to petition the Chinese throne for imperial approval prior to the dispatch of Minister Min. Li claimed that the Korean notification

[7] Li Hung-chang at first approved Yüan's dethronement plan and readied a military expeditionary force for Korea but, at the last minute, called off the plan. *Li's Navy Communications*, Ch. 2, pp. 5a–5b; *Li's Telegrams*, Ch. 7, pp. 34b–35a.

[8] *Li's Communications*, Ch. 18, pp. 34b–35a.

violated the established rules and was not acceptable.[9] Nevertheless, Li took no further punitive steps at this time.

Korea's next attempts to send envoys abroad were not so lightly regarded. Yüan had warned the Korean king directly that any important question of foreign affairs must first be approved by Li Hung-chang; so when the king dispatched Pak Chŏng-yang to the United States as minister plenipotentiary, Yüan prevented the envoy from departing. When the Korean government belatedly petitioned the Chinese government for permission to send the Pak mission and a comparable mission to Europe, permission was granted with the provision that Korean representatives observe three rules; (1) the Korean minister must report his arrival at his post first to the Chinese legation; (2) at any official reception, he must yield precedence to the Chinese representative; and (3) regarding any important question, he must first consult the Chinese representative.[10] After over two months of Chinese harassment, the Korean government was willing to pledge full compliance with these rules.

Pak Chŏng-yang, on arrival in Washington, however, chose to defy the Chinese and was received by the United States secretary of state without the presence of the Chinese minister. Such furor was raised by his act that the European-bound envoy, Cho Sin-hi, returned home on a pretext of poor health, and his replacement, Pak Che-sun, never left for his post. It was not until after China had been defeated by Japan in 1895 that Korea appointed another envoy to Europe.

The episode caused further damage to the traditional tie between Korea and China, in that Korea's submission to China no longer stemmed from willingness to recognize Chinese superiority, in accord with their traditional relationship. Korea, by 1890, was *forced* to submit, thus subverting the Confucian relations between the two nations that hinged upon "the personal allegiance of the

[9] *T'ongmun'gwanji* [Records of the Office of Interpreters], ed. Kim Kyŏng-mun (Seoul, *ca.* 1900), *Kwŏn* 12, p. 11. There is no record of this exchange in *Li's Collected Writings*.

[10] *Li's Telegrams, Ch.* 9, pp. 6b–9a. An English translation of "the three rules" appears as an enclosure to Dinsmore's dispatch to Bayard, November 17, 1887, U.S. Dept. of State, *U.S. Foreign Relations,* 1888, Part I, pp. 441–442.

lesser ruler" to the Chinese throne.[11] In the face of China's superior power, Korea could not openly defy China. But Korea's will to defy was subtly manifested in various moves to oust Yüan who personified Chinese control in the Korean capital. In 1888 and again in the following year, the Korean government requested Yüan's recall but Li rejected these pleas. In his memorials to the Chinese throne, Li argued that Yüan's unpopularity in Korea was in itself a proof of his efficiency and thoroughness in carrying out China's policy, which the Korean king and some foreign representatives did not view with favor.[12] Yüan remained in Korea as Li's faithful agent until the Japanese virtually forced him out in 1894.

In the latter half of the 1880s the Korean economy was experiencing the usual dislocation attendant on throwing open an economically backward area to the concession-seekers and mercantile interests of superior financial and technological powers. The sudden introduction of foreign goods and merchants to the trade centers of Korea, particularly in Seoul, was not long ignored by the native merchants. In 1890 the powerful merchant guilds in Seoul held protest rallies demanding the expulsion of all foreign traders from the capital; especially vociferous were the wholesale merchants in cotton goods and in general merchandise who marched, in hundreds, to the Foreign Office to demand the expulsion of Japanese and Chinese competitors from the city. There were about 80 Chinese business establishments and an equal number or more of Japanese wholesale and retail stores in Seoul. The demonstrators threatened to close their own shops in protest should their demands go unheeded by the government. Mindful of the legal and unofficial financial contributions made by these merchants for the expenses incurred by the government or by the officials in the government, the Foreign Office had to promise to open negotiations with foreign representatives.[13]

The opening of Seoul to foreign merchants had been one of the

[11] Nelson, pp. 176–177 et passim.

[12] See *Li's Communications*, Ch. 19, pp. 20a–20b, 24b–26b, 49b–50b; *Li's Memorials*, Ch. 67, pp. 4a–5a; Ch. 74, pp. 46a–47a.

[13] Kondō (in Seoul) to Aoki (foreign minister), January 30 and February 2, 1890, *NGB*, XXIII, 159–165.

most unpalatable consequences of Korea's decision to join the modern family of nations. Since the rights of the other foreign nations were based on the trade rights first obtained by the Chinese, it was essential to negotiate first with China for the withdrawal of foreign merchants. China flatly refused; Seoul stayed open, and the native merchants slowly lost ground in competition with the Chinese and Japanese.

The plight of the Seoul merchants was only one of the serious economic difficulties that confronted Korea. Public finances faced ever-greater deficits. In addition to the increasingly unfavorable balance of trade in the 1880s, Korea incurred heavy foreign financial obligations — indemnities owed to Japan which amounted to 110,000 yen ($88,000), expenses of the Korean diplomatic missions, and salaries for highly paid foreign employees. Above all, the various "modernization" projects undertaken during the 1880s added considerably to the already over-burdened treasury. The first steamer was bought from the Japanese in 1886; a government hospital, schools, a powder mill, a mint, a bank, and modern weapons, to name but a few, had to be paid for out of the meagre government revenues.[14]

The imposition of heavy taxes upon the populace, made more intolerable by official corruption, caused a few uprisings in the years between 1885 and 1893; but the taxes were inadequate for the sudden and large increases in government expenditures. The only recourse was foreign loans.

In 1885 the Chinese government constructed the first telegraph line that linked Inch'ŏn, Seoul, and Peking and appointed a Chinese official to superintend its operation. Japan immediately made a demand for a concession to construct a telegraph line that would link Seoul with Pusan, and eventually with Japan. Korea, probably with China's support, rejected the Japanese demand and undertook to construct the southern line itself. Lacking the necessary financial resources, Korea obtained a 210,000 *tael* loan from the Chinese Merchant Marine Company. The Chinese loan was soon followed by a 100,000 Mexican dollar loan from a German

[14] Horace N. Allen, *Korea: Fact and Fancy* (Seoul: Methodist Publishing House, 1904), p. 170 *et passim*.

firm. Thus began a period of irresponsible borrowing from foreign powers.

In 1887 Korea showed interest in a Japanese offer of half a million yen but recoiled when Japan demanded long-term — fifty years or longer — mining rights in Korea. Meanwhile the king and his close advisers solicited foreign loans on their own without going through regular governmental channels. As the years went by, the interest charges alone required more foreign loans. Although it was almost impossible to determine the sum of Korea's indebtedness, the best estimate in the middle of 1889 was approximately 1.3 to 1.5 million yen, the creditors being the Germans, Americans, Japanese, and Chinese.[15]

In an effort to consolidate its debt obligations, the Korean government attempted to negotiate large loans from France and later the United States. Both attempts were successfully blocked by the Chinese. At the same time, Li ordered Yüan to make it known to the Korean government that China would favorably consider a Korean application for a loan. The reason for China's objection is plain; Yüan and Li wanted to reinforce China's political control over Korea with a monetary tie. The Korean king, weary of Chinese interference, did not wish to borrow from China; but when the non-Chinese sources failed, he was forced to accept 200,000 *tael* from China in 1892. Korea had become a debtor to China as well as a semiprotectorate.

Meanwhile, Japanese commerce in Korea suffered a relative decline due to the inner cohesion and cooperation among their Chinese competitors and also to the financial weakness and personal depravity of the Japanese merchants. An illustration of cooperative group action among the Chinese is the inauguration of a regular liner service by the Chinese Merchant Marine Company in 1888 that broke the Japanese monopoly of shipping services to and from Korea. When the Nihon Yūsen Kaisha (the N.Y.K.) continued to mistreat its Chinese patrons, the Chinese merchants in Korea, with active encouragement from Yüan and

[15] Yüan's estimate was 1.3 million yen. See Yüan to Li, July 1, 1889, *Li's Telegrams*, Ch. 11, p. 30a. The Japanese chargé in Seoul estimated 1.4 to 1.5 million yen. See Kondō to Ōkuma (foreign minister), June 9, 1889, *NGB*, XXII, 439–440.

Li, invited the Chinese company to run a steamer once a month between Inch'ŏn and the Chinese ports of Shanghai and Chefoo and guaranteed the shipping company against loss. Once the Chinese liner service began, the Chinese commercial community in Korea completely boycotted the Japanese ships.[16] As for the business and personal qualifications of the Japanese residents in Korea, the Japanese officials themselves had little if any good to say of them. Lack of capital, business skill, and experience plagued the small-scale, independent merchants from Japan.

In addition to these considerations, Japanese trade with Korea was handicapped by the relatively high cost of the merchandise which Japan sold to Korea. In the case of both Japanese and Chinese merchants the most important items they imported into Korea were the cotton goods of English origin. Both groups made their purchases in Shanghai markets; however, since the Japanese had to route the commodities through Japan, they were clearly at a disadvantage in relation to their Chinese rivals. Moreover, Chinese political influence in Korea reached its zenith in the years 1885–1894, thus spurring Chinese economic activities.

As a result of these factors, China's trade with Korea, particularly Chinese exports to Korea, showed a significant gain. From 1885 to 1892 China's share in Korea's import trade increased from 19 percent to 45 percent, while that of Japan declined from 81 percent to 55 percent.[17]

Aside from the question of Sino-Japanese rivalry, it is not difficult to see that such increases in Korea's importation of foreign commodities led to basic changes in the nation's economic and social life. Korean handicraft industries suffered an irreparable setback; new consumer goods affected the lives of men of humble circumstances as well as those of the well-to-do. Moreover, the presence of Chinese, Japanese, and Westerners amidst the tradition-bound Koreans occasionally gave rise to violent clashes between the natives and the foreigners.

[16] See *Li's Telegrams, Ch.* 9, pp. 30a–33a. See also *NGB*, XXI, 311–326.

[17] Korean exports to foreign markets were predominantly agricultural products, particularly food grains such as rice and beans, sold to Japan. In the years 1885–1892, Japan bought 91 to 98 percent of the total Korean exports. Conroy, p. 460.

One such dispute, which became known as the "bean controversy," gave rise to a diplomatic crisis. The 1883 trade agreement between Japan and Korea explicitly reserved to Korea the right to proclaim an emergency grain embargo provided the local Korean authorities gave notice to the appropriate Japanese consular official one month in advance of the effective date of the embargo.[18] Japan imported most of the food grains Korea had for exportation, and in the 1880s more and more Japanese grain dealers established themselves at such treaty ports as Pusan and Wŏnsan. From these ports a number of Japanese agents fanned out into the interior to purchase grain, which often resulted in preemptive buying prior to actual harvesting. The lure of foreign-made consumer goods in addition to the perennial impoverishment of the Korean peasantry often led the Koreans to accept a cash loan from the Japanese buyers in return for a promise to hand over the prescribed portion of the autumn harvest to the creditor. The Japanese creditors invariably charged high interest rates for the loan and offered low prices for the grains, but the debtors were in no position to drive a hard bargain.[19] From this description it should be apparent that any obstruction placed on the movement of grain would disrupt and jeopardize the commercial interests of many Japanese merchants. Furthermore, during the period under study, Japanese commercial interests in Korea were faced with an increasingly serious challenge from China; Japan, therefore, could ill afford any embargo that hurt Japanese commerce.

In 1889 the governor of the northeastern province of Hamgyŏng issued an embargo decree that technically violated the trade agreement by putting the embargo into effect before the required one-month warning period expired. On this basis, plus some doubt as to the actual need for the embargo, the Japanese chargé d'affaires in Seoul protested. Although the Korean government ordered the embargo withdrawn, the Japanese merchants who had been adversely affected by the embargo demanded large sums for damages.

[18] Article 37 of the Korean-Japanese Trade Agreement signed on July 25, 1883. For the text, see *NGB*, XVI, 283–289.

[19] Hatada, p. 179.

The Japanese minister in Seoul, Kajiyama Teisuke, who presented the demands for damages in December 1891 considered the sum excessive. Kajiyama, however, was under instructions to collect the full sum "even if the negotiations should take a long time."[20] Wearisome negotiations in Seoul ensued. Min Chongmuk, president of the Korean Foreign Office, was criticized at home for offering to pay at all, while the Japanese Foreign Office was berated by the afflicted Japanese merchants and also by the opposition party members in the Diet who used the controversy to attack the government. No settlement could be reached until Prime Minister Itō of Japan sent an urgent request to Li Hungchang to use his influence with the Koreans in order to avoid a diplomatic rupture between Japan and Korea.

After a year and a half of diplomatic wrangling, Japan won the bout and forced Korea, with the help of an ultimatum, to pay 50,000 yen more than what Korea had originally offered. In view of the modest sum involved, it may seem that Japanese persistence was unreasonable if not absurd. However, the "bean controversy" was not, in the final analysis, a bargain over the amount of the damage payment.[21] Since the time of the Progressives' coup in 1884, Japan's political influence in Korea had waned. Even in the economic realm, Japan was gradually losing ground. The Korean embargo and Korea's resistance to Japan's demand for satisfaction epitomized the secondary position Japan had come to occupy on the Korean scene. In short, Japan lost much of its influence in Korea — temporarily at least — while China succeeded in converting the peninsula into a semiprotectorate. The fact that Japan won the victory in the bean controversy through Chinese intervention was in itself an indication of the deteriora-

[20] Kajiyama to Min, December 7, 1891; Kajiyama to Enomoto, April 14, 1892, NGB, XXV, 295–296, 303–307. The quoted passage is taken from Enomoto to Kajiyama, May 5, 1892, ibid., p. 309.

[21] A recent publication prepared under the supervision of the Japanese Foreign Office states that the real issue in the bean controversy was to force Korea to abandon its attitude of contempt toward Japan. See Nichibei Tsūshinsha (ed.), Shinsei Nihon Gaikō Hyakunenshi [Diplomatic History of the Newly Born Japan During One Hundred Years] (Tokyo, 1953), p. 45.

tion of Japan's position in Korea. Japan no longer sent warships and troops, as it did in 1876 or in 1882, to force the Koreans to their knees. In 1885, when he signed the Tientsin Treaty, Itō Hirobumi probably did not correctly foresee the developments of the years to follow. History, however, placed him at the helm when Japan forcibly challenged China in Korea in 1894–1895.

5.

Rebellion, War, and Reform, 1894-1895

The decade of Chinese supremacy in Korea was suddenly brought to an end when Japan forced China to a military contest in 1894 and won a resounding victory. From the defeated came an abject renunciation of any claim to a special position in Korea; to the victor belonged the power and the opportunity to remake Korea in his own image. A whirlwind of reforms swept through the peninsular kingdom under Japanese auspices, promising much but accomplishing very little. Korea emerged from under the Chinese shadow but doggedly resisted the Japanese. The dramatic reversal in Korea's relations with her two neighbors in 1894–1895 developed in the wake of large-scale popular uprisings in southern provinces of Korea led by a group of religionists known as the *Tonghak Tang.*

During the first few years of the 1890s, Korea on the surface presented a picture of a quiescent society in spite of occasional diplomatic crises; but restiveness permeated the nation. It was the restiveness of the poor and the persecuted, who comprised the great majority of the population. It was the discontent of those who viewed the decadent luxury and corruption of the royal family and high officials with scorn and resentment. It was no secret that Queen Min frequently called into the palace witches, sorceresses, singers, dancers, acrobats, and other lowly individuals for diversion and entertainment of a questionable nature.[1] It was

[1] Homer B. Hulbert, *The History of Korea*, 2 vols. (Seoul: The Methodist Publishing House, 1905), II, 248–249.

a matter of common knowledge that the most powerful of the
Mins, Min Yŏng-jun, had amassed an enormous fortune by illicit
means. He allegedly possessed more wealth than the royal family
itself.[2] Public offices, both at the national and local levels, coud
be procured by the well-to-do who reaped the dividend for their
"investment" by ruthlessly exploiting those below them either in
the political hierarchy or in social status. Ultimately the heavy
burden of supporting the privileged classes rested on the peasantry. Such a sad state of affairs warranted the lamenting memorial submitted in 1893 by a retired official in the censorate who
compared the nation to an aged tree, the inside of which had
been rotten to the core and which was nothing but a standing
shell of bark.[3]

The *Tonghak* Rebellion of 1894 was essentially a political
protest against these evils of Korean society. It failed, but not
until after it had served as a catalyst for a Sino-Japanese war.
The *Tonghak* movement had started in 1860 as a new religion
promising salvation on earth. Its founder, Ch'oe Che-u, was a
native of Kyŏngsang province whose mother was a concubine of
an impoverished member of the local *yangban* class — a circum-
stance which probably made it virtually impossible for him to
seek a career in the government or as a full-fledged member of
the *yangban* class regardless of his own educational qualifications. Following a divine revelation during a time of "a super-
natural sickness" Ch'oe began preaching the new doctrine called
Tonghak or Eastern Learning in contrast to Western Learning
or Catholicism. The new religion combined features from Confucianism, Buddhism, and Taoism, and in time it developed its
own scriptures and rituals. Magical powers, particularly in heal-
ing the sick, were ascribed to its prayer phrase and a charm (a
curved, bow-like figure resembling a cosmological symbol which
was widely used in Korea). The new faith became popular among
the peasants in the populous southern provinces of Kyŏngsang,
Chŏlla, and Ch'ungch'ŏng despite official persecution of this

[2] Chŏng Kyo, *Han'guk Kye'nyŏnsa* [History of the Last Years of the
Yi Dynasty] 2 vols. (Seoul, 1957), I, 66. Chŏng Kyo (1856–1925) was a
scholar-official from Chŏlla Province in the last decades of the Yi dynasty

[3] *Taedong Ki'nyŏn* [Korean Chronicles] (Shanghai, 1905), p. 97.

"wicked learning." In 1866 Ch'oe himself was executed, but his followers carried on the proselytizing work among the people.[4]

As the *Tonghak* movement grew so did the intensity of the official persecution of it. In 1892 and 1893, the *Tonghak* believers held mass rallies to petition the government for an end to suppression and for clearance of the name of Ch'oe. By a show of force, the government managed to persuade them to disband but only for a short while. The movement by then was causing widespread political agitation, demanding expulsion of foreigners and corrupt officials.[5]

In February 1894 a militant *Tonghak* leader, Chŏn Pong-jun, staged an uprising in the rural town of Kobu in Chŏlla province. Within two months, the rebellion spread throughout the province and involved several thousand armed peasants. Wherever possible, the rebels seized the government granaries and returned the tax grains to the peasants from whom they had been collected. The provincial troops literally melted away before the rebel forces, and the reinforcements rushed from Seoul in May were not in time to save the provincial capital. What ensued was not a decisive defeat of the poorly armed peasants, but a negotiated truce by which the government officials apparently promised to stop anti-*Tonghak* persecution in return for an orderly evacuation of the provincial capital by the rebels. An unsupported *Tonghak* source suggests that 12 sweeping social and political reforms were demanded at this time by the rebels and were finally agreed to; these included official toleration of the *Tonghak* religion, punishment of the pro-Japanese, improvement of the treatment of the seven-vile-occupation groups, abolition of slavery, land redistribution, tax reform, and punishment of corrupt officials and arrogant *yangban*.[6] It is rather unlikely that a government negotiator

---

[4] Charles Allen Clark, *Religions of Old Korea* (New York: Fleming H. Revell Co., 1932), pp. 145, 158–176; Murayama Chijun, *Chōsen no Ruiji Shūkyō* [Quasi-Religions in Korea] (Seoul, 1935), pp. 1–44. See also Benjamin B. Weems, *Reform, Rebellion, and the Heavenly Way*, the Association for Asian Studies, Monographs and Papers, No. XV (Tucson: University of Arizona Press, 1964), chap. 2.

[5] *Ibid.*, chap. 3; Murayama, pp. 1–44.

[6] The *Tonghak* source mentioned in the text refers to O Chi-yŏng, *Tonghaksa* [History of the *Tonghaks*] (Seoul, 1940), pp. 126–127. Weems's

could have accepted all of these demands. However, it is highly probable that the above-mentioned *Tonghak* source has correctly pointed to the long-standing popular grievances which were at the root of the rebellion.

The truce lasted a little over four months. The rebels had not been defeated; their strength had actually grown in these months and they came to exercise quasi-governmental authority in certain parts of Chŏlla province. In October, a few months after the outbreak of the Sino-Japanese war, the *Tonghak* forces, recruited from all the southern provinces and numbering in the tens of thousands, marched toward Seoul but suffered a decisive defeat at the hands of combined Korean and Japanese forces. Some of the rebel leaders, including Chŏn, perished at the executioner's hands, and for the time being the *Tonghak* organization ceased to be a political force.

The mass rebellion thus ended as abruptly as it had begun. A major factor contributing to its failure was foreign intervention, first by the Chinese as we shall presently discuss and later by the Japanese. Another obvious factor was the lack of unity and discipline among the rebels, who were divided and uncoordinated during the periods of armed campaign and especially during the few months following the truce. Less obvious was the determined resistance they encountered from the well-entrenched *yangban* class, which, upon perceiving the elements of class warfare in the rebellion, threw its support to the side of the government and organized local self-defense corps to fight the rebellious peasants. Above all the *Tonghak* leaders lacked ideological conviction and revolutionary strategy; they rode the tiger of peasant antipathy but possessed no master plan to control and direct it.

The irony of the *Tonghak* movement, which had a distinct anti-foreign overtone, was that it gave rise to foreign armed interventions leading eventually to the Sino-Japanese War of 1894–1895. On June 1, 1894, shortly before the truce in the rebellion, the Korean government unofficially requested Chinese assistance through Yüan Shih-k'ai, the Chinese Resident in Korea. A formal written request was delivered to Yüan two days later. The Chinese

work above, in chapter 3, quotes O and other Korean sources. See also Tabohashi, II, 241–269, for a description of the uprising.

government promptly complied, dispatching 1,500 soldiers and two warships. At the same time, Li Hung-chang notified the Japanese government, in accordance with the Tientsin Treaty of 1885.[7] Li may have been under the impression that Japan would not object to, if not welcome, the use of Chinese troops to help suppress the rebellion in Korea, because Yüan had reported to him that the Japanese representative in Seoul had expressed a desire for Chinese military intervention.[8] The first Chinese soldier landed at Asan, about 80 miles south of Seoul, on June 8. Soon thereafter, the first phase of the rebellion ended before the Chinese forces were ready to move out to the rebel territory.

The dispatch of Chinese soldiers to Korea was a direct cause for the Japanese government to do the same. On June 10, 400 Japanese marines arrived in Seoul. Within a matter of several days, over 4000 Japanese troops were concentrated in the Seoul-Inch'ŏn area, while one-half that many Chinese soldiers were stationed at Asan. Alarmed by the presence of the two rival foreign forces, the Korean government publicly announced the recovery of the rebel-held provincial capital and demanded the withdrawal of all foreign troops. Li Hung-chang, equally alarmed by the Japanese move, notified Tokyo of China's willingness to recall its troops from Korea. The Japanese response was to send an additional infantry regiment to Korea in the last days of June.[9]

[7] *Li's Telegrams*, Ch. 15, pp. 33b–34a; *NGB*, XXVII, Part II, 168. For details on the Korean request for withdrawal of the Japanese and Chinese troops, see *ibid.*, pp. 190–191; *Li's Telegrams*, Ch. 15, pp. 40a–40b. Korea also sought the good offices of Western representatives in Seoul for such withdrawal, see Spencer J. Palmer (ed.), *Korean-American Relations*, vol. II, *The Period of Growing Influence, 1887–1895* (Berkeley and Los Angeles: University of California Press, 1963), p. 340.

[8] References to the alleged Japanese solicitation for Chinese intervention in Korea appear in Li's report to the Tsungli Yamen, June 1 and 5, 1894, *Li's Telegrams*, Ch. 15, pp. 32b–33a. The Japanese official later refuted Yüan's version of his conversation with Yüan, see Conroy, pp. 236–239. What is important for our purpose is not what the Japanese had actually said but what Li believed he had said. The American minister in Seoul observed in 1893 that Japan was deliberately encouraging China to assert suzerain controls over Korea in order to obviate the danger of intervention by Western powers when Japan should fight China for supremacy in Korea; see Nelson, pp. 205–206.

[9] Tabohashi, II, 288–352.

Japan had resolved to risk a war to regain her position in Korea.

In Japan, dissatisfaction with the policy of the Tokyo government in dealing with Korea had been voiced for some time by various individuals and groups. In 1890 Foreign Minister Aoki Shūzō wrote that "Korea should be made a part of the Japanese map." [10] Some opposition party members in and outside the Japanese Diet took delight in embarrassing the government by advocating the "tough" line in foreign policy. Japanese supporters of the 1884 Progressives' coup in Korea revived their interest in Korean affairs in 1894, after the exiled Kim Ok-kyun, chief architect of the coup, was murdered in a Shanghai hotel. An ostentatious memorial service held in Tokyo by the "Friends of Mr. Kim" aroused popular indignation against the Min-controlled government of Korea and Li Hung-chang, the suspected perpetrators of the assassination plot.

The most decisive influence for the aggressive policy of Tokyo in the summer of 1894, however, was the Japanese army general staff which was controlled by General Kawakami Sōroku, an ardent advocate of continental expansion. The army had maintained a close watch on the Korean situation for some time through a separate intelligence system of its own. On the last day of May 1894, an officer on the army general staff returned from a trip to Korea and apparently confirmed General Kawakami's suspicion that the rebellion could provide a welcome opportunity to send Japanese soldiers to Korea to carry out "reforms" and establish Japanese predominance. The army general staff thereupon made a formal proposal to the cabinet for a decision to send an army unit. The army proposal, the impending movement of Chinese troops into Korea, a parliamentary crisis within Japan, and the popular demand for strong action in Korea converged to create an atmosphere of extraordinary tension leading to the decision of the Japanese cabinet, on June 2, 1894, to send a "mixed brigade." Foreign Minister Mutsu Munemitsu was the most vocal advocate of a militant policy among the civilian leaders of the government. It was with his connivance that the army staff chose to represent the strength of the proposed expeditionary force as a

[10] Aoki's memorandum was written under the title of "The Balance of Power among the East Asian Nations." See *NGB*, XXIII, 538–543.

"mixed brigade" (which could contain as many as 8000 men in contrast to a normal brigade of 2000 men) in order to secure the acquiescence of Prime Minister Itō who might have opposed sending a large force of more than a few thousand soldiers.[11]

One day after the arrival of the Japanese troops, the *Tonghak*-led rebels began to disperse in Chŏlla province thus eliminating the need for Japanese or Chinese soldiers. Japan's objective, however, was not confined to a mere restoration of the status quo; it had by then become impossible for Japan to be content with any situation that permitted continued Chinese domination over Korea. Japan needed a new pretext to maintain a strong military force in Korea to counterbalance, if not overcome, the Chinese influence. The Tokyo government proposed a joint Sino-Japanese reform of Korea's financial, administrative, and military systems. China rejected the Japanese proposal as Tokyo had anticipated, on the ground that it constituted an interference with Korea's domestic affairs.[12]

But such an interference was precisely what Japan had in mind and, in the first days of July, the Japanese minister Ōtori Keisuke, supported by 4000 Japanese troops in the vicinity of the capital, made the reluctant and dismayed Korean government appoint a commission to carry out the reforms he proposed. When hostilities commenced in the last week of July between the Japanese and Chinese forces in Korea, Japan's declaration of war charged China with circumventing and thwarting efforts to promote Korean reforms.[13]

One of the first military moves of Japan was to occupy the royal palace in Seoul and create a new Korean cabinet excluding the Min ministers. The new cabinet promptly renounced the traditional tie with China and established a quasi-legislative council to draft reform measures. The Japanese cabinet resolved to pursue a policy that would allow Korea to remain "nominally independ-

[11] Tabohashi, II, 292–293; Mutsu Munemitsu, *Kenkenroku* [Memoirs] (Tokyo, 1933), p. 16. See also Chong-sik Lee, *The Politics of Korean Nationalism* (Berkeley and Los Angeles: University of California Press, 1963), pp. 36–37, for details on the Mutsu-Kawakami conspiracy to mislead Itō.

[12] Mutsu, pp. 33–37; *NGB*, XXVII, Part II, 206–207, 234.

[13] *Ibid.*, Part I, pp. 578–580, 584, 586; *ibid.*, Part II, pp. 264–266.

ent," subject to "direct or indirect, permanent or long-term protection and assistance" by Japan.[14] On August 20, 1894, Japan
forced Korea to sign "Provisional Articles" which, among other
things, obligated Korea to accept Japanese advice on internal
reforms (Item 1).[15] The task of advising the Korean government
was entrusted to Count Inoue Kaoru, the minister of home affairs
and a powerful member of the Japanese oligarchy.

The energetic Count Inoue arrived in Seoul in late October as
the new Japanese minister, and immediately submitted a lengthy
proposal for reforms. In the first month of 1895 the Korean king
(escorted by blue-coated Japanese policemen) swore before the
"Holy Spirits" of the royal ancestors to safeguard national independence and terminate forever the bondage to China. He pledged
that he would complete and perfect the laws of the state and promote efficient administration. He announced before an assembly
of the queen, the *Taewŏn'gun*, and other members of the royal
family and ministers of state that his consort and relatives would
no longer be permitted to interfere in the affairs of government.[16]

The new governmental machinery set up devoid of the Min
faction was modeled after the Japanese cabinet system. Pak
Yŏng-hyo, a chief conspirator of the coup of 1884 who had subsequently escaped to Japan, was invited back and appointed minister of home affairs. Also a noted pro-Japanese, Sŏ Kwang-pŏm,
was made minister of justice. The cabinet met three times a week
under the titular presidency of the monarch, but in the presence
of Count Inoue, to pass resolutions. Altogether, 421 new proclamations, decrees, and other acts directed toward reform were
announced in the period between November 22, 1894, and
June 30, 1896.[17] Meanwhile, Japan forwarded to the Korean
court a 3,000,000 yen contribution to finance the reforms.

These numerous and detailed reform measures covered almost
all aspects of Korean life. By a stroke of the pen, the royal house-

[14] Mutsu, pp. 134–139.

[15] *NGB*, XXVII, Part I, 653–655.

[16] *NGB*, XXVIII, Part I, 378–380; Conroy, p. 276. For an English
rendition of the full text of the oath, see Palmer, p. 351.

[17] The figure is compiled from W. H. Wilkinson, *The Corean Government; Constitutional Changes, July 1894 to October 1895* (Shanghai: The
Statistical Department of the Inspectorate-General of Customs, 1897).

hold was separated from the government, and members of the royal family (especially the queen and the *Taewŏn'gun*) were forbidden to interfere in the affairs of the state. The king himself was to act only in consultation with and on the advice of his ministers. The traditional Six Boards were replaced by the eight ministries (Home Affairs, Foreign Affairs, Finance, Military Affairs, Justice, Education, Public Works, and Agriculture and Commerce) with clearly defined jurisdictional authorities. Ministers headed these executive establishments while the prime minister, renamed *ch'ongni taesin* — an obvious imitation of the designation used for the Japanese prime minister — presided over the ministries. The centuries-old discrimination against military officials was to come to an end; equality between the civilian and the military branches of the government service was provided for. In the important areas of military organization and tax administration, new and hopefully more efficient systems were promulgated.

Probably the most significant of all the reform measures at this time was a declaration ending the monopoly of public offices by the *yangban* class, accompanied by the discontinuation of the old examination system that had helped perpetuate the elitist existence of this privileged class. Further egalitarian innovations were the abolishment of the slavery system, outlawing of discrimination against those engaged in "the vile callings," and lifting of the ban on the remarriage of widows. There were also regulations encouraging Korean men to cut off their traditional top-knots, wear black garments rather than the traditional white ones, and smoke short pipes rather than long ones. At the same time, a new Japanese postal service was organized. In southern Korea the Chinese telegraph was taken over by Japan so that the line from Seoul to Pusan was operated as part of the Japanese government system with Japanese forms, words and seals.[18]

The zeal with which the work of reconstruction was pursued was reminiscent of the first years of the Meiji restoration in Japan, but the Korean reforms lacked the necessary support from the various strata of society. Powerful traditionalist forces within and

[18] H. B. Hulbert, "Korean Reforms," *Korean Repository*, II (1895), 1–9.

outside the government, including commoners as well as officials and the *yangban* class, objected to these sudden drastic changes. Their well-founded suspicion of Japanese authorship of these innovations lent additional support to their opposition.[19] Nor was the Korean government united in its commitment to the cause of modernization. The reform advocates were soon divided among themselves into roughly two groups, the pro-Japanese group and the pro-Western group. The latter group came to be known as the Chŏngdong Club and comprised relatively young officials who had been to Western nations. As an American editor of the *Korean Repository* lamented at the time, "everybody believes in reforms as long as his prerogatives are not questioned." [20] There was a universal antipathy to the reforms. As an English student of Far Eastern affairs wrote at the time, "From the palace to the hovel, the new programme was met with an obdurate conspiracy of resistance that only a slow-witted and lethargic people could put forth." [21]

The Japanese victory over China and the conclusion of the Treaty of Shimonoseki in April 1895 did not go beyond formal recognition of the termination of Chinese influence in Korea which had been accomplished by force of arms in the summer of 1894. Korea was declared fully and completely independent and "the payment of tribute and the performance of ceremonies and formalities" which reflected Korea's inferior status to China were to cease. On the other hand, the Triple Intervention by Russia, Germany, and France, which followed immediately the signing of the Shimonoseki Treaty, not only reduced Japan's prestige by forcing her to retrocede Liaotung Peninsula to China, but also bound Japan to honor her avowed policy of aiding Korea's independence.[22]

[19] American Minister John B. Sill reported from Seoul on September 24, 1894, that the provincial governors and district magistrates in Korea "disregard the orders of the King, saying that His Majesty is a helpless prisoner" in Japanese hands. See Palmer, p. 347.

[20] *Korean Repository*, II (1895), 270.

[21] George N. Curzon, *Problems of the Far East*, rev. ed. (Westminister: Constable & Co., 1896), pp. 194–195, 379.

[22] The three European powers argued that Japan's possession of Liaotung would be a "constant menace to the capital of China, *would at the same*

Confronted with such unsettling international developments and the hazardous uncertainties of Korean politics, the Japanese cabinet decided on May 25, 1895, to reverse its Korean policy and give up the year-old project of reforms in Korea.[23] The chief Japanese agent in Korea, Count Inoue, was suddenly ordered home "for consultation." As he reflected on his brief but eventful career in Korea, Count Inoue had to admit the failure of the reform. He attributed this to (1) the selfishness of the Japanese in Korea who were only looking after their individual gains and were offensive in their dealings with the Koreans, (2) the confusion of responsibility within the Korean court and lack of cooperation by the disunited Korean cabinet, and (3) the Triple Intervention.[24]

As Count Inoue prepared to resign his post, the Korean king undid one of the most important changes Inoue had introduced; the monarch declared the resumption of his power to appoint or dismiss high officials at will without advice from the cabinet. At the same time, those of the Min faction that had been purged from the government were granted royal pardons. The brief era of Japanese domination ended abruptly. So did the ambitious and forceful reform projects that Japan had sponsored in Korea.

time render illusory the independence of Korea." (Emphasis added.) NGB, XXVIII, Part I, 17.

[23] Tokyo considered but dropped the plan to notify interested foreign powers of this decision. The unused draft note stated that Japan would not bear the burden of maintaining Korean independence alone because it was a matter of common concern. Ibid., pp. 434–435.

[24] See New York Herald, October 17, 1895, for the interview of Inoue by John H. Cokerill. See also Itō Hirobumi, ed., Chōsen Kōshō Shiryō [Materials on Negotiations with Korea], 3 vols. (Tokyo, 1936), III, 112.

6.

The Russo-Japanese Rivalry, 1895–1904

The Sino-Japanese conflict stimulated Russia's interest in the areas adjacent to its Far Eastern possessions. For the first time since 1860, Russia adopted an aggressive policy of expansion; Manchuria and Korea became focal points of Russian attention. In view of Japan's long-standing political and economic interests in Korea, it was inevitable that the two nations should become rivals in the peninsular kingdom. During the first few years following the Treaty of Shimonoseki, Japan was exhausted and too weak to challenge Russia, while the latter was unprepared to take full advantage of the situation. Therefore, both powers were willing to accept the status quo in a series of temporary agreements. During these same years, Korea chose to seek Russian assistance primarily because of her experience with Japanese intervention; and Russia enjoyed a period — albeit a relatively brief one — of predominance in Korea. The *modus vivendi* between Japan and Russia, however, did not last any longer than the preceding one between Japan and China. Ten years after the Sino-Japanese War, the Russo-Japanese War broke out. Unlike 1895 Japan's predominance in Korea after its victory over Russia was not challenged by foreign powers.

Within Korea during these ten years of Russo-Japanese rivalry, the endemic partisan strife continued, but with the passing of the queen in 1895 and of the *Taewŏn'gun* in 1898, new factions and hitherto little-known individuals came to the fore. More important, a nascent form of nationalism began to develop accompanied by the introduction of mass communication media and mass political movements.

One of the immediate reactions to Japan's newly adopted policy of nonintervention in Korean affairs was open defiance of Tokyo's decision by Japanese officials in Korea. None other than Inoue's successor, Lieutenant-General Miura Gorō, was responsible for the murder of the Korean queen in her own palace on October 8, 1895. Miura was a professional soldier with no diplomatic experience or sophistication.[1] He viewed the settlement of the tangled Korean problem "merely as a matter of prompt and vigorous action." [2] He was enthusiastic about the prospect of rectifying Japan's Korea policy which he thought had failed because there had not been established "a firm, unalterable guideline." [3]

The Korean situation when Miura arrived in Seoul, however, was not amenable to simple "vigorous" treatment based on a "firm guideline." A coalition cabinet of the queen's faction and a newly emerging pro-Russian faction had been organized in August 1895 under Prime Minister Kim Hong-jip. A cordial, cooperative relationship developed between the two, and the pro-Japanese faction was almost without political power. In early October the court began preparations for disbanding a Japanese-trained Korean infantry regiment in Seoul.

Miura felt that he had to act swiftly to remedy the situation, even though the Tokyo government's policy had been one of extreme caution for several months. Not only had Japan stopped pressuring Korea for reforms, she had even decided to withdraw her troops from Korea except for a limited number of guards for

[1] Miura Gorō (1846–1926) fought with Inoue against the Shogunate forces in 1864–1868. Under the Meiji government, he stayed in the army and became a lieutenant-general in 1878. In 1886 he retired from the army and was a member of the House of Peers in the Japanese Diet when he received the diplomatic assignment. See Yamamoto Shirō (ed.), *Miura Gorō Kankei Bunsho* [Documents related to Miura Gorō], mimeographed (Tokyo, 1960), pp. 123–137.

[2] Homer B. Hulbert, *The History of Korea*, 2 vols. (Seoul: The Methodist Publishing House, 1905), II, 286.

[3] Miura's memorandum to the Japanese Foreign Office, August 17, 1895, *NGB*, XXVIII, Part I, 483–484.

the legation and the military telegraph lines.[4] Repeated requests
from Miura for instructions concerning measures to counteract
the favorable developments in Korea went unanswered. Rather
than wait to see Russia eclipse Japan at the Korean court, Miura
decided to take matters into his own hands. The first secretary
of the legation, Sugimura Fukashi, who had long experience
(since 1891) in Korean politics, was Miura's chief of staff in
the plot.[5] Sugimura did not see any impropriety in Miura's resort
to drastic measures on his own authority since "there have been
precedents set by [Miura's] predecessors" (perhaps referring to
the events in 1884 and 1894.)[6]

Beginning at the end of September, Miura and Sugimura discussed tactics and decided to use the *Taewŏn'gun* for their purpose. A cautious and indirect inquiry revealed that the ex-regent
"was indignant enough to plan a coup." But he was willing "to
see Mr. Miura personally to discuss ways to save the situation,"
and was ready to cooperate. In fact the prince wanted revenge for
his years of suffering at the hands of the Mins. The date was set
for October 10 and for the deed Miura and Sugimura selected a
score of Japanese *sōshi* (adventuresome civilian extremists), set
aside ten Japanese consular policemen, and alerted the Japanese
garrison commander and the Japanese instructors of the dis-
affected Korean regiment.

The moment of action came two days earlier than had been
planned because of information that the queen was pressing for
disarmament and dispersal of the Korean regiment which had
caused serious concern to the royal family.[7] During the early
hours of the morning of October 8, 1895, a group of *sōshi* and
plain-clothed Japanese policemen went to the *Taewŏn'gun's*
country home in the southwestern suburb of Seoul and escorted
the prince to the palace. On their way they were joined by Japanese and pro-Japanese Korean soldiers. The Korean palace guard

[4] Prime Minister Itō's memorandum on Korea dated October 21, 1895,
Chōsen Kōshō Shiryō, III, 158–162.
[5] Sugimura admitted his central role in the conspiracy. See Sugimura's
diary as reproduced in part in Conroy, p. 318.
[6] Sugimura's testimony, *Chōsen Kōshō Shiryō*, II, 526.
[7] Yamamoto, pp. 84–86.

was powerless. The king and his son were held captive. The queen was murdered and her body burned. Shortly before daybreak, Miura and Sugimura went to the palace on royal summons and feigning innocence ordered the withdrawal of the invaders.[8]

Within a few days the king was coerced into appointing pro-Japanese individuals to key posts in the government and issuing a decree that demoted the (late) queen to commoner status. At the time no mention of her passing was made. The palace was guarded by the mutinous Korean soldiers. The king became a prisoner in his own palace and lived in daily fear for his life.

Tokyo received its first news of the October 8 incident through a report from the military attaché in Seoul. Acting Foreign Minister Saionji immediately demanded full particulars from Miura, especially on the question of Japanese complicity. Miura's first report, arriving late in the afternoon of October 8, misrepresented the incident by stating that it involved a clash between Korean soldiers and the palace guards, while the Japanese army unit had become involved by guarding the palace in order to "calm things down." Dissatisfied, Tokyo pressed for more details. By October 10, Miura conceded that the Japanese garrison troops had aided the rebellious Korean soldiers and also that some of the *sōshi* invaders had in fact taken an active part in the coup.[9]

Tokyo reacted quickly. It was quick in conveying to the Russian government the innocence and sense of "abhorrence" of the Japanese government. Tokyo instructed the Japanese minister at St. Petersburg to explain the government position and express the hope that Russia would not "misunderstand." On October 17 the Japanese cabinet decided to recall Miura to face trial and appointed Komura Jutarō to succeed him. Inoue Kaoru was also ordered to Korea to aid in the settlement.[10]

[8] This account is based on Japanese Consul Uchida's report, *NGB*, XXVIII, Part I, 552–562; the decision of the Hiroshima court in Hulbert, *History of Korea*, II, 289–296; Fred Harvey Harrington, *God, Mammon, and the Japanese: Dr. Horace N. Allen and Korean-American Relations, 1884–1905* (Madison: Univ. of Wisconsin Press, 1944), pp. 267–268.

[9] See the telegraphic exchanges between Tokyo and Seoul, October 8–10, 1895, in *NGB*, XXVIII, Part I, 491–498.

[10] *Ibid.*, pp. 517–523. The Hiroshima district court tried Miura, Sugimura, and 46 others and confirmed the conspiracy and the invasion of the

The Russian and American representatives in Seoul, suspecting correctly that the Korean king was under duress, organized a boycott by the entire foreign diplomatic corp of all decrees issued by the new regime in Seoul. Small contingents of Russian and American marines were called to the Korean capital, and the Westerners provided asylum for those Koreans who feared persecution by the pro-Japanese regime.

Some of the Korean refugees soon plotted a counter-putsch to rescue the king and overthrow the existing regime. During the night of November 27–28, several hundred members of the now disbanded palace guards attempted to invade the palace. The Japanese later alleged that the counter-putsch group had intended to seize and murder all the cabinet ministers. The pro-Westerners' attempt ended in a complete failure because of the stiff resistance of the new palace guards.

The leaders of the unsuccessful putsch did not abandon their project. In February 1896 they succeeded in smuggling the king and the crown prince out of the palace; the Korean sovereign sought and received asylum at the Russian legation in the capital of his own kingdom. This unusual development occurred one day after 150 Russian marines equipped with a cannon had arrived in Seoul, an indication of Russian foreknowledge of the impending development. Immediately after reaching the safety of the Russian legation, the king decreed death sentences for several leaders of the pro-Japanese regime, particularly those who controlled the army and the police. Deprived of the royal authority that had justified their positions, the pro-Japanese cabinet ministers were exposed to the mercy of angry mobs. While most of the confirmed pro-Japanese collaborators managed to escape with Japanese assistance, the opportunistic Prime Minister Kim Hong-jip and the Minister of Treasury Ŏ Yun-jung, together with the unpopular Minister of Agriculture Chŏng Pyŏng-ha, were murdered in savage mob assaults. Overnight, the political tables were turned; Japan lost its tenuous hold on the Korean government, while the

palace. But the court acquitted all defendants for lack of evidence regarding their actual participation in the acts of violence; Hulbert, *History of Korea,* II, 193.

Russian legation suddenly became host to the royal family and the government of Korea.[11]

The Japanese government's response at this turn of events was surprisingly meek, although Minister Komura at one time considered using force to bring the king back to his palace.[12] Japan's desire to settle the issue through diplomatic accommodations became evident when Saionji expressed to Russian Minister Mikhail Hitrovo the wish for a Russo-Japanese understanding.[13] The proposal was favorably received in St. Petersburg, and agreement was reached in the Komura-Waeber Memorandum signed on May 14, 1896. By the terms of this agreement, (1) the Korean king was to return to the palace at his own discretion, control of the sōshi being guaranteed by the Japanese; (2) the present members of the Korean cabinet were to be recognized and accepted by Russia and Japan; (3) Japan was to continue for the time being to guard the Japanese telegraph line between Seoul and Pusan; and (4) Japanese soldiers were to be temporarily stationed in Seoul, Pusan, and Wŏnsan for the protection of Japanese settlements, while Russia was entitled to keep an equal number of guards at those places for the protection of the Russian legation and consulate.[14]

By this memorandum Japan formally acknowledged that Russia had as much right as Japan to be interested in Korea. Politically it was a defeat for Japan. In return for a vague Russian promise to advise the king to return to the palace, Japan agreed to reduce its troops in Korea; acknowledged the past wrongdoings

[11] For details see *Korean Repository*, III (1896), 81–94; Komura to Saionji, February 11, 13, and 17, 1896, *NGB*, XXIX, 687–693; Hwang Hyŏn, *Maech'ŏn Yarok* [Unofficial Records of Hwang Hyŏn] (Seoul, 1955), pp. 195–197.

[12] Komura to Saionji, February 11, 1895; *NGB*, XXIX, 682. Komura, however, emphasized that Japan's use of force would inevitably lead to a Russo-Japanese clash.

[13] For the Saionji-Hitrovo conversations, see *ibid.*, pp. 731–733. Komura had earlier voiced the desirability of an agreement that would provide for a joint Russo-Japanese guarantee of Korean independence and joint supervision of Korean reforms. See Komura to Saionji, February 18, 1895, *ibid.*, pp. 729–730.

[14] From an English text in Frederick A. McKenzie, *Tragedy of Korea* (London: Hodder and Stoughton, 1908), pp. 299–300.

of her nationals, the *sōshi*; agreed to accept the anti-Japanese cabinet as being "liberal and moderate"; and above all, conceded that Russia, too, could dispatch troops to Korea. The willingness with which Saionji and Komura accepted the Russian proposals was in itself symbolic of the Russian ascendency in Korea.

The Komura-Waeber Memorandum, however, dealt with specific issues in Korea without any agreement on the more basic question of what should be done with Korea. Japan decided to entrust this important assignment to Yamagata Aritomo, one of the most powerful members of its oligarchy. Yamagata had favored, even prior to the conclusion of the Shimonoseki Treaty, a Russo-Japanese understanding based on a mutual recognition of each other's interests in Korea.

Early in 1896, Yamagata went to Russia officially as a member of the Japanese delegation to attend the coronation ceremony of Czar Nicholas II. In Moscow, he had four secret sessions with Russian Foreign Minister A. B. Lobanov-Rostovsky. The fourth meeting witnessed the signing of the Protocol of Moscow by Lobanov and Yamagata dated June 9, 1896. Both countries were to aid Korea's financial reform with loans and to leave to Korea the formation and maintenance of an armed force for the preservation of internal peace. It was also agreed that Japan would continue to administer the telegraph lines. At the suggestion of Prince Lobanov, the agreement included a secret article providing that, should Russia and Japan decide at any time to send their troops into Korea, each would define the area to be occupied so that a buffer zone would be created to prevent conflict between them. A second article confirmed the Komura-Waeber agreement on the stationing of foreign troops in Korea and continued the "present arrangement" for the protection of the king, pending the organization of new palace guards.

Yamagata's primary objective — a joint Japanese-Russian guarantee of Korea's independence — had not been attained. Japan, whose economic interests in Korea were far greater than those of any other nation, willingly conceded to Russia an equal status with regard to loans for Korea. On the question of the training of the Korean armed forces, Japan's objective to leave it in the hands of a neutral power had been frustrated; instead, a vague promise to leave it to the Koreans themselves was substituted. Otherwise, the Protocol of Moscow was merely a higher-level confirmation of the Komura-Waeber Memorandum with the notable exception of the novel and untested proposition for a partition of Korea into two spheres of influence.[15] One comforting discovery for Japan was, however, the Russian government's apparent disinterest in any drastic alteration of the status quo at this time.

Also present in Moscow for the coronation ceremony was a Korean envoy. Min Yŏng-hwan, a close relative of the late queen, journeyed to Moscow with a letter from the king. He presented it to the czar in a private audience, and subsequently Min and Lobanov signed a secret agreement assuring Russian protection for the Korean king, and Russian military and financial aid. The Russian government also agreed to connect the telegraph lines of the two countries.

Perhaps more important was an agreement on a defensive alliance. In response to Min's written request, Lobanow agreed with the approval of the czar to provide military and other assistance to Korea in case of serious internal disturbances or violation of Korean independence by a foreign power (Japan?).[16] In line with this agreement and in violation of the spirit of the Yamagata-Lobanov Protocol, in the summer of 1896 Russia sent to Korea two representatives of the newly created Russo-Chinese Bank, together with a small group of Russian military personnel. By the end of October 1896 a Colonel Potiata, three other officers, and ten men from the Russian army arrived in Seoul to train the newly reconstituted royal guard unit. The Russian economic expert Pokotilov concluded a secret loan agreement with the Korean government by which the Russo-Chinese Bank was to lend three million yen to Korea, on the security of the customs receipt, for the purpose of repaying a Korean debt to Japan. Russian eco-

[15] For the French and the Japanese texts of the Protocol, see NGB XXIX, 815–817, 817–818.

[16] See the gist of Lobanov's memorandum to Min Yŏng-hwan in Japan, the Ministry of Foreign Affairs (ed.), Komura Gaikōshi [History of Komura Jutarō's Diplomacy], 2 vols. (Tokyo, 1953), I, 95. Hereafter cited as Komura Diplomacy.

nomic penetration also took the form of a timber concession along the Yalu River which the Korean government granted to a Russian, Jules Bryner, in late August 1896.[17] The Japanese government protested but without effect.

The rapid decline of Japanese influence in the course of 1896 made the Russian ascendancy even more apparent. According to the provisional articles signed between Korea and Japan in August 1894, Japan was to construct the Seoul-Pusan and Seoul-Inch'ŏn railways; but in 1896 Korea granted the concession for a Seoul-Inch'ŏn railway to an American. In July another railway concession, for a Seoul-Uiju line, was granted to a French syndicate. Thereupon, Japan decided to begin the construction of the Seoul-Pusan railway, but Korea rescinded its earlier grant because of the intervention of the Russian Minister Waeber.[18]

Japan's cause, however, had not been competely lost. Within Korean political circles, distrust of Russian influence and particularly of pro-Russian Korean collaborators began to develop. Some of the old conservative politicians and the younger, enlightened but nationalistic officials who had been pro-Russian against the Japanese only a short time before began to urge the king, early in 1897, to return to the palace. When the king decided to leave the Russian legation in February 1897, there was no strong objection from the Russian minister. The Korean king stayed in the Russian legation a little over a year.

In March 1897, Japanese Foreign Minister Ōkuma made public the Komura-Waeber Memorandum and the open articles of the Yamagata-Lobanov Protocol. He also informed the Korean government of these agreements including the secret articles of the protocol dealing with the possible future partition of Korea in order to discredit Waeber's profession of altruistic friendship toward Korea. It seems that the Korean government did not fully realize the seriousness of the Russo-Japanese scheme to divide Korea into two spheres of influence. The Korean Foreign Office merely acknowledged the receipt of the Japanese notification and expressed the hope that nothing in the protocol would compromise the sovereign integrity of the country. It was not an indig-

[17] *Komura Diplomacy*, I, 93.
[18] Hara to Ōkuma, November 17, 1896, *NGB*, XXIX, 656–657.

nant protest but a feeble supplication for favor. Some Korean officials privately showed their resentment of the Russo-Japanese agreement made without Korea's knowledge.[19]

Meanwhile, following the king's departure from the Russian legation, a series of discordant notes began to sound in Korean-Russian relations. When Waeber suggested that 160 Russian military personnel be employed as instructors for the Korean army, Korea refused.[20] What proved to be most serious, however, was the replacement of Waeber, whose diplomatic tact had won him the royal favor and the goodwill of many foreign diplomats, by Alexis de Speyer, an overly aggressive man who had dealt arrogantly with the Koreans when they sought Russian help in 1885.

The gradual growth of sentiments hostile to Russia and Speyer among those Koreans who were politically articulate and the sudden shift in Russia's own Far Eastern policy to the so-called "Port Arthur Orientation" brought about a sudden collapse of Russia's predominance in Korea in 1898.[21] Early in January 1898 Russia intimated a desire for an agreement with Japan to terminate "continual friction" in Korea on the basis of Russian recognition that Japan had greater interests in Korea than Russia.[22] The conciliatory attitude of Russia was partly due to her concern over Japan's hostile reaction to the Russian lease of the Liaotung Peninsula. The possibility of an Anglo-Japanese entente against Russia could not be ruled out, nor could Russia afford to ignore the rapidly developing military capabilities of Japan.[23]

While the Russian government was more willing to explore the

[19] Andrew Malozemoff, *Russian Far Eastern Policy 1881–1904* (Berkeley and Los Angeles: Univ. of California Press, 1958), p. 91. See also *Komura Diplomacy*, I, 91–92; *NGB*, XXX, 384–386.

[20] Malozemoff, pp. 89–90.

[21] The "Port Arthur orientation" as used here refers to the propensity of Russian policy to concentrate its efforts on developing the ice-free ports of Port Arthur and Talien (Dairen) and on linking southern Manchuria by rail with northern Manchuria, and the like, thus deemphasizing its interests in Korea. The expression is taken from Malozemoff, pp. 107 ff.

[22] Hayashi to Nishi, January 7, 1898, *NGB*, XXI, Part I, 109–110.

[23] For a comparison of the military capabilities of Russia and Japan, see Malozemoff, pp. 108–109.

possibilities of an agreement with Japan, the new Russian minister in Seoul, Alexis de Speyer, was undermining the Russian position in Korea by his display of intemperate aggressiveness. In February 1898 he forced the reluctant Korean government to grant a lease for a Russian coaling station on Chŏllyŏng-do (Deer Island) in southern Korea, brushing aside unanimous objection of other foreign representatives in Seoul. However, it was a victory without substance, because Japanese agents were quick (and quiet) in buying up all possible sites for a coal depot on the island. It was also a Pyrrhic victory because Speyer's overbearing tactics invited vigorous protests from many Korean officials and especially from the Independence Club, an organization of reformists who demanded an end to all foreign interference. (More will be said of this club in the next chapter.) Impatient with these and other signs of resistance to Russian encroachments, Speyer threatened in March 1898 to end the service of Russian advisers unless the Korean government would unequivocally declare its pro-Russian orientation by punishing anti-Russian Korean officials. When the government, obviously irritated by the tactless Speyer, refused to comply, he fell into his own trap and was forced to withdraw all Russian employees of the Korean government.[24] The Russian influence in Seoul that had been skillfully and patiently cultivated by Waeber was thus destroyed overnight.

In view of the abrupt shift in the Russo-Japanese balance of power in Korea, the Japanese Foreign Office revised its terms for agreement with Russia. The new conditions stated that "the duty of extending such aid and assistance [as Korea would require] should be left to Japan," in return for Japan's willingness to consider Manchuria as being outside of Japan's sphere of interest if Russia would reciprocate with regard to Korea.[25] The proposal later became well publicized as a "plan to exchange Manchuria for Korea." The Russian response, however, was much firmer than Japan had anticipated. In Tokyo the Russian minister Rosen declared that "we cannot admit the exclusion as a matter of

[24] Chŏng Kyo, I, 176–178, 182–183; Lee Chong-sik, p. 62; Katō to Nishi, March 3, 8, 13, and 17, 1898, NGB, XXXI, Part I, 140, 143, 147, 155–157, 194.

[25] For Nishi's note verbale to Rosen dated March 19, 1898, see ibid., p. 153. See also Komura Diplomacy, I, 98.

principle of all influence of Russia who cannot divest herself of all concern in the destinies of a State adjacent to her frontier." [26]

For nearly a month, the Japanese foreign minister Nishi and Rosen continued bargaining until an agreement was finally worked out. The Russo-Japanese protocol signed on April 25, 1898, known as the Nishi-Rosen Agreement, covered three main points: (1) both countries recognized Korean independence and sovereignty and would refrain from direct interference in internal affairs, (2) both parties would refrain from nominating military and financial advisers to Korea without a prior mutual agreement, and (3) Russia would not interfere with Japanese commercial and industrial interests in Korea.[27] Japan could not yet exclude Russia from Korea but had at least regained an equal status in the matter of political influence over the Korean government. Moreover, Japan had obtained Russia's reluctant admission that Japan's economic interest in Korea was "large." [28] Although the new agreement was in essence similar to the 1896 agreements, the situation in Korea in 1898 was markedly different from that of two years before. Irrespective of the working of the diplomatic documents, the Russian tide had begun to recede from its high watermark of 1896–97.

The six years that followed the Nishi-Rosen Agreement of 1898 saw Japan and Russia coexist in Korea but with little pretense of hiding their suspicions of each other. Economically, Japan continued to enjoy the position of predominance, while Russia was ill prepared even to utilize the concession rights it possessed. Beginning with its occupation of Manchuria in 1900, Russia's interest in Korea had only secondary importance for its policy-makers, with the exception of a few periods of short dura-

[26] *NGB*, XXXI, Part I, 163–164.

[27] The French text, an English translation, and the Japanese text of the Nishi-Rosen agreement appear in *ibid.*, pp. 182–183, 183–184, 184–185.

[28] In 1898 Japan's share in Korea's export and import trade was (in values) 79.2 percent and 57.4 percent, respectively, while those of Russia were 1.0 percent and 0.9 percent. See Nohara Shirō, "Kinsei Shina Chōsen o meguru Nichiro no Kankei" [Russo-Japanese Relations with Regard to China and Korea in the Recent Period], in *Sekai Rekishi Taikei* [An Outline of World History], 25 vols. (Tokyo, 1934), IX, 402–403.

tion. Japan, on the other hand, became more than ever aware of Korea's strategic significance for Japanese security against the suspected southward thrust of Russian expansionism. The intensification of Japan's political interest in Korea was accompanied by an improvement of her international position as signified by the Anglo-Japanese Alliance of 1902. Russia, however, refused to make a complete renunciation of its political interest in Korea, thus making a Russo-Japanese conflict inevitable. Unlike the period that followed the Tientsin Treaty of 1885, Korea was now a relatively free agent and attempted to balance one powerful neighbor against another.

The tangible manifestations of Russo-Japanese rivalry were the struggles for concessions — leases for the use of Korean lands, railway constructions, and exploitation of timber and fishery resources. In 1899 Russian Minister A. I. Pavlov undertook to lease a strip of land near Masan, an ideal harbor site to the west of Pusan. A strong Japanese protest and the preemption of the most desirable pieces of land by the Japanese defeated Pavlov's plan. However, in 1900 Pavlov succeeded in persuading Korea to pledge that the island of Kŏje in the Masan area would not be leased to any foreign power.[29] With regard to Korean railroads, Japan finally obtained the right to construct the Seoul-Pusan line in September 1898 through an application of strong diplomatic pressure. In the following year, after the Seoul-Inch'ŏn line had been completed by an American, the Japanese government provided the funds for a Japanese group to purchase the line. Japan also showed great interest in acquiring the Seoul-Uiju line which the original French concession holder had financially been unable to construct. The Korean government refused both Japanese and Russian applications in 1903 to build the line. Instead, Korea declared its intention to build the railroad under its own management.

Japan was more successful in monopolizing the modern banking system of Korea. Beginning in May 1902, the Korean branch

[29] For the text of the Russo-Korean agreement on nonalienation of Kŏje Island see Hayashi Gonsuke (Japanese Minister in Seoul) to Aoki, April 4, 1900, *NGB*, XXXIII, 221.

of the Japanese Daiichi Bank issued the so-called Shibuzawa notes which soon became unofficial legal tender, in spite of objections from the Korean government. In March 1899 a Russian named H. Keyserling acquired whaling rights in the waters off the Korean east coast. In the following year a similar whaling concession was granted to a Japanese.[30]

The most controversial of all was the timber concession granted to a Russian in 1896 for Ullŭng Island in the Sea of Japan and for the Tumen and the Yalu river regions. After years of inactivity that threatened the expiration of the concession, in 1898 the well-known Russian expansionist A. M. Bezobrazov became interested in the prospect of using the concession to develop Russian political and economic influence in the lower Yalu region. Starting with a fund provided from the personal treasury of the Czar, the Yalu operation grew into a serious economic and military project by the end of 1903. This furthered the already rapid deterioration in relations between Japan and Russia.[31]

On the whole, Japan reaped far more than Russia in these battles for concessions. Additional evidence of Japan's success in the economic sphere is Japan's continuing predominance in Korean trade [32] and the overwhelming numerical superiority of Japanese over Russian residents in Korea.[33] (See Appendix, Tables V and VI).

Russia's inferior economic position in Korea was partly due to her increasing commitments in Manchuria, especially after the outbreak of the Boxer Rebellion. From June to October 1900 Russian troops occupied Manchuria, and it appeared that Russia

[30] K. Asakawa, *The Russo-Japanese Conflict* (Boston and New York: Houghton, Mifflin and Co., 1904), pp. 282–283.

[31] Many references to the Yalu timber concession appear in *ibid.*, pp. 285 ff; Hulbert, *History of Korea*, II, 346 ff; Malozemoff, chaps. 8–9.

[32] Japan's share in Korea's foreign trade maintained a high level of over 61 percent (in value) of imports to Korea and over 76 percent of exports from Korea in the years from 1899–1904. During the same period, Russian trade with Korea was almost negligible. See Nohara, *Sekai Rekishi Taikei*, IX, 402–403.

[33] In 1901, the number of Japanese residents in Korea was nearly 17,000, of which 2,360 persons were in Seoul; in 1899, Seoul had 1,764 Japanese and only 9 Russians. See *Korea Review*, I, 310; Conroy, p. 466.

would not stop short of establishing firm political control over these Chinese provinces. Simultaneously there were indications that Russia might make a political retreat from Korea.

In January 1901 Russia proposed to Japan "a scheme for the neutralization of Corea under the joint guarantee of the Powers." [34] Japan turned down the proposal with an acid remark that Russia's occupation of Manchuria had made Korean independence illusory, as Japan's occupation of the Liaotung Peninsula in 1895 had been so regarded by Russia.[35] Japan desired to maintain and expand her "preponderate" position in Korea and to induce Russia to give her a free hand in Korea in return for recognition of Russian interests in Manchuria.[36] Thus the plan to "exchange" Korea for Manchuria which Foreign Minister Nishi had proposed in 1898 was revived. The primacy of Japan's interest in Korea and her willingness to let Russia incorporate Manchuria, if need be, were clearly stated by the Japanese minister in London, Hayashi Tadasu, to British Foreign Secretary Lansdowne in July 1901: "[Japan] was above all things interested in Corea, and it was a matter of life and death for them to keep Russia out of it. Their [Japanese] interest in Manchuria was only secondary, and due to the fact that encroachments in Manchuria might lead to enroachments in Corea." [37]

The official Russian position was that Russia could not renounce its interest in Korea altogether and that Manchuria could not be considered as a *quid pro quo* for Korea. The Russo-

[34] Baron Rosen made the proposal on January 7, 1901, to Foreign Minister Katō Takaski. See *NGB*, XXXIV, 521.

[35] Katō to Chinda (St. Petersburg), January 17, 1901, *ibid.*, pp. 526–528. The Korean government had entertained some hope for an internationally guaranteed neutralization of their country and had made inquiries in 1900 regarding the Russian and Japanese responses. See Yamaza (Seoul) to Katō, January 11, 1901; Hayashi (Seoul) to Aoki, September 14, 1900, *ibid.*, pp. 523–524.

[36] Komura stated this as his personal view. See Komura to Kurino (St. Petersburg), September 19, 1902, *ibid.*, XXXV, 392–394.

[37] See Lansdowne to Whitehead (in Tokyo), October 16, 1901, *in* Great Britain, the Foreign Office, *British Documents on the Origins of the War, 1898–1914*, ed. G. P. Gooch and Harold Temperley, 11 vols. (London: H. M. Stationery Office, 1926–1938), II, 97.

Japanese controversy that was to lead to open hostilities stemmed from such differences.

Hopes and efforts to narrow these differences existed in both Japan and Russia. In Japan, Itō Hirobumi was foremost in advocating an understanding with Russia by a sort of demilitarization of Korea. In the latter part of 1901 he traveled to St. Petersburg to seek an agreement that would give Japan a free hand regarding political, industrial, and commercial relations in Korea in return for a promise not to use the Korean peninsula for any military purpose. The Japanese cabinet headed by General Katsura Tarō was not entirely pleased with Itō's private project in St. Petersburg; Katsura and Foreign Minister Komura Jutarō believed, as did Katsura's patron, Yamagata, that a war with Russia would be inevitable in the long run and that Japan needed an ally — Great Britain — to win the war. Preliminary negotiations between Japan and Great Britain were in progress in London, and they feared Itō's Russian trip would ruin the London talks by making the British suspect Japan's good faith.

Itō's project came to a sudden end with the signing of the Anglo-Japanese Treaty of Alliance on January 30, 1902. The alliance was a logical outcome of British concern over Russian intentions regarding the British spheres of interest in China proper and of the Japanese fear of the Russian menace directed against Korea. As far as Japan was concerned, therefore, the new alliance was primarily for the purpose of keeping Russia out of Korea. Prime Minister Katsura suspected that Russia would attempt to seize Korea after Manchuria.[38]

In the course of the negotiations for the alliance Japan revealed that she wanted something more than prevention of the absorption of Korea by a third power. Japan's intention was to have the British underwrite Japan's freedom of action in Korea. The first article read in part: "Japan . . . is interested in a peculiar degree, politically as well as commercially and industrially, in Korea." This admission of Japan's "peculiar" interests in Korea was preceded by a joint disavowal of any aggressive intention

[38] This was stated in a memorandum written by Katsura that explained his decision to authorize the negotiations for the treaty of alliance. See a reproduction of the memorandum in *Komura Diplomacy*, I, 257–259.

against China and Korea and was followed by a reciprocal recognition of each other's right to intervene in either China or Korea. If such measures of intervention should lead to a war for either contracting party, the other was to remain benevolently neutral. If a third power should join the war against one of the allies, the other party to the alliance was to aid its ally.[39]

The Korean government was greatly alarmed when it learned of the Anglo-Japanese alliance. It feared that Japan was now ready to fight Russia — with unpleasant consequences for Korea. It also feared that Japan would interfere more actively in Korean affairs than she had during the past several years. The Korean emperor told Japanese Minister Hayashi Gonsuke in March 2, 1902, that he (the emperor) would henceforth make stronger efforts for domestic reforms, as if this gesture were all that was needed to keep Japan from resorting to aggressive actions in Korea.[40] In August 1903 Korea formally requested the Japanese and Russian governments to consider Korea as a neutral country in case of war and to spare Korea from the hostile military operations of either belligerent.[41]

The Korean plea was of little import to Tokyo and St. Petersburg. In the summer of 1903 direct negotiations were underway for the settlement of the explosive issues between Japan and Russia. Japan sought Russia's recognition of her "preponderant" interests and a complete freedom of action in Korea. Russia, however, was not willing to go that far; Russia's counterproposal confined Japan's right to assist Korea with "advice and instructions in the interests of reform and good government in Korea," and

[39] For the full text, see Great Britain, the Foreign Office, *British and Foreign State Papers*, XCV, 83–84; or *NGB*, XXXV, 20–21. An English diplomatic historian writes, "The British prevented any Japanese combine with Russia and strengthened the barrier against any further Russian advance. The price they paid was small: . . . their only sacrifice was Korea, and that was only a sacrifice of principle." See A. J. P. Taylor, *The Struggle for Mastery in Europe, 1848–1918* (London: Oxford University Press, 1954), p. 400.

[40] Hayashi to Komura, March 2, 1902, *NGB*, XXXV, 31–32. The emperor's pledge of reforms was not carried out. See Nelson, p. 247.

[41] Hayashi to Komura, June 8, and August 26, 1903, *NGB*, XXXVI, Part I, 464, 542.

provided for a neutral zone in Korea from the thirty-ninth parallel northward to the Yalu-Tumen border. Even the right to dispatch Japanese troops to Korea was to be subject to "a notification to Russia" in advance.[42]

Although Russia was ready to admit Japan's "preponderant" interests in Korea, its insistence on the neutral zone and on the prohibition against using Korea for military purposes remained unchanged until the end of the torturous negotiations in February 1904.[43] With active military preparations in progress on both sides, suspicion bred suspicion leading to hostilities.

War between Russia and Japan finally broke out early in 1904, and on the first day the Japanese navy scored a one-sided victory in Korean waters immediately outside Inch'ŏn harbor, a Korean neutrality declaration of January 21, 1904, notwithstanding.[44] The battle of Inch'ŏn signalized the end of Russo-Japanese rivalry in Korea. It also signalized the beginning of exclusive Japanese control over Korea, unrestricted and uncontested by a third power.

[42] For a partial reproduction of the czar's note of August 29, 1903, see Malozemoff, pp. 239–240. For a Japanese rendition of the Russian counter-proposal dated October 3, 1903, see *Komura Diplomacy*, I, 334–335.

[43] For details on the amendments and counteramendments exchanged between October 3, 1903, and February 5, 1904, see *ibid.*, pp. 335–360; Malozemoff, pp. 241–249.

[44] For a text of the Korean neutrality declaration, see *NGB*, XXXVII, Part I, 310–311.

7.

The Reform Movement and Its Aftermath, 1896-1904

While Korea was serving as the pigskin during these years of international football between Japan and Russia, other contests for power within her borders occupied much of her attention. The most phenomenal development in Korean politics in the few years that followed the murder of the queen was the growth of a new political party called *Tongnip Hyŏp'hoe* (Association for National Independence) or the Independence Club. It drew its inspiration from Sŏ Chae-p'il, a young revolutionary of 1884 who had spent over ten years in the United States and who had returned to Korea in January 1896 as an American citizen and a physician with the Anglicized name of Dr. Philip Jaisohn.[1] He had accepted the position of an adviser to the Korean Privy Council (*Chungch'uwŏn*) which had replaced the more active Reform Council in December 1894.[2] The pro-Japanese cabinet headed by Kim Hong-jip was anxious to draw Jaisohn into the cabinet, but he declined the honor because of his wish to remain free from partisan politics and devote his energy to popular enlightenment.[3]

[1] For a brief account of his life see Jaisohn's autobiography "Ch'aemi Osipnyŏn" [Fifty Years in America] appended to Min T'ae-wŏn, *Kapsin Chŏngpyŏn kwa Kim Ok-kyun* [The Coup of 1884 and Kim Ok-kyun] (Seoul, 1947), pp. 86–92.

[2] Wilkinson, *The Corean Government*, p. 2. Due to a shift in Minister Inoue Kaoru's policy, the Privy Council possessed no real power and it was to remain a weak sinecure organization.

[3] Yi Sŏn-gŭn, *Han'guk Tongnip Undongsa* [History of Korean Independence Movement] (Seoul, 1956), p. 200; Philip Jaisohn, "What Korea Needs Most," *Korean Repository*, III (1896), 108–110.

In order to educate the masses, Jaisohn started the first private newspaper *Tongnip Sinmun*, or the *Independent*, in April 1896. The *Independent* was published in four pages; the last page was written in English while the other three were in Korean written with Korean phonetics instead of the more conventional Chinese characters. The editorial policy was "Korea for Koreans."[4] The first issue of the *Independent* carried an editorial written by Jaisohn which proclaimed emphatically the editor's intention to speak in the interest of Korea and nothing else and to serve all Koreans, high or low in social status, in Seoul or elsewhere in the country.[5]

Almost simultaneously with the founding of the *Independent*, Jaisohn helped a small group of 30-odd reform advocates, some in the government and many ex-officials, to organize the Independence Club. Jaisohn himself declined formal membership but became an adviser to the club. Later in the same year, the new organization began publication of a journal twice a month to promote patriotism, reforms, and Western knowledge.[6] In addition to the printed words, the Independence Club sought to arouse nationalistic pride by erecting a stone arch, the Gate of Independence, near the western limit of the capital where the Gate of Welcoming [Chinese] Blessing had once stood. The name of a building that had been used to entertain Chinese envoys in the days of the tributary relations was changed from the Hall of Adoration of China to the Hall of Independence and the club used it to hold public debates. To these weekly Sunday meetings came some high officials riding in sedan chairs and escorted by several servants in strict accordance with the long-standing conventions. They betrayed their ignorance when such topics as street lights to prevent crimes were discussed.[7]

[4] *Ibid.*, p. 171. It was published four times a week at first but later became a daily publication.

[5] See a reprint of the editorial in *Sin-dong-a* [New East Asia] (Seoul), a supplement to the January 1966 issue, pp. 36–37.

[6] Paek Sun-jae, "Tongnip Hyŏp'hoe Wŏlbo wa Kajŏng Chapji" [The Independence Association Monthly and Home Magazines], *Sasangge* (September 1965), pp. 270–274.

[7] For a description of one of these discussion meetings, see Yun Hyo-jŏng, *P'ung'un Hanmal Pirok* [Secret Records of the Turbulent Last Years of Korea] (Seoul, 1937), pp. 183–186.

As long as Jaisohn and his friends in the Independence Club confined their activities to discussions on issues of lesser importance such as street lights, they posed no threat to those in power. Within a relatively short time, however, these reformists were voicing their views on matters of greater significance. Their slogan of complete national independence was at first welcome to the king and the Korean government. The anomaly of the royal residence within the Russian legation in 1896–1897 was a damaging blow to the dignity of an independent Korea, and Jaisohn and some leading members of the Independence Club were among those who implored the king to return to his palace. In March 1898, as Speyer's behavior became increasingly highhanded, the Independence Club sponsored a mass rally in downtown Seoul to demand the expulsion of all Russian advisers and the resignation of the pro-Russian foreign minister. Following Speyer's anticlimactic retreat the Korean government summarily terminated Jaisohn's contract and forced him to leave Korea as an indirect expression of its disapproval of the mass rally tactics of the Independence Club. By this time Jaisohn's untiring and outspoken advocacy of libertarian reforms and his blunt remonstrations to the Korean sovereign had made him unwelcome.[8]

Indeed the political reforms Jaisohn was advocating in 1896–1898 envisioned radical changes in the political system. In the fourth issue of the *Independent* we find him advocating popular elections to select local officials up to the level of the provincial governor.[9] At about the same time, writing in an English language journal published in Seoul by American missionaries, he urged dismissal of two-thirds of the government officials to save money and contended that the remaining one-third could fill the gap by working more diligently.[10] Discounting a certain amount of emotionalism in these few illustrations, we should nevertheless note that Jaisohn's program was ultimately to lead to some form of representative government under a constitutional monarch. It is not surprising, therefore, that the conservative forces in the

[8] Hulbert, *History of Korea*, II, 310; Kim To-t'ae, *Sŏ Chae-p'il Paksa Chasŏjŏn* [Autobiography of Dr. Sŏ Chae-p'il] (Seoul, 1948), pp. 211–212.

[9] Chong-sik Lee, *The Politics of Korean Nationalism*, p. 60.

[10] Philip Jaisohn, "Korean Finance," *Korean Repository*, III (1896), 166–168.

government and the king, the natural and devoted champion of the traditional absolute monarchy, should view Jaisohn and his reformist supporters in the Independence Club with increasing hostility.

In these few years following the king's escape to the Russian legation, the conservatives were in the ascendancy in the government. In sharp contrast to the rising voice for reforms outside the government, the officials in power were gradually undoing earlier reform measures. After the hegira one of the first royal decrees rescinded the unpopular anti-topknot ordinance, thereby serving notice of reversion to the old status quo. In September 1896, the governmental structure was changed back to the old *uijŏngbu* (the council of state) from the modern *naegak* (the cabinet) system. The council headed by a chancellor (*ŭijŏng*) was to deliberate and pass resolutions on matters of state, but its resolutions became enforceable only with the royal approval. Moreover, the king could even give his assent to a motion that had received support only from a minority in the council. In other words, the Inoue-sponsored reform to curtail the abuse of the royal prerogatives was replaced by a renewed assertion of royal authority. In October the minister of education published a book, *The Warp and Woof of Confucianism*, which heaped abuses on the "barbarious teachings" of Christianity, on Westerners, and on the Japanese while acclaiming China as "the center of Civilization."[11]

The regressive tendency of the royal court continued after the return of the king to the palace. A foreign observer grieved, in May 1897, over the "complete" and "pathetic" collapse of the reform sentiment in the Korean government.[12] The Independence Club was foremost in sounding public warnings. One of the few occasions in 1897 when the nationalistic reformists and the conservatives could see eye to eye was the elevation of the royal title from that of a king (*wang*) to emperor (*hwangje*). The name of the country was also changed, in October, from *Chosŏn* to *Taehan*

[11] *Ibid.*, p. 421; Horace N. Allen, *Korea: Fact and Fancy* (Seoul: Methodist Publishing House, 1904), p. 198. Due to protests from Western representatives, the book was suppressed soon after publication.

[12] "Reformation, Revision, Regulation," an editorial, *Korean Repository*, IV (1897), 192.

("Great Han"); the new official name of the nation thus became
Taehan Cheguk (the Empire of Great Han).[13]

By the time of Jaisohn's dismissal, the Independence Club had
grown into a potent radical organization. It was no longer a simple
debating society; it had become an active political pressure group
that had successfully mobilized several thousands in anti-Russian
and anti-corruption rallies. Although the exact figures are not
available, the club membership had increased. The few high
officials who had joined the club in the early days of its existence
(such as Yi Wan-yong, a pro-Russian official who later became
pro-Japanese and presided over the extinction of an independent
Korea) had quit the club, and a new breed of young activists
(such as the young Yi Sŭng-man, or Syngman Rhee) had joined
the ranks. As Jaisohn departed for the United States, the presidency of the club was entrusted to the hands of Yun Ch'i-ho, a
34-year-old former official in the Ministry of Education who had
traveled and studied in Japan and the United States.[14] Under
Yun's leadership, the club devoted most of its attention to domestic reforms.

Accusations of the corrupt and the greedy in officialdom followed and Cho Pyŏng-sik, the vice-president of the Privy Council,
resigned under fire from the Independence Club. Yun Ch'i-ho, at
an imperial audience, requested that his club be recognized as a
vital link between the government and the people. A cleaning of
the imperial household to expel the palace favorites was vigor-
ously demanded. In an apparent move to appease the radicals,
Yun Ch'i-ho and three of his club members were appointed members of the Privy Council in early July.

Conspiracies of all kinds followed one another. Various groups
schemed to force abdication in favor of the crown prince, or
sought to increase the power of other members of the court. Even
an attempt to poison the emperor was made — unsuccessfully —
and his fear for safety made him authorize the American adviser
Greathouse to recruit 30 Westerners in Shanghai — "European
and Americans ruffians" as the Japanese described them — to

[13] Allen, *Korea: Fact and Fancy*, p. 201. Japan, Russia, and the United
States recognized the new title for the Korean sovereign.

[14] See Hulbert, *History of Korea*, II, 316.

form an imperial bodyguard. Opposition from the Independence Club and from within the government caused the cancellation of the project after considerable money had been spent.[15]

It was against the backdrop of such political chaos that the supporters of the Independence Club clashed with those in the government. In early October 1898 the club began demanding the dismissal of several high government officials. The first target was the conservative minister of justice who had written the antiforeign tract on Confucianism in 1896 during his tenure as minister of education. He was accused of reintroducing the old torture system in dealing with suspects. Soon public lectures and a stream of petitions and memorials to the government from the club demanded the resignation of six ministers. On October 11, the club mobilized students in various foreign language and missionary schools and staged a mass demonstration in front of the palace. The emperor succumbed to this display of mass strength and dismissed the accused ministers.

Their success perhaps whetted the enthusiasm of the reformers. On October 14, the leaders of the club held a joint conference with the key officials of the government and presented a revolutionary request that the Privy Council be reconstituted to admit 25 popular representatives, or one-half of the enlarged council membership. According to a later resolution, the representatives were to be elected by a "people's assembly" from among those who were 27 or more years old and who were knowledgeable and talented in politics and law.[16] For the first time in Korean history, a demand for something approaching popular participation in the government was voiced.

The emperor became disturbed enough by the audacity of the club to issue a rebuke for "the wanton discussion of governmental affairs" by a private organization.[17] On the same day, the club sponsored a new mass organization, *Manmin Kongdonghoe* (Ten Thousand People's Cooperative Association), or what an Ameri-

[15] Chŏng Kyo, I, 236–239; Katō to Ōkuma, October 5, 1898, *NGB*, XXXI, Part II, 395–397.

[16] *Ibid.*, Chŏng Kyo, I, 261–263, 288. Chŏng Kyo, having been a leading participant in this episode, gives the most detailed account of it.

[17] *Ibid.*, p. 266.

can observer chose to call "a people's assembly," perhaps to widen the base for its popular support.[18] Agitation by the radicals continued with scant regard for the imperial rebuke. On October 29 the club held another mass rally to which came not only the club members but also the ministers of the government, students from missionary and language schools, many newly organized quasi-political groups, a women's organization, and even a butchers' guild. This "meeting of the government and citizenry" adopted six resolutions which included a pledge not to rely on foreign aid, a demand for more strict control of contracts with foreigners, a demand for a fair public trial for "important offenders," a demand requiring the sovereign to appoint ministers only with the concurrence of the majority of the cabinet, a demand for a unitary system of taxation administered by the ministry of finance and for publication of annual estimates and balances, and a demand for the faithful and impartial enforcement of the existing laws and regulations. In spite of the pledge to endeavor to strengthen "the imperial power," the majority of the resolutions were demands for a curtailment of the arbitrary powers of the sovereign; they reflected a popular protest against misgovernment by an absolute monarch.[19]

The weak and indecisive emperor and his undistinguished Council of State must have been impressed with the intensity and the scope of the protest, but they could not immediately resort to forceful suppression because the Council or the cabinet was neither united nor powerful, subject as it was to an almost daily change in its membership due to the pressures and counterpressures upon the emperor, and because the soldiers and the police were sympathetic to the protesters. The emperor had become highly displeased, if not actually terrified, by these developments. On October 25 he had appointed a former military officer as the vice-minister of justice; this official had been busy mobilizing the notorious peddlers. Korean history had seen precedents in which the disciplined and militant peddlers armed with cudgels

[18] Allen, *Korea: Fact and Fancy*, p. 206.

[19] For an English text of the resolutions, see Hulbert, *History of Korea*, II, 319. A Japanese text appears in Hioki to Ōkuma, November 8, 1898, *NGB*, XXXI, Part II, 404–405.

acted as para-military mercenaries in the service of the government.[20] Until these peddlers could be brought into the capital, however, the government had to appease the radicals and procrastinate. The emperor formally approved the six-item resolution adopted at the mass rally. On November 2 the Privy Council was formally reorganized to provide equal representation between the government appointees and the "popular delegates" selected by the Independence Club. In reality the government was only waiting for an opportune moment to crush the reform movement.

On November 5, a few days after the entry into Seoul of the peddlers, the government declared the Independence Club subversive and arrested a number of its leaders, although its president, Yun Ch'i-ho, managed to go into hiding. A formal decree from the throne ordered the club to disband. The club had been quiescent for the preceding few days while preparing to elect 25 new members to the Privy Council. The apparently treacherous shift of government policy accompanied by the reentry of the foes of the club into the cabinet angered the supporters of the club, which now included a large number of merchants and other occupational groups. A huge mass demonstration followed, while the stores closed their doors. In the name of the "people's assembly," protests were made which forced the government to release the radicals after a sham trial held on November 10. The assembly wanted more; it demanded punishment of the ministers responsible for the act of betrayal. Near anarchy reigned in the city while the emperor had to banish "the five evilsome" ex-ministers.[21]

In ten days the counteroffensive by the peddlers began. Unarmed demonstrators were attacked by the peddlers on Novem-

[20] Peddlers were known as *pubosang*; they sold earthen wares, textiles, and other household goods carried either in shoulder bags or on wooden racks borne on their backs. For nearly 200 years they had maintained a tightly knit guild organization which was officially declared illegal by a reform decree of 1894. In 1882, at the time of the mutiny, the peddlers sided with the Mins and threatened the shortlived regime of the *Taewŏn'gun*. See Hwang Hyŏn, p. 60; "The Peddlers' Guild," *Korea Review*, III (1903), 337–342; Japan, Chōsen Chūsatsu Kempeitai Shireibu, *Chōsen Shakaikō*, p. 60.

[21] Pak Yŏng-hyo sent a considerable sum of money from Japan for the radicals, according to Chŏng Kyo, I, 327–328.

ber 21 resulting in heavy casualties. The enraged citizenry fought battles of revenge in and near the capital on the following days with slingshots, stones, and sticks.[22] Before the mob fury subsided, the homes of their foes had been laid waste. Again the emperor attempted reconciliation by changes in the government, but the tension did not dissipate quickly. As a last resort and acting upon strong urging from the foreign representatives, the emperor personally appeared before the crowd of demonstrators and exhorted them to cease agitations and disperse.[23] He also ordered the peddlers group to do the same. The unprecedented imperial plea was effective; although memorials and countermemorials continued to pour into the government for some more weeks, the threat of revolutionary uprising subsided. By the end of the year, the people's assembly disbanded itself.

The Independence Club failed to obtain many of its stated objectives in spite of the massive popular support which at times was strong enough to force the government to grant political concessions.[24] It failed despite the sympathy and encouragement given it by the foreign community in Seoul, particularly the American missionaries. Compared to the earlier attempts at reform — the coup of 1884 and the 1894–95 reforms — it had the advantage of having no stigma of foreign (Japanese) sponsorship. Compared to the *Tonghak* rebellion, it had the advantage of a relatively enlightened and socially respectable leadership. Above all, the activities of the Independence Club were not encumbered by international complications that had jeopardized those earlier reform movements and popular protests against the corrupt regime. Its failure, therefore, was a more serious indication of the dysfunctionality of the Korean body politic and dealt a more crippling blow to the progress of modernization.

[22] An eye witness description of the sticks-and-stones battle appears in William F. Sands, *Undiplomatic Memories* (New York: Whittlesey House, 1930), pp. 152–154. See also Chŏng Kyo, I, 331–341.

[23] The emperor also intimated his approval of the demonstrators' demands. See *ibid.*, pp. 351–352; Hulbert, *History of Korea*, II, 323.

[24] Although Independence Club activities had been confined largely to Seoul, there had also been certain preparations for spreading the movement to other areas of Korea by organizing local branches of the club. See Chŏng Kyo, II, 1–2.

It appears that the failure of the 1898 reform movement can be attributed to four major causes. The first is the organizational weakness of the movement. The popular assemblies were ad hoc organizations and lacked discipline and structural cohesion. They could display impressive outbursts of emotional energy in occasional mass rallies but did not have sufficient organizational strength for sustained political action. Furthermore, the leaders of the movement lacked experience and skill in guiding a mass movement; they mobilized the crowd but could not direct it, especially following the peddlers' attack on the demonstrators. Secondly, there were errors of strategy and tactics. The Independence Club and its supporters failed to exploit fully their initial advantages. They were beguiled by the intermittent gestures of appeasement of their opponents; they relaxed their vigilance and weakened their organizational strength at crucial junctures such as the first few days of November, thereby giving the conservative officials the necessary time to prepare a counterattack.

The third and probably the most basic weakness was the inability or unwillingness of the reform leaders to recognize the need for drastic changes in the existing political institutions, including the monarchy. They concentrated their energy on removing and punishing a handful of high officials whom they accused of corruption and treasonable acts. They requested one-half of the seats in the reconstructed Privy Council for "people's delegates," but the council was merely an insignificant appendage to the central governing machinery; it is doubtful that it would ever have developed into a genuine representative assembly even under more favorable circumstances. What Korea needed in 1898 for national revitalization was not only new faces in the government or a new advisory council but an entirely new political framework that would have cleared away the debris of the past for construction of a new edifice. Mere patchwork was bound to fail when drastic surgery was called for. The Independence Club was seeking "reform from above" relying on the dim prospect of converting the ruler to its cause. However, to strengthen the imperial power, as the club loudly proclaimed, was to strengthen the force of reactionary conservatism. The absolute monarchy wedded to the traditional institutions and values was hardly a likely source of support for reform. Perhaps our analysis here asks too much of Yun Ch'i-ho and even Jaisohn; their *yangban* origin may have been an insurmountable limitation on their political outlook. It seems clear that as long as these reformists were unable to do much more than petition and remonstrate, their cause was doomed to failure.

This leads us to examine the fourth reason for the defeat of the reformists: the strength and the tactics of the antireform elements in the government, especially the emperor himself. The Korean monarch and his top advisers had vested interests in the prolongation of the traditional system of government, with minor modifications if necessary, which emphasized the Confucian virtue of unquestioning loyalty of the subjects to the ruler. They naturally condemned "the wanton discussion of governmental affairs" by the people. The emperor was not a man of progressive outlook despite his earlier interests in things foreign and novel — an interesting contrast to his counterpart in China who was instrumental in the so-called One Hundred Days Reform movement in the same year, 1898. Since his ascension to the throne in 1864, the Korean monarch had chafed under irksome pressures on him by his father (the *Taewŏn'gun*), his queen, the Japanese, the Chinese, and the Russians. He was at last free (at least temporarily) from all of them and was not willing to allow the Independence Club or anyone else to curtail his arbitrary powers.[25] When the arrest of the leaders of the Independence Club was ordered on November 5, the conservative Cho Pyŏng-sik had charged them with conspiracy to establish a republican government in which Yun Chi'i-ho was allegedly the vice-president designate.[26] At the height of the mass demonstrations it was the emperor acting on the advice of the conservative officials who had allegedly readied the corps of peddlers. It was he who dismissed and reappointed, banished and pardoned one after another high official in order to gain time for the eventual suppression of the Independence Club. In the course of these kaleidoscopic shifts in his position, the demonstrators became confused and divided.

[25] The *Taewŏn'gun* died early in 1898, Chŏng Kyo, I, 173.
[26] *Ibid.*, pp. 289–290.

There is no question that the Independence Club had failed, just like the earlier reform attempts of 1884 and 1894–1895. It nevertheless deserves a prominent mention in the history of modernization in Korea. The club was unique in that it represented the first genuine reform movement of Koreans themselves without active foreign interference. In two decades following Korea's "opening" in 1876, there had been gradual intellectual awakening among some impressionable members of the *yangban* class, particularly among those few who had traveled abroad. Men like Yun Ch'i-ho fit this characterization. However, there were others in this movement who had no direct exposure to Western civilization; Chŏng Kyo, a former county magistrate, played an active role as a key member of the Independence Club and wrote a detailed account of the reform movement which was valuable to the present authors. For Chŏng and others like him, modernization was desirable perhaps not so much for the sake of modernization per se but for what it promised in the way of ridding the government of official corruption and of strengthening the country to safeguard its independence. If Yun was more of a modernizer and Chŏng, a nationalist, the younger activists in this period who had held no governmental positions before were to inherit both of these trends in the reform movement; Yi Sŭng-man (Syngman Rhee) was typical in this group. Many of the club members were later to become leaders in politics, education, and journalism in Korea, and for most of them the 1898 episode was the catalystic experience.

One more unique aspect of the Independence Club activities was the quasi-legal methods it employed in its reform campaign. It did not resort to a palace coup (as in 1884) or a massive uprising (as in the *Tonghak* revolt which, as we have seen, was strongly colored by political and social egalitarian reformism); publication, public debate, petition, and largely peaceful demonstrations were the principal means of the reformists' political actions unlike any previous reform attempts in Korea. In short, the Independence Club was the first native and modern political party for the cause of modernization and reform which, despite its obvious failure in 1898, served as a training ground for future leaders.

The years between 1899 and 1904 were to demonstrate what Korea could do for itself in the relative absence of pressure from foreign powers. As a result of the failure of the 1898 reform movement, the emperor was left relatively free for five years to direct affairs in accordance with his own ideas and judgement. A simple description of the Korean scene during these five years prior to the outbreak of the Russo-Japanese War is that the political, economic, and social conditions of the nation continued to deteriorate under an absolutistic regime dominated by petty, rapacious, and irresponsible court favorites. There were no large-scale convulsions; it was a gradual process of system decay.

On the surface many modern innovations were introduced. In September 1899, the Seoul-Inch'ŏn railway was opened for traffic part of the way and was completed, following the construction of the modern bridge over the Han River, in July 1900. About a year later the Japanese began constructing the Seoul-Pusan railway. The capital city acquired new foreign-style buildings, one of which was a library within the palace. Electric streetcars ran through the streets of Seoul beginning in 1899, and by the summer of 1901 electric lights were available for its residents. Schools, a modern hospital, and a few factories — a mint, a rice mill, porcelain works, and so forth — were built. Foreign mail service opened in January 1900, followed by the inauguration of parcel post to Japan the following year. Modern bank notes to replace the cumbersome copper coins for transactions involving moderate to large sums of money were issued, albeit by the Daiichi Bank of Japan, for the first time in April 1902.[27]

Following the resumption of diplomatic relations with China, a Chinese minister, Hsu Shou-peng, arrived in September 1899, bearing a letter from "the great emperor of the Great Ch'ing" to "the great emperor of the Great Han (Korea)."[28] In the course

[27] Allen, *Korea: Fact and Fancy*, pp. 209 ff.

[28] Hwang Hyŏn, pp. 232-233; Allen, *Korea: Fact and Fancy*, pp. 209, 221.

of 1901 Great Britain and France elevated the ranks of their representatives in Korea to that of minister resident.[29]

Behind these seemingly hopeful signs of progress, however, there was a tendency to reinforce and perpetuate the old attitudes and institutions. In March 1899 the imperial court appointed ten new senior scholars (*paksa*) to the government-supported Confucian College (*Sŏnggyun'gwan*) in the hope of reviving the study of orthodox Confucianism.[30] Early in 1903, many Confucian scholars sent in memorials in support of the one submitted by Cho Pyŏng-sik — one of "the five evilsome" ministers accused by the Independence Club — which advocated the restoration of the old and discredited civil service examination system. The emperor was disposed to approve the memorial although he was eventually dissuaded, allegedly by foreign representatives.[31] The palace attracted the greedy favor seekers who catered to the vanity of the emperor. Among those were foreigners as well as Koreans. To quote from an American adviser to the imperial household at this time, "the court was full of idle, hungry native place hunters" while "each legation chief and diplomatic consul . . . maintained an organized native group within the palace."[32] Sorcerers and witches were among the frequent visitors to the palace. Agents sent out from the palace roamed the country selling public offices and exacting special taxes in addition to the regular land tax.[33]

In this game for imperial favor, the most ruthless and cunning won. Against the abuse of power by the emperor and his infamous ministers, the commoners had no defense. Advocates of reforms in the tradition of the Independence Club were hunted down and suppressed throughout these years. The peasants in the southern provinces of Chŏlla and Kyŏngsang organized secret societies known as *hwalpindang* ("help-the-poor party") in order to resist the tax collectors and the landowning *yangban* class. The *Tong-*

---

[29] *Ibid.*, pp. 217, 221.

[30] Hwang Hyŏn, p. 235.

[31] *Ibid.*, p. 289; *Korea Review*, III, 168–172.

[32] Sands, pp. 54–56.

[33] See a memorial by Chancellor Yun Yong-sŏn in 1900 which deplored these baneful practices, Hwang Hyŏn, pp. 247–248.

hak followers were reported to be still active in parts of southern Korea in 1900.[34] The most serious of these spontaneous uprisings of the exploited took place in the island of Cheju in 1901. It was a year of famine in most parts of southern Korea. The imposition of a new system of taxation upon the islanders and the official favoritism shown to the Christian (Catholic) converts were the cause of the rioting. A massive display of force subdued the rioters without a serious encounter, but the Cheju uprising symbolized the popular discontent against the oppressive regime.[35]

With the exception of these incidents, the nation was in a state of tranquil decadence. The Boxer uprisings in China caused some alarm in Korea, but the peninsula was spared the tribulations that its neighbor had to suffer. This period of Korean quietude was due primarily to the effectiveness of the 1896–1898 understanding between Russia and Japan. When Russo-Japanese relations began to show signs of strain in the early years of the twentieth century, Korea could not escape their disturbing impact. It is difficult to believe that Korea could have survived the Russo-Japanese conflict without suffering the fatal consequence that was in store, even had she been governed by a more enlightened regime. On the other hand, it is quite certain that the regressive and venal regime under the personal rule of the emperor had not prepared the nation to face the extraordinary situation of 1904–1905.

At the outbreak of the Russo-Japanese War in February 1904, Japan moved powerful military forces into Korea. For the second time in ten years, Koreans saw their capital city and a large part of their native land occupied by the alien army. The captive government in Seoul was forced to give up, step by step, its sovereign powers. Japan did not act as impetuously as she did in 1894–1895, nor was she to encounter any serious opposition

[34] *Ibid.*, pp. 248, 250–251, 259; Allen, *Korea: Fact and Fancy*, p. 220; McKenzie, *Tragedy of Korea*, pp. 100–101.

[35] *Korea Review*, I, 256–267; "The Disturbance on Quelpart," tr. from the *Revue de l'Extrême Orient* by E. Martel, *ibid.*, pp. 539–542; Hwang Hyŏn, p. 271. For Sands' own account of his experience in this island of "the Amazons" see Sands, pp. 163–178. Sands suspects that the rioters had been instigated by the Japanese.

from a third power. In the years of 1904–1910, the last act of the demise of the kingdom of Korea unfolded. Under the shadow of the Japanese bayonet, Korea became a Japanese protectorate in 1905 and five years later was reduced to a colony of the expanding empire of Japan. In the remaining chapters we will examine the instruments and the techniques of Japanese control and the record of desperate Korean efforts to resist Japan in these final years.

PART III

JAPANESE PROTECTORATE IN KOREA

8.

The Protectorate Treaty

From the very first day of the Russo-Japanese hostilities, the Japanese army held complete military hegemony in the peninsula; Russian military activities in Korea were negligible. From this time onward, Japan maintained at all times a powerful army in Korea; and this military superiority enabled Japan to induce the reluctant Korean government to conclude a series of agreements in 1904–1905 culminating in the treaty of November 17, 1905, which established a Japanese protectorate. Under the treaty Japan created the Residency-General in Seoul to take charge of Korea's external affairs; however, Japan did not confine itself to overseeing foreign relations alone. Matters of internal administration were also brought under Japanese control, thus turning its role into that of a de facto ruler.

A fortnight after the Japanese declaration of war on Russia, Japan obtained the first set of treaty rights that legitimated, step by step, her absorption of Korea. A protocol was signed in Seoul on February 23, 1904, that permitted Japan to take necessary measures to combat the threat to Korea caused by foreign aggression or by an internal disturbance. Korea was obligated to provide full facilities to the Japanese army and allow Japanese occupation of "such places as may be necessary" for strategic purposes (Article IV). This open-ended concession provided an ex post facto justification for Japanese military actions already taken. Far more important were the future consequences of this provision. The protocol also obligated Korea to accept Japanese advice and assistance for improvement of its administration (Article I). "Advice and assistance" easily became interference and supervision with the passage of time. A provision preventing Korea from seeking any outside assistance to defy Japan was also included in the protocol. This protocol was indeed "the first step in subordinating Korea" to Japan.[1] In light of these provisions, Japan's renewed pledge to safeguard the Korean imperial house and Korea's independence and territorial integrity (Articles II and III) must have sounded hollow.[2]

The protocol was the result of two-month-long negotiations initiated by Japan. The first draft of the protocol was designed as a mere affirmation of mutual friendship and cooperation, but the Korean emperor, on the advice of key court officials, refused to give his approval. Following the entry of four Japanese army battalions into Seoul and the Japanese naval victory off the port of Inch'ŏn, however, Japan presented a set of stronger demands. Present at the negotiation session was the commanding general of a Japanese army division who was also asked by the Japanese minister in Seoul to take "appropriate measures" against anti-protocol Korean officials.[3] Korea at last had to yield and the protocol was signed by the acting foreign minister.

Although bombs were thrown into the homes of the acting foreign minister and his assistant, and a few high officials memorialized the throne in protest, Korean reactions to the protocol were not as serious as one might expect. It seems that the full import of the concessions contained in the protocol escaped public attention. It is possible that many Koreans may have thought that Japanese domination of their country would be only temporary as it was in 1894–1895. Some court officials also believed in an ultimate Russian victory in the war and so advised the emperor.[4]

What Japan intended to do in Korea with the help of the protocol was soon made clear. At the end of May 1904, the Council of Elder Statesmen and the cabinet in Tokyo resolved,

[1] Quoted from Komura Diplomacy, II, 255.

[2] For the text of the protocol see NGB, XXXVII, Part I, 345–346.

[3] See a memorandum entitled "Protection and Annexation of Korea" prepared by the Japanese Government-General in Korea in 1917, reprinted in Kim Chŏng-myŏng (ed.), Nikkan Gaikō Shiryō Shūsei [Collection of Sources of Diplomatic Relations Between Japan and Korea], VIII, 13–16.

[4] Ibid.

in unequivocal terms, that Japan was "to take possession of the real powers of protection in political and military matters of Korea and to promote the development of our [Japanese] economic rights and interests in Korea." In other words, Japan was to establish a de facto protectorate. Also decided at this meeting were specific steps to implement the above objectives. Military occupation of Korea would continue even after the conclusion of peace with Russia; Korea's conduct of foreign affairs would be subject to Japanese supervision and veto, and Japan would make the Korean government hire an adviser for foreign affairs who would in turn take his orders from the Japanese foreign office; Korea would employ a Japanese adviser on financial affairs; Japan would construct and manage major railroad lines and telecommunication system and would encourage her farmers to emigrate to Korea; and it would also acquire additional forest, mining, and fishery concessions in Korea.[5] All of these steps and more were eventually carried out except for the plan to seek a lease for the state-owned wasteland in Korea for the use of Japanese farmer-settlers.[6]

The first significant step for Japanese exercise of "the real powers of protection" was an agreement signed on August 19, 1904, whereby Korea was to employ advisers on financial and foreign affairs as recommended by the Japanese government; the former post was to be occupied by a Japanese national and the latter by a national of a third power. These foreign advisers were to be consulted on all important matters of finance and foreign affairs of Korea. A high official of the Japanese Ministry of Finance and an American, Durham W. Stevens, were subsequently appointed to these posts. (Stevens had been a loyal employee of the Japanese foreign office and was chosen apparently in order to improve the chances for favorable foreign reactions to Japan's new role in Korea.)

[5] *NGB*, XXXVII, Part I, 351–356.

[6] A former high official of the Japanese ministry of finance applied for the lease of "the wasteland, hills and forests, grasslands and all other uncultivated lands," but he gave up the project when the Japanese government, because of very strong Korean resistance, decided to postpone it for the time being. See *ibid.*, pp. 600, 607; McKenzie, *Tragedy of Korea*, p. 115; *The Korea Review*, IV, 289, 344–350.

Japan's special concern over the possibility of Korea's secret dealings with foreign powers was manifest in another agreement signed on August 22, 1904. The new agreement stipulated that Korea would consult the Japanese government in advance in "concluding treaties and conventions with foreign powers and in dealing with other important diplomatic affairs, such as the grant of concessions to or contracts with foreigners."[7] The Korean government had shown much reluctance to accept the terms of these agreements, particularly the last named, but it did not — perhaps, could not — flatly reject the Japanese demands; it merely tried to amend and procrastinate.

Meanwhile, Japan held a tight military control over Korea. The Japanese army and navy occupied and constructed many military establishments throughout the country. In the process, many local residents were ejected without proper compensation.[8] The Japanese gendarmes began to exercise police power in suppressing any anti-Japanese agitation. By late December 1904, Japanese policemen were assigned to supervise Korean police organizations at national and provincial levels. At about the same time, in another agreement acceded to by the Korean government, the Japanese gendarmes were formally authorized to enforce the regulations issued by the Japanese military command concerning the political activities of Koreans.[9]

Japan made further gains in 1905. In January, Japanese-sponsored financial reforms were put into effect and Japanese currency was given legal recognition. An agreement signed on April 1 transferred the postal, telegraph, and telephone services to Japanese management with the additional stipulation that, "when it is deemed necessary by the Japanese government, . . . [it] may appropriate land and buildings" to expand the communication system.[10] In the name of budgetary economy, Korean

[7] See the texts of the two agreements in NGB, XXXVII, Part I, 365, 368–369.

[8] See a series of Japanese documents in ibid., pp. 613–640.

[9] Ibid., pp. 478–482, 485, 489; Korea Review, V, 31.

[10] "Agreement for the Transfer of Postal, Telegraph and Telephone Services of Korea to Control of Japan (April 1, 1905)," in Carnegie Endowment for International Peace, Korea: Treaties and Agreements (Washington, D.C., 1921), pp. 38–40. For the texts of three Korean im-

troops were reduced to six battalions and three companies (311 officers and 8,214 men) by October 1905.[11] In August Japan obtained the right to engage in coastal trade and commercial navigation on the rivers of Korea.[12]

In summary, it is clear that Japan was highly successful in seizing the control of important functions of the Korean government even without a protectorate treaty. Also, Japan, in 1904–1905, made little pretense of reforming Korea as she did in 1894–1895. Its aim now was establishing effective control. Japan did not advocate any drastic change in the administrative structure of the Korean government.[13]

If the Japanese policy of seizing "the real power of protection" needed the presence of a large Japanese force, consolidation of the newly won position required careful diplomatic maneuvers to obtain acquiescence of interested foreign powers. Japan remembered the Triple Intervention of 1895 and the subsequent rise of a rival power in Korea. Months before the end of the Russo-Japanese War and the Korean Protectorate Treaty, Japan sought assurances for her freedom of action in Korea from the governments of the United States and Great Britain.

President Theodore Roosevelt had favored Japanese control of Korea even prior to the Russo-Japanese conflict.[14] In January 1905 Roosevelt told the Japanese minister to the United States that Japan had the right to place Korea under its sphere of influence. When the Japanese envoy communicated Japan's wish

perial ordinances promulgated on January 19, 1905, legalizing the use of the Japanese currency in Korea see *NGB*, XXXVIII, Part I, 726–727.

[11] "First General Report on Korean Finance [October, 1904–1905]," enclosed in Morgan to Root, November 27, 1905, U.S. Department of State, *The Records of the Department of State, National Archives, Korea: Dispatches*, XXII. Hereafter cited as *K.D.*

[12] *NGB*, XXXVIII, Part I, 471–481.

[13] See *ibid.*, XXXVII, Part I, 286–298.

[14] As early as 1900, Roosevelt wrote to his German friend, Speck von Sternburg, that he would "like to see Japan have Korea" because Japan deserved it in order to check Russia. In May 1904 he told Sternburg to inform the Kaiser that the United States was willing to see Japan take Korea. See Howard K. Beale, *Theodore Roosevelt and the Rise of America to World Power* (Baltimore: The Johns Hopkins Press, 1956), p. 314.

to provide "protection, supervision and guidance" to Korea, the American president fully concurred.[15] The reasons for Roosevelt's ready approval was, in his own words, that "We [the United States] cannot possibly interfere for the Koreans against Japan. They [the Koreans] could not strike one blow in their own defence."[16] Six months later, American Secretary of War William H. Taft conferred with Prime Minister Katsura Tarō in Tokyo and gave additional assurance of American approval of the Japanese policy. In a memorandum Katsura disavowed any aggressive Japanese designs against the Philippines and emphasized Japan's resolve that "a complete solution of the peninsula (Korean) question should be made as the logical consequence of the war." Taft admitted the "justness" of Katsura's comments and remarked that "the establishment by Japanese troops of a suzerainty over Korea to the extent of requiring that Korea enter into no foreign treaties without the consent of Japan was the logical result of the present war and would directly contribute to permanent peace in the East." Roosevelt shortly gave unqualified consent to Taft's words.[17] Early in November Katsura informed Roosevelt in strict confidence that Japan planned to take charge of Korea's external relations.[18]

The British government expressed similar willingness to accept the new role of Japan as protector in Korea. In the course of negotiations for the second Anglo-Japanese Alliance in the summer of 1905, Japan sought British support for her plan to establish a protectorate over Korea. Britain had no basic objection and was willing to support Japan in return for a Japanese pledge of cooperation regarding future British plans in India. It was a typical diplomatic *quid pro quo* arrangement, a Japanese Korea

[15] See Komura's instructions to Minister Takahira in Washington, January 22, 1905, and a record of Takahira's conversation with Roosevelt on January 24, 1905, in *NGB*, XXXVIII, Part I, 216–217.

[16] See Komura to Takahira, January 3, 1905, and Takahira to Komura, January 8, in *ibid., Supplement on the Russo-Japanese War*, V, 203–204, 206–207.

[17] For a text of the Taft-Katsura agreement see *ibid.*, XXXVIII, Part I, 450–451; see also Dennett, *Roosevelt*, pp. 112–114. For Roosevelt's reactions see Beale, p. 157.

[18] Katsura to Takahira, November 6, 1905, *NGB*, XXXVIII, Part I, 529.

for a British India. Britain's only concern was for Japan to honor the treaty rights of foreign powers. British commercial interests in Korea were minimal, but Britain feared involvement, under the terms of the alliance, in a Japanese war with a third power resulting from reckless Japanese actions against foreign interests in Korea. After three months of negotiation, the alliance treaty was signed on August 12, 1905. Japan accepted the extension of the alliance to cover India, and Britain recognized Japan's right "to take such measures of guidance, control, and protection in Corea as she may deem proper and necessary" to promote her "paramount political, military, and economic interests." Japan, however, was not to violate "the principle of equal opportunities for the commerce and industry of all nations" in Korea. A significant omission from the treaty text was any mention of Korea's independence and territorial integrity that had been explicitly recognized in the first Anglo-Japanese Alliance of 1902.[19]

In addition to American and British acquiescence, Japan obtained a Russian recognition of her intentions in Korea in the form of the Treaty of Portsmouth of September 5, 1905, concluding the one-and-a-half year war between Japan and Russia. At Portsmouth the Russian delegation had made a half-hearted attempt to include in the treaty a guarantee for the sovereign rights of the Korean emperor; Count Witte, the chief Russian delegate, confided to his Japanese counterpart that Russia wished to avoid the onus of any collusion with Japan against the independence of Korea. Japanese Foreign Minister Komura Jutarō, representing his government at the peace conference, summarily rejected Witte's proposal. On this occasion, Komura also made a significant remark to the effect that Korea had already suffered a partial loss of her sovereign rights as a result of the agreements between Japan and Korea signed in 1904 (undoubtedly referring to the protocol of February 1904 and the agreements on advisers made in August 1904, among others). The final text of the Ports-

[19] For Japanese documents on the Anglo-Japanese negotiations see *ibid.*, pp. 1–96. British documents appear in Great Britain, Foreign Office, *British Documents on the Origins of the War: 1898–1914*, edited by G. P. Gooch and Harold Temperley, V, 120–169.

mouth Treaty contained no reference to Korean independence; instead, Russia recognized Japan's "predominant" interests in Korea and disavowed any Russian interference with Japanese measures of "direction, protection, and supervision" (Article II).[20]

These diplomatic maneuvers had been the prelude to Japan's formal assumption of complete control and management of Korea's external affairs. As early as April 8, 1905, the Japanese government had decided to seek a bilateral agreement with Korea that would legitimate such partial transfer of Korean sovereign rights. This decision by the Japanese cabinet, however, stipulated that the protectorate treaty should be negotiated "at an opportune moment after adequate measures have been taken to avoid as much external complications as possible."[21] By the late fall of 1905, the danger of foreign interference with the Japanese plan had been eliminated; the American, British, and Russian blessings had been obtained. On October 27 the Japanese cabinet decided to act and adopted a draft treaty and the basic strategy. Additional troop reinforcements were to enter Seoul before the negotiations with the Korean government, and the general in command of the Japanese forces in Korea was ordered to provide the necessary assistance for successful consummation of the negotiations. If the Korean government should persist in rejecting the treaty, Japan, as the last resort, would simply make an unilateral declaration of the establishment of Japanese protectorate over Korea and so notify the foreign powers as well as the Korean government.[22]

The responsibility of negotiating the treaty was assigned to Itō Hirobumi. Itō arrived in Seoul on November 9, 1905, with a letter from the Japanese emperor advising the Korean sovereign to "follow the directions of the Marquis [Itō], and come to an agreement with him, as it was essential for the maintenance of peace in the Far East."[23] The Korean government was not fully

[20] *NGB, Supplement on the Russo-Japanese War*, V, 400–436, 528–538.
[21] See the text of the Japanese cabinet decision in *ibid.*, XXXVIII, Part I, 519–520.
[22] The text of the decision appears in *ibid.*, pp. 526–527.
[23] McKenzie, *Tragedy of Korea*, p. 131.

aware of the purpose of the Japanese envoy but was gripped with fear to see a person of Itō's prestige appear at this time. The next day a reception was held in his honor at the Korean court, but the Korean emperor, pleading illness, declined to receive Itō in formal audience. When the delayed audience was finally granted on November 15, Itō presented a draft treaty of protection and demanded immediate acceptance by the Korean government. When the Korean sovereign spoke of the need to maintain some outward semblance of Korea's diplomatic independence, such as the exchange of diplomatic representatives with treaty powers, Itō categorically refused to consider it and ominously hinted at unpredictable consequences of Korean rejection. On the other hand, the Japanese ambassador explained that the treaty would not only ensure peace in East Asia but would also maintain the safety and dignity of the Korean imperial family. He also guaranteed that Korea's sovereign rights in internal affairs would not be at all affected by the treaty.[24]

Itō accomplished little in the nearly five-hour conference. Thereafter, the Korean emperor refused to grant audience to the Japanese envoy. Itō then decided to persuade the members of the Korean cabinet, individually and as a group. On the following day they were summoned to the Japanese legation, and Itō and Hayashi Gonsuke, the resident Japanese minister in Seoul, preached the need for the treaty, claiming that it was inevitable under the existing circumstances. The Korean officials tried to dissuade the Japanese from imposing the formal protectorate when Korea had already been deprived of any substantive freedom of action in foreign affairs. Acting Prime Minister Han Kyusŏl was most strongly opposed, while the other ministers including Foreign Minister Pak Che-sun, remained reluctant. Pak also referred to the danger of assassination of the Korean ministers if they were to accept the treaty. Hayashi hastened to guarantee the personal safety of these ministers. At the end of the inconclusive meeting, Hayashi reported to Tokyo that the Korean officials understood the inescapable fate awaiting their nation, but they were

[24] See a detailed account of the audience in *NGB*, XXXVIII, Part I, 499–503.

trying to extricate themselves by passing on the responsibility for the decision to their sovereign.[25]

Meanwhile, the Japanese troops in Seoul were staging an impressive display of military might. "On the main street leading to the old Palace," an American eyewitness reported, "half a regiment of artillery, 3 batteries with 18 guns were maneuvering, dashing to and fro, unlimbering their pieces. . . . The street was full of excited people with an unusually large number of Japanese police and gendarmes about." [26] Despite the Japanese effort to keep the negotiations secret, the news had leaked out and was published in the November 17 issues of two newspapers published in Seoul.[27]

The mounting tension made it imperative for Itō to conclude the negotiations quickly by any device. In the afternoon of November 17, a meeting of the Korean cabinet in the imperial presence failed to reach any conclusion. Han and Pak urged rejection of the treaty, but the emperor, opposed as he was to the treaty, could not decide to risk provoking Japanese anger. Itō, accompanied by the commanding general of the Japanese forces, hurried to the palace in the evening. Because the emperor declined to receive him, Itō met only with the Korean ministers and demanded that each of them clarify his position. Three ministers expressed opposition and the remaining four favored the treaty with some modifications. At the end of this unusual roll call, Itō declared that the treaty stood approved by a vote of five to two (having twisted the essentially negative vote of Foreign Minister Pak, who had perhaps inadvertently stated that he would sign the treaty if the emperor so ordered). Itō then agreed to

[25] See Hayashi's report to Katsura, November 17, 1905, in *ibid.*, p. 531; see also a record of Itō's conversations with Korean ministers, *ibid.*, pp. 488–491.

[26] Quoted from Willard Straight's diary entry for November 17 reproduced in Herbert Croly, *Willard Straight* (New York: Macmillan, 1924), pp. 178–179; see also McKenzie, *Tragedy of Korea*, p. 134.

[27] *The Korean Daily News*, a British-operated paper, and the *Hwangsŏng Sinmun*, a Korean paper, printed the news; see Hayashi to Katsura, November 18, 1905, in Japan (in Korea), *The Japanese Archives in Korea*, the 1894–1910 series, photographed for the Hoover Institution, Stanford University, No. 194, pp. 78–79. Hereafter cited as *JA (Korea)*.

make a few minor changes as requested by Yi Wan-yong, one of the four assenting ministers. One exception, however, applied to a phrase that would have expressly prohibited Japan from interfering in the internal affairs. According to the official Japanese account, the Korean emperor then gave his approval to the majority decision of the cabinet. The emperor, however, denied later that he had ever approved the treaty. The Protectorate Treaty was signed at one o'clock on the morning of November 18 by Foreign Minister Pak and Minister Hayashi.[28]

The treaty, officially dated November 17, contained five articles. Japan, through the Japanese Foreign Ministry, was to have control and direction of the external relations of Korea (Article I), and Korea was to make no international agreement except through the medium of the Japanese government (Article II). A Japanese resident-general was to be stationed in Seoul "primarily" for the purpose of managing diplomatic affairs and was to enjoy the right of private and personal audience with the Korean emperor. Japan was to station residents at the treaty ports and other places in Korea wherever necessary (Article III).

The final text of the treaty was essentially the same as the original Japanese draft. Changes made on Korean request were in the Preamble, Article III, and the addition of Article V. In the Preamble, a vague and ineffectual time limit for the duration of the treaty was inserted: ". . . until the moment arrives when it is recognized that Korea attained national strength." In Article III, the word "primarily" was added to the effect that the Japanese resident-general was to function primarily in the area of diplomatic affairs; as has already been mentioned, Itō refused to make a binding commitment that the resident-general would not interfere in the internal affairs, and the addition of this ambiguous adjective was the extent of his compromise. The newly added Article V contained Japanese pledge to maintain the welfare and dignity of the Korean imperial house — a face-saving gesture which Japan was willing to concede.[29]

[28] See the official Japanese accounts of these meetings in *NGB*, XXXVIII, Part I, 503–507, 534–536.

[29] For the text of the treaty, see *ibid.*, pp. 532–533, 543–545. See also *ibid.*, pp. 536–537 for a list of amended passages.

It took only three days to "negotiate" this momentous treaty. The process hardly deserves the term "negotiation"; it is probably more accurate to call it an act of "imposition." The Japanese exercised uncontested military control over Korea including the city of Seoul which was virtually under Japanese martial law. The Japanese negotiator pressed the Korean government relentlessly. He intimidated the Koreans with a threat of "unpredictable consequences."

The Korean ministers were fully aware that the Japanese would establish a protectorate with or without the treaty; therefore, a majority of them could not reject the treaty outright but tried to save, by amendments, the semblance of independence. When Itō pressed for a final decision by the Korean government, however, neither the emperor nor his ministers wished to assume the onerous responsibility of decision-making. The resultant uncertainty was resolved by the rude imposition of Itō's will on these Korean leaders.

The reason for Itō's haste was undoubtedly his fear of violent and massive resistance by the Korean people that might wreck the entire project. Because of the speed of the treaty-making process and the secrecy that surrounded it, antiprotectorate demonstrations did not take place until after the signing of the treaty. Following the delayed announcement on November 23, a considerable number of officials and ex-officials, including some of the most prominent members of the ruling elite, submitted memorials to the throne. They denounced the treaty and demanded severe punishment of "the Five Traitors" including Foreign Minister Pak who had been the last to accede to the Japanese demand. The tone of these memorials was passionate. The memorialists stood vigilance outside the palace gates. Some officials gave up their offices in protest. Min Yŏng-hwan, a highly respected official and currently the chief aide-de-camp to the emperor, committed suicide leaving behind an impassioned plea for independence. Cho Pyŏng-se, a former prime minister, also took his own life in protest when his memorials had proven futile. The news of these suicides caused spontaneous public rallies in the streets but were dispersed by the Japanese gendarmes; dozens of the demonstrators were arrested. Storekeepers put up their shutters as a sign of mourning.[30] The *Hwangsŏng Sinmun*, a daily paper in Seoul, printed an inflammatory article against the treaty and asked: "Is it worthwhile for any of us to live any longer? Our people have become the slaves of others. . . ."[31] Even Foreign Minister Pak, who signed the treaty, attempted to kill himself in the presence of Minister Hayashi, blaming the latter for making him turn traitor to his country; Hayashi stopped him and rushed him to a hospital for treatment. Japanese bodyguards were assigned to protect the five Korean ministers who had voted for the treaty.[32]

These protests produced patriotic martyrs but did not alter the Japanese plans. Official notifications of the treaty were sent to the governments of the United States, Great Britain, Germany, France, and other foreign powers. The foreign diplomatic corps in Seoul began leaving Korea. The United States was the most prompt; Secretary of State Root ordered the withdrawal of the American legation on November 24.[33]

Meanwhile, in Tokyo plans were being drawn up for the organization of the Residency-General and the local residencies. Some Japanese leaders favored a plan for a military government. Others favored a civilian rule and they prevailed.[34] The final plan was for the resident-general to issue orders to the commander of the Japanese garrison forces whenever the use of troops should become necessary. This grant of direct authority over the military to a civilian official was an unprecedented development in Meiji Japan. A complicated system of hierarchical relationships was

[30] This account is based on Hayashi's reports to Tokyo in *ibid.*, pp. 952–957, and Chŏng Kyo, II, 178–205. Also see McKenzie, *Tragedy of Korea*, pp. 137–141.

[31] Quoted from *ibid.*, pp. 140. The original Korean language text contains a few allegorical references to past events in Korean history which McKenzie omits in his otherwise faithful translation of the editorial.

[32] *Ibid.*, p. 137; also see Hiratsuka Atsushi (ed.), *Itō Hirobumi Hiroku* [Unpublished Papers of Itō] (Tokyo, 1929), I, 323–334. Hereafter cited as *Itō Hiroku*.

[33] Root to Takahira, November 24, 1905, *U.S. Foreign Relations*, 1905, pp. 613–614.

[34] See a series of telegrams exchanged between the Japanese foreign ministry and Foreign Minister Komura who was on a temporary tour of duty in Peking at this time in Kim Chŏng-myŏng, Vol. VI, Part I, pp. 100–104.

created with the home government. The resident-general was to be directly responsible to the Japanese emperor, thereby freeing him from the jurisdictional control of the cabinet ministers in Tokyo. However, he was to channel his applications for the emperor's sanction through the foreign minister in Tokyo on all matters of diplomacy and through the prime minister on all other matters. It was obviously a compromise between the desire of the resident-general-to-be for a large area of discretionary authority and the need of the Tokyo leaders to supervise the Japanese agencies in Korea.

The functions of the resident-general, as set forth in the Japanese imperial ordinance of December 20, 1905, went considerably beyond those stipulated in the Protectorate Treaty. He was empowered to take steps to maintain peace and public order in Korea through the use of Japanese troops. Conceivably, a broad interpretation of the protocols of February 1904 could provide a legal basis for this policing authority. He could more directly intervene in the internal administration of Korea "if necessary for the purpose of discharging responsibilities under the treaties"; he could demand that the Korean government take certain administrative actions or he could even issue an order directly to the local Korean authorities merely notifying the Seoul government afterward. He was to supervise all Japanese officials in Korea, including those employed by the Korean government. Ordinances could be issued on his authority carrying penalties of imprisonment or fine.

At the local level, the Japanese resident was to exercise the powers of issuing directives to the Korean authorities, promulgating regulations that carried minor penalties for infraction, and ensuring public order, if necessary, by requesting the assistance of the Japanese garrison forces.

In addition to the regular Japanese army units and the gendarmes, a police force was to be attached to the Residency-General and each local residency; the size of the residency police was to be decided by the resident-general.[35]

[35] See Imperial Ordinance No. 267 issued on December 20, 1905, over the countersignatures of the prime minister and the minister of war in *NGB*, XXXVIII, Part I, 564–567.

On February 1, 1906, the Japanese Residency-General was formally opened in Seoul, replacing the Japanese legation that had been in existence since 1880. The Korean Foreign Ministry had already been abolished as of January 18. Itō Hirobumi, as the first resident-general, arrived in Seoul soon thereafter to take up his new duties. He held in his hands an impressive array of powers to control Korea's internal as well as external affairs. At his command were Japanese civil servants, a powerful garrison army, the gendarmerie, and a police force. The protocol of February, 1904, the Protectorate Treaty, and other agreements signed by Korea during the Russo-Japanese War provided a legal basis for the powers he was to assume. In his relations with Tokyo he enjoyed a wide discretionary freedom. Japan's new role in Korea had received diplomatic blessings from major foreign powers. Resident-General Itō was the new de facto ruler of Korea.

9.

The Expansion of the Resident-General's Role

On December 21, 1905, Itō was appointed resident-general. He was the logical choice for this very delicate and onerous job, and it could very well have been that he himself wanted the position to see his "safe and sane" Korean policy put into execution and act as a check on increasing militarist pressure for quick action. Then, too, the Katsura cabinet was about to resign in favor of Saionji. Saionji could not form a cabinet entirely devoid of the Yamagata faction; but as a supporter of Itō and his policy, Saionji was ready to stand behind Itō.[1] Japan's aim in Korea now was to consolidate her position rather than to conquer new territory. The complexity of problems was overwhelming, and quick and orderly solutions were urgent. Itō had prestige as one of the great statesmen in Japanese history.

The *Mainichi Shimbun* stated, "Marquis Itō now goes earnestly resolved to make his mission a glorious climax to his long and useful career. . . ."[2] Itō might have wanted the job for other reasons as well. He may have wanted to play the role of a restorer of Korean faith in Japanese justice and of sympathies alienated

[1] *Itō Hiroku*, I, 313–316; the *Hōchi Shimbun*, July 7, 1908, in Nakayama Yasumasa (ed.), *Shimbun Shūsei Meiji Hennenshi* [History of the Meiji Era by Newspapers], 15 vols. (Tokyo, 1934–1936), XIII, 448 (hereafter cited as *Meiji Shimbun Shūsei*); Tokutomi Iichirō (ed.), *Kōshaku Yamagata Aritomo Den* [Biography of Prince Yamagata Aritomo], 3 vols. (Tokyo, 1917), III, 724–725.

[2] The *Japan Times* (Tokyo), February 3, 1906, enclosed in Wilson to the Secretary of State, February 13, 1906, No. 3, in *U.S. Foreign Relations*, 1906, p. 1032.

by the military regime.[3] For Itō insisted that he, as a resident-general in Korea, should also be given the authority of a commander-in-chief in Korea. Without this unity of command he threatened to refuse the appointment. It was Itō, and he alone, who could overrule the opposition by the military.[4]

On the eve of his departure for Korea, Itō outlined his policy in a speech before the leading journalists of Tokyo. On the question of Korean administrative reform, he said, "It will be the duty of the Government of this Empire to take it upon itself in accordance with the protocol, but governmental corruption is of remote origin, and to reform it in a day is no easy task. . . . Of course," he continued, "to revise laws and thus effect superficial reforms is a matter presenting no difficulty, but such, I believe, is not by any means the way to achieve the object of administrative reform."[5] Undoubtedly, this was an enormous task, and Itō conceived that gradualism was a prerequisite for success. Touching on the poverty of the Koreans in the same speech, Itō said, "If it be neglected and no means devised for relieving it, this Empire will not only be violating its responsibility as protector of Korea, but will also itself have to suffer in the end."[6] Therefore, the Protectorate Treaty to Itō also meant that Japan should promote the economic development of the country.

Itō's speech was received with hearty endorsement. The Nichinichi went one step further and favorably compared the Japanese policy in Korea with what it felt to be the enlightened and advanced colonial policy of the American government in dealing with the Philippines. This paper was confident that the public would join in its appreciation of Itō's great service to the country. The Asahi and the Mainichi also praised Itō as resident-general. Above all, however, both of them pointed out the deep-rooted hatred that existed between the Koreans and the Japanese residents in Korea, a feeling partly caused by the unpleasant and

[3] Morgan to Root, November 22, 1905, K.D. XXII.

[4] Itō Hiroku, I, 313–316; the Mainichi-Asahi Shimbun, February 24, 1906, in Meiji Shimbun Shūsei, XIII, 40.

[5] Marquis Itō's speech as reported in the Japan Daily Mail of Yokohama, February 3, 1906, enclosed in Wilson to the Secretary of State, U.S. Foreign Relations, 1906, p. 1030.

[6] Ibid.

overbearing manners of the latter group. These papers urged in their editorials that Itō do something to remedy the unfriendly relationship between the two peoples.[7]

Itō's policy statement carried meanings and implications far surpassing the Japanese role in effect in Korea at the time. On another occasion, Itō stated that the step which Japan took in the enforcement of the protectorate over Korea was only a formal solution of the Korean problem and that the solution in reality — the realization of the community of interests between Japan and Korea — still belonged to the future. He also observed that Korea did not submit herself willingly to Japan as had the other colonized areas, because the Japanese imposition of the Protectorate Treaty meant the loss of Korean independence. Therefore, in order to win sincere allegiance of the Koreans to Japanese overlordship, he said, "We must . . . make her understand that Japan's protection is not for the purpose of harming her independence." [8]

Itō was apprehensive of possible Korean opposition. In one of his speeches, he stated that "from Japan's point of view we certainly have had a most painful experience with regard to Korea, yet from Korea's point of view she doubtless believes that she too has been subjected to great pressure, and that she certainly does not submit to us willingly. . . ." [9] Furthermore, as the one who negotiated the Protectorate Treaty with the Korean court, Itō experienced the obstinacy of the Korean emperor. Many episodes in connection with the treaty negotiation have been related already, but the following quotation from a statement by Itō himself sheds more light on succeeding events in Korea. Addressing various newspaper editors he had invited to luncheon in Seoul after the conclusion of the Protectorate Treaty, Itō admitted: "His Majesty [the Korean emperor] expressed and seemed profoundly moved by the fact that even in the days when

[7] From the *Japan Times* (Tokyo), February 3, 1906, *ibid.*, enclosed in Wilson to the Secretary of State, No. 3, p. 1031.

[8] From the *Japan Daily Mail*, February 8, 1906, enclosed in Wilson to the Secretary of State, February 13, 1906, *ibid.*, pp. 1032–1033.

[9] From the *Japan Daily Mail*, February 8, 1906, enclosed in Wilson to the Secretary of State, February 13, 1906, No. 4, *ibid.*, pp. 1032–1033.

Korea used the Chinese almanac and was in effect a tributary of China she nevertheless retained the control of her own foreign affairs, whereas now in the reign of His Majesty, after his dynasty had continued for five hundred years, he was asked to sign a convention which would destroy his empire and render him guilty in the sight of his ancestors. . . ." [10]

Itō obviously knew that the Korean emperor was not going to sit still until the moment of eventual Japanese annexation, because the survival of his kingdom was of great import to him, if for nothing else than the retention of his monarchical prerogatives. The Korean emperor might have cherished a sincere wish to strengthen his kingdom. He was well versed in court politics and international manipulation through his long experience in the Korean "wars of the roses," but he was confused politically, weak in personality, and obsessed by "his lifelong and well-grounded fear of personal violence." [11]

Resident-General Itō's administration in Korea was characterized by the introduction of Japanese "advisers" into virtually every office of the Korean government at the national and the local levels. It was a government by "advisers," with the exception of foreign affairs, military defense, and communications, which had been placed directly under Japanese management and control. The various ministries, including the Ministry of the Imperial Household, hired Japanese advisers, councillors, or assistant councillors. At the local level, each province had Japanese councillors, financial councillors to advise the provincial tax supervisors and assistant councillors to advise the tax assessors in important districts.

A complicated police system, consisting of three or possibly four distinct police forces, was developed by the end of 1906. The Japanese gendarmerie was under the immediate control of the commander-in-chief of the Japanese garrison forces in Korea. This military police unit was to guard the railroads and the tele-

[10] From the *Japan Daily Mail* (Yokohama), November 30, 1905, enclosed in Wilson to the Secretary of State, February 13, 1906, No. 1, *ibid.*, p. 1029.

[11] W. F. Sands, "Korea and the Korean Emperor," *Century*, LXIX (1905), 581.

graph lines in addition to regular police functions for both ordinary and political crimes. The gendarmerie soon proved to be the
most dreaded of all the Japanese agencies of repression in Korea.

The second force was the old Japanese consular police now
renamed Residency Police. The third force had come to be known
as the Advisory Board Police, many of them of supervisory ranks.
They were nominally within the Korean police hierarchy under
the Ministry of Home Affairs and served in the national and provincial police organization. The native police force consisted
mostly of patrolmen who took orders from the Japanese inspectors and captains in the "advisory police." [12]

The Residency-General itself was an ever-growing bureaucracy
which, by early 1907, had become a miniature government except
for military affairs. Behind these civilian organizations, the Japanese army in Korea in the years of 1905–1907 stood at the level
of one and a half to two divisions that could be ordered into action
by the resident-general.[13]

With such impressive machinery of control at his command,
Itō in 1906 was clearly in a position to impose whatever he willed
on the Korean government. The Korean cabinet, headed by Pak
Che-sun since his promotion to acting prime minister in November 1905, was unable and perhaps unwilling to resist Itō's bid-
ding. The Korean emperor had been reduced to a protesting
but powerless figurehead, especially after July 1906 when the old
palace guards were replaced by Japanese policemen. The issuance of passes to permit only those "who had legitimate business
with the Court" to enter the palace isolated the anti-Japanese
sovereign from the outside.[14]

Itō's policy of controlling the Korean government through
advisers without instituting any sudden drastic innovations in its
structure, however, was subject to increasing pressures from two
opposite directions. On the one hand, the frankly chauvinistic

[12] Based upon Japan, Residency General in Korea, *Annual Report on
Reforms and Progress in Korea, 1907* (Seoul: H.I.J.M.'s Residency General, 1908), pp. 4–5, 31–35 *et passim*. Cited hereafter as *Annual Report*.

[13] *Ibid.*, p. 34.

[14] Quoted passage from *ibid.*, p. 14. See also Kaneko Kentarō *et al.*,
Itō Hirobumi Den [Biography of Itō Hirobumi], 3 vols. (Tokyo, 1940),
III, 719–725.

Kokuryūkai (the Amur Society) in Japan and their collaborators in the *Ilchinhoe* in Korea (a pro-Japanese society) felt that Itō was overly cautious and slow moving. The Japanese extremists wished for a speedy and complete absorption of Korea, while the openly pro-Japanese Koreans of Song Pyŏng-jun's kind wished to take over the Korean cabinet from the hands of Pak Che-sun and others now in power with Itō's blessing.[15] On the other hand, Itō had to contend with the various anti-Japanese agitations in Korea, which at times became so serious that Itō wrote in 1906 to his immediate family members giving instructions as to what to do in case of his untimely death.[16] However, the year 1907 proved to be much more turbulent than 1906. In 1907 Japan set out on a definite course of annexation of her neighboring peninsular kingdom.

As nearly as can be determined, the Russo-Japanese conversations in 1907 mark the beginning of Japan's effort to obtain foreign approval for the annexation of Korea. Perhaps more important, they provided the first occasions for important officials of Japan to reveal, in official papers, their belief in eventual annexation. Russian Foreign Minister A. P. Izvolsky took the initiative in February 1907 in suggesting to the Japanese minister to Russia, Motono Ichirō, the desirability of a Russo-Japanese entente in Northeast Asia so that Russia could devote her full attention to the European scene.[17] Within a few days, the government in

---

[15] Uchida Ryōhei, the guiding spirit of the Amur Society, became an adviser to the *Ilchinhoe* in October 1906, while he was technically an official without portfolio of the Residency-General. Even after Uchida had to quit the advisership because of its incompatibility with his official position, he continued to help and advise the Korean group. An example of Uchida's criticism of the Residency-General is his letter written in January 1907 to his friend and sponsor, Sugiyama Shigemaru, which stated that the "reforms" in Korea were in reality "regressions" and urged an early merger of Japan and Korea. See Kuzū Yoshihisa, *Nikkan Gappō Hishi* [Secret History of the Merger of Japan and Korea], 2 vols. (Tokyo, 1930), I, 41, 55–56, 74–95. See also Conroy, pp. 418–423. For an example of the *Ilchinhoe's* ranting criticism of the Pak cabinet see its "open letter of impeachment" published in May 1907, in a monthly magazine published by the Amur Society. Kuzū, I, 206–238.

[16] Kaneko, III, 715–718.

[17] Motono to Hayashi, February 6, 1907, *NGB*, XXX, Part I, 98–100.

Tokyo headed by Saionji responded favorably to the Russian overture, partly as a result of Itō's urging that this was a welcome opportunity to negotiate for Russian agreement to "a complete solution of the Korean question" as well as to a more satisfactory arrangement in Manchuria.[18] On February 20 Izvolsky handed a draft agreement to Motono which provided for a mutual guarantee of each other's rights in China and for mutual assistance, by pacific means, for "maintenance and legitimate exercise" of such rights.[19] Motono, however, considered the Russian proposal too general and suggested to Foreign Minister Hayashi Tadasu that Japan should obtain, among other things, a Russian pledge of the territorial inviolability of China in the Mongolian region and also an unqualified Russian admission of Japan's right to annex Korea. Motono argued that "we have to gradually move toward the goal of annexing Korea since there is no other way of insuring the establishment of tranquility in Korea." [20] By April the negotiations clearly showed Russia's willingness to let Japan annex Korea in return for Japan's renunciation of any interest in Mongolia. Itō, who had been kept closely informed on the progress of the St. Petersburg negotiations, felt that Japan should accept the Russian terms without hesitation and so advised Hayashi on April 11.[21] Furthermore, Itō endorsed Motono's suggestion that there should be a separate secret article on Korea that would explicitly state that the annexation of Korea was contemplated by Japan. He also added, in this telegram to Hayashi on April 13, that "the annexation will become more difficult every year. Therefore it is important that we [Japan] clarify where our intentions lie and obtain the Russian acquiescence in advance." [22] Itō explained on April 25 that the spread of Christianity and the growth of anti-Japanese sentiment in Korea made delay undesirable.[23] However, Hayashi and particularly Komura (former foreign minister and now ambassador to Great Britain) felt that the total

[18] Itō to Saionji, June 11, 1907, *ibid.*, pp. 153–154. For the favorable response of Tokyo to the overture of Izvolsky, see Hayashi to Motono, February 8, 1907, *ibid.*, pp. 101–102.

[19] For the Russian draft see *ibid.*, p. 107.

[20] Quoted from Motono to Hayashi, February 21, 1907, *ibid.*, p. 105.

[21] *Ibid.*, p. 122.

[22] *Ibid.*, p. 124.   [23] *Ibid.*, pp. 132–133.

renunciation of Mongolia was too high a price to pay for Russian support of the annexation, and the negotiations dragged on, in spite of frequent and strong urgings from Itō.[24]

After months of protracted negotiations, on July 30, 1907, Izvolsky and Motono signed a convention, a secret convention, and an additional secret article. The first contained declarations of mutual obligation to honor each other's rights in China and to uphold the Open Door principles in China; the second was prefaced by an expression of the mutual wish "to eliminate any cause of misunderstanding or conflict" between Russia and Japan concerning Manchuria, Korea, and Mongolia and included the original Japanese proposal that spoke of the "further development" of "the relations of political solidarity existing between Japan and Corea" as well as Japan's pledge not to interfere with Russian "special interests in Outer Mongolia." [25]

The date these agreements were signed was significant because Article II of the secret convention had been modified at the last minute to read in part: "Russia, recognizing the relations of political solidarity existing between Japan and Korea in consequence of the conventions and agreements *actually in force* between them . . ." (italics added) instead of "conventions and agreements of 1904 and 1905." Seven days prior to the signing ceremony at St. Petersburg, Korea had signed another agreement with Japan, as will be explained, permitting the Japanese to exercise direct authority on matters of internal affairs. The last minute revision of Article II of the secret Russo-Japanese convention, therefore, meant Russian recognition of Japan's virtually complete take-over of Korean sovereignty in both external and internal affairs.

The emperor opposed this latest agreement of 1907. Already in the spring of that year, the *Korean Daily News* printed what it claimed to be a message secretly sent by the Korean emperor to the sovereigns of various foreign powers, denouncing Japan's

[24] On June 11, Itō bypassed Hayashi and sent a telegram directly to Prime Minister Saionji eloquently arguing that it was a serious mistake to sacrifice the solution of the Korean question, which was the most urgent of all questions involved in Russo-Japanese relations, for the sake of restraining Russian freedom of action in Mongolia. See *ibid.*, pp. 153–154.

[25] For the texts of these agreements see *ibid.*, pp. 173–175.

encroachments on Korea's freedom and asking for foreign assistance in regaining independence. When Itō questioned the emperor
on this, the latter denied any knowledge of it. Itō accepted the
emperor's apologia, but far more serious repercussions developed
from the uninvited appearance of Korean envoys at the Hague
Peace Conference of 1907. Itō was informed of this Korean plot
by the French consul general in Seoul, whose help in planning
had been sought by a Korean, Yi Yong-ik.

Since the office of the Residency-General was informed of the
Korean secret mission to The Hague, Hulbert, who was serving
as the mission's adviser, was under strict surveillance.[26] He left
Korea for The Hague via Russia in the latter part of May; and
on June 27, 1907, three Koreans led by Hulbert presented their
credentials to the Hague conference and asked for recognition. As
Korea was legally a Japanese protectorate, their credentials were
refused, and they then tried to mobilize world public opinion for
the cause of Korean independence.[27] Itō decided to use this incident as a pretext for putting an end to the anti-Japanese activities
of the Korean emperor. When the Koreans at The Hague earnestly
claimed they had duly signed credentials from the emperor, Itō
declared that the incident constituted an open expression of
Korean hostility against Japan and that Japan now had reason
to declare war on Korea. The emperor again declared his personal innocence, but Itō rejected the disclaimer. The new Korean
cabinet, headed by Yi Wan-yong and including a notoriously
pro-Japanese member of the *Ilchinhoe*, Song Pyŏng-jun, was
extremely subservient to Itō, and feared that Japan might now

[26] Itō to Hayashi, May 19, 1907, *JA (Korea)*, No. 392, pp. 126–128;
for the check on Hulbert's activity see *ibid.*, 29–44, 371–370. See also
Japanese Foreign Office (microfilms) MT 2.4.1.9, 2433 sheets.

[27] Suzuki to Hayashi, transmitted to Itō, July 2–4, 1907, *JA (Korea)*,
No. 267, pp. 4–13; also the same to the same, September 7, 1907,
Japanese Foreign Office (microfilms), MT 2.4.1.9., 105. The three Koreans
at The Hague were Yi Sang-sŭl, ex-vice premier; Yi Chun, former police
magistrate of the Supreme Court of Korea; Yi Wi-jong, ex-secretary of the
Korean legation at St. Petersburg. For the "Petition to The Hague by Korean delegation (June 27, 1907)," see Donald G. Tewksbury, compiler,
Source Materials on Korean Politics and Ideologies (New York: International Secretariat, Institute of Pacific Relations, 1950), pp. 34–35.

take the final step in terminating even the semblance of Korea's independence. Since the cabinet had been out of sympathy with the emperor anyway, it decided to hold the emperor strictly accountable for the Hague affair in the professed hope of saving the nation; conceivably, they had political considerations of their own. Yi Wan-yong hinted at the possibility of the emperor's abdication when he talked to Itō on July 6. Itō promised Yi that the question would receive his serious attention. Itō was primarily concerned lest the blame be placed upon Japan in case of a mishap in the dethronement project. Aside from the question of what to do with the emperor, Itō believed that Japan should seize this opportunity to strengthen its control.[28]

In Tokyo the elder statesmen and the cabinet decided on July 12 that (1) Japan should seize all governmental powers for the internal administration of Korea by such appropriate means as Itō would choose; (2) if the above plan should prove unfeasible, Japan should at least order Korea to appoint its high officials, including the prime minister, only with the consent of the resident-general and also to appoint Japanese nationals nominated by the resident-general as cabinet ministers or other high officials of Korea; and (3) the above arrangement should be formalized in an agreement between the two governments, instead of a unilateral decree by the Korean emperor. However, if Korea should refuse to sign an agreement embodying these changes, Japan was to take steps for annexation.[29] In order to explain the Tokyo decision to Itō, Foreign Minister Hayashi was ordered to Korea where he arrived on July 18, 1907.

Meanwhile, within the Korean government, Song Pyŏng-jun had been foremost in advocating the emperor's abdication. He persuaded Prime Minister Yi Wan-yong that Itō had decided upon the abdication and that Japan could not be appeased in any other way. The unprecedented visit of Japan's foreign minister to Korea strengthened Song's argument. On July 17, the cabinet ministers went before the throne to present their request that the emperor abdicate. The emperor angrily rejected it. The following

[28] Itō to Hayashi, July 7, 1907, *JA (Korea)*, No. 392, pp. 454–455.

[29] Hayashi to Itō, July 12, 1907, and the appended documents in *ibid.*, pp. 455–456.

day, the harassed emperor called in Itō, hoping to obtain some support from him. Itō coldly refused to give any reassurance and stated that the matter lay beyond the concern of an alien like himself.

On the evening of July 18, the Korean ministers went again before the emperor to repeat their request. Prime Minister Yi Wan-yong and Song Pyŏng-jun exhorted their sovereign to avert a national crisis by giving up the throne as an expression of his regret and apology for the Hague affair. Hayashi's arrival that same evening lent an air of urgency to their request. Early in the morning of July 19, after hours of pleading, and after the emperor had had emergency consultations with nine former high officials, the cabinet won. The emperor reluctantly decreed that he would order the crown prince to act in his stead, but he explicitly denied that his decision was that of abdication.[30]

However, the Korean cabinet and Itō chose to interpret the decree as one of abdication and held a court reception on July 20 at which occasion the new emperor received congratulatory salutations from high government officials and foreign consuls in Seoul. Because of violent anti-abdication demonstrations in the city which resulted in the prime minister's home being burned and numerous clashes between the Korean demonstrators and scores of Korean soldiers on the one hand and the Japanese police and soldiers on the other, a large Japanese guard protected the palace while the ceremony was being conducted. The Korean ministers also had Japanese guards to protect them from the angry mob. Following the new emperor's first audience, the cabinet requested and received the ex-emperor's approval for the use of the term "emperor" in referring to his 34-year-old son.[31]

It goes without saying that the retirement of the 56-year-old emperor pleased Japan. The ex-emperor was a source of anti-Japanese agitation, while the new emperor was "feeble of intellect" and docile. Japan was no longer to encounter any difficulty

[30] Kuzū, I, 295–310; Shakuo Shunjō, *Chōsen Heigōshi: Ichimei, Chōsen Saikinshi* [History of Korean Annexation: Modern Korean History] (Keijō, 1926), pp. 347–355.

[31] *Ibid.*, pp. 355–367. See also Itō to Chinda (vice minister of foreign affairs), July 20, 1907 (six telegrams), *NGB*, XXXX, Part I, 469–471.

in obtaining his assent to whatever Japan willed; the new emperor was to be the figurehead of a sham government.[32] A few days after his ascension, Itō presented the draft of an agreement between Korea and Japan by which the latter was to extend its control over the internal affairs of Korea. Itō and Hayashi prepared the draft, and on the day it was handed to Yi Wan-yong, it was signed by Yi and approved by the new emperor.

By the terms of the Japanese-Korean agreement of July 24, 1907, Korea consented to act under the guidance of the resident-general in all administrative matters — all reforms, laws, ordinances, and regulations — and to appoint as high officials the Japanese subjects or other foreigners recommended by the resident-general. Judicial affairs were to be set apart from ordinary administration. Unannounced at the time was the signing of a memorandum by Itō and Yi on the same date which bound Korea (1) to appoint Japanese judges and prosecutors to all the courts of law throughout the country as well as to appoint Japanese as the wardens and guards at nine penitentiaries in Korea; (2) to disband the Korean army except for a battalion to guard the palace; and (3) to appoint Japanese nationals as vice-ministers in each ministry of the government, as the chief of the Police Bureau in the Home Ministry, as the chief secretary of the cabinet, and other officials in key posts at national and provincial levels.[33]

On the next day, addressing the officials in the Residency-General, Itō was again his cautious self and warned against hasty action on the part of the Japanese officials in Korea and tried to dispel the rumors of annexation. But Sammons, the American consul general in Seoul, expressed the well-founded fear: "Prince Itō's policy of peaceful and paternal dealing with the Koreans

[32] Quoted passage taken from Frederick A. McKenzie, *Korea's Fight for Freedom* (New York: F. H. Revell Co., 1920), p. 124.

[33] Itō to Chinda, July 25, 1907, *NGB*, XL, Part I, 498. For the text of the memorandum, see *ibid.*, pp. 494–495. It should be noted that the establishment of eight district and 113 county courts throughout Korea under effective Japanese control necessarily involved the weakening of the Korean officials at the provincial and local levels who had enjoyed a high degree of autonomy in dispensing justice. See Shakuo, p. 410.

may be modified or more fully abandoned in favor of the exercising of greater military authority. Prince Itō's critics have maintained that this would be ultimately necessary and should have been, in fact, resorted to following the Russo-Japanese war, both in Korea and South Manchuria." [34]

With the news of the Korean secret mission to The Hague, the Japanese press widely criticized the lenient policy of Itō toward Korea, stating in essence, "I told you so." *The Japan Advertiser* of Tokyo, presented in its editorial what was the most *realistic* argument at the time on the dilemma of Japan's Korean policy: it claimed that world opinion would support Japan more readily if she forthrightly deposed the "puppet monarch" and declared Korean independence "incompatible" with Japanese security.[35] As early as April a proposal of the Waseda University debating society in Tokyo to adopt the dethronement of the Korean emperor as a topic reflected much Japanese thinking.[36] Japanese Prime Minister Saionji also warned Itō of the prevalence of such sentiments among the Japanese public, and the Japanese residents in Korea contributed to the surge of opinion advocating a stronger policy in Korea.[37]

On August 27, 1907, a ceremony for the crowning of the new emperor, Sunjong, was conducted. His traditional top-knot was cut off despite the pleas of a group of old court officials not to abandon the old way, and he dressed in a new imperial gown which had been displayed in the streets around the palace. All the pag-

[34] Sammons to O'Brien, October 28, 1907, U.S. Department of State, *Records of the Department of State, Archives, Japan: Dispatches*, CXLV, case No. 1166. Hereafter cited as *J.D.*

[35] "The Korean Fiasco," The *Japan Advertiser* (Tokyo), July 14, 1907, enclosed in Wright to Root, July 24, 1907, *J.D.* CXLV, case No. 1166.

[36] "Korea," the *Japan Daily Mail*, April 10, 1907, enclosed in Wright to Root, April 12, 1907, *J.D.*, CXLV, No. 1166; see also "Kankoku Chihō Seikyō" [Local Political Situation in Korea], Itō to Hayashi, June 22, 1907, *Japanese Foreign Office* (microfilms), MT 1.5.3.11, 122–138.

[37] Chinda to Itō, July 19, 1907, *JA (Korea)*, No. 267, pp. 77–78; P'yŏng'yang Japanese Residents Association to Itō, July 19, 1907, *ibid.*, No. 267, pp. 79–80; Yūkōkai Giin Ichidō to Itō, July 13, 1907, *ibid.*, No. 320, pp. 43; and for proposals presented by some Japanese political leaders see *Japanese Foreign Office* (microfilms), MT 2.4.1.9, 163–164.

eantry emphasized a new Korean way under Japanese tutelage. The old kow-tow ritual was replaced with a simple bow. "The music was no longer the ancient Korean, but modern airs from the very fine European trained band attached to the palace." [38] Emperor Sunjong was then removed to the *Ch'angdŏk* Palace on November 13, 1907, against the wish and over the objection of his father, who was left behind in the old palace of *Kyŏng'un*, his permanent residence.[39]

[38]McKenzie, *Korea's Fight for Freedom*, pp. 127–131.

[39] *The Keijō Shimpō*, November 14, 1907, in *Meiji Shimbun Shūsei*, XIII, 341.

10.

Repression and Control

Following the treaty of July 24, 1907, the preponderance of Japanese nationals in top official positions in Korea became more obvious than before. The former Japanese advisers to the Korean government were incorporated in the Korean central administrative system as vice-ministers in the respective ministries, and other Japanese were employed in various capacities by the Korean government. The resident-general's official report of December 31, 1908, reveals the number of Japanese and their distribution and proportion to the number of Korean officials. There were more Japanese officials than Korean in the ministries of Finance, Justice, and Agriculture, Commerce, and Industry. No Japanese officials were listed in the Ministry of the Army, but the reason was obvious. Most of the Korean army units were disbanded in August 1907, and the few Koreans still in the Army Ministry as of December 1908, were eventually dismissed *in toto* with its abolishment on July 31, 1909. The reason for more Korean than Japanese officials in the Ministry of Home Affairs could have been the predominance of Korean local government officials under the jurisdiction of that ministry. Altogether, no less than 40.7 percent of all officials employed by the Korean government at the end of 1908 were Japanese nationals.[1]

[1] For details see C. I. Eugene Kim, "Japanese Rule in Korea (1905–1910): A Case Study," *Proceedings of the American Philosophical Society*, CVI (February 1962), 53–59.

Equally significant as this introduction of a large number of Japanese officials into the Korean government was the phenomenal growth in the number of officials and other employees of the Japanese Residency-General. When it formally opened in 1906, the Residency-General had a staff of only 74 persons in its Seoul office while a smaller staff was assigned to each local residency. In addition there was a small police force of 250 constables headed by a chief inspector and 20 captains attached to these Japanese agencies in Seoul and elsewhere in Korea.[2] A generous estimate of the total number of personnel serving under the resident-general in 1906 would not probably exceed 500. By 1909, the corresponding figure rose to 4,781.[3] (The latter figure includes some 2,000 Korean employees — interpreters, letter-carriers, daily laborers, and other petty employees.) This ten-fold increase in the number of employees of all categories is an unmistakable indication of the rapidly expanding role of the Japanese control agencies in Korea.

As the rate of growth in the number of Japanese officials and civil servants in Korea, employed in either the Korean administrative structure or the office of the Residency-General, increased rapidly in 1907, 1908, and 1909, almost "unlimited employment" of the Japanese was complained of by the Koreans and even by some Japanese in the Korean government service.[4] Meanwhile, many Korean bureaucrats were expelled from their offices.[5] Moreover, priority given to Japanese-speaking Koreans in the Korean government service, regardless of their administrative knowledge, was bitterly denounced by the educated Koreans, and especially by those educated in the United States.[6] Some Koreans also looked askance at the higher salary and other material inducements afforded the Japanese employed in government service. They

[2] The second *Annual Report* (1908–1909), p. 9.

[3] The *Annual Report* (1907), p. 31.

[4] Furutani to Ishizuka, October 31, 1908, *JA (Korea)*, No. 384, pp. 44–45.

[5] Furutani to Ishizuka, *ibid.*; also from the *North China Herald*, October 2, 1909, quoted in "Kenki" [Gendarmerie Secret Report], October 16, 1909, *JA (Korea)*, No. 357, pp. 179–181.

[6] "Kenki," March 20, 1909, *ibid.*, No. 352, p. 106.

were paid more than those in Japan; for the high officials the rate
was 50 percent higher and for subordinate officials 80 percent
higher than those of equivalent rank in Japan.[7]

The rate of change was necessarily slower at the local and village level. The Japanese authority in Korea stated, "By various
reform measures and by the appointment of competent Japanese
to important offices, the administration of the Central Government
and the Imperial Household has been brought into fairly good
shape. . . . The progress of reforms in local administration,
however, is slow, in spite of the fact that a number of reform
measures have been introduced."[8]

By an imperial ordinance of Sepeptember 28, 1906, the local
administration was reorganized into 13 provinces, 11 prefectures,
and 333 districts (Seoul was one of the 11 prefectures). By December 1909 there were 13 provinces, 11 prefectures, 317 districts and 4,322 myŏn as administrative units, with Seoul classified as a special prefecture.[9] To the Japanese authority in Korea,
these local administrative divisions existed simply for the purpose
of administration by the central government and could scarcely
be said to possess local autonomy. Therefore, at the beginning,
reforms were undertaken in order to bring the local management
of taxing, judiciary, and policing powers under the control of
the agencies of the central government.[10] Despite this evidence
of structural centralization, however, there was no systematic
and effective planning to place pro-Japanese Korean elements
at the local level.[11] The Japanese authority in Korea had to
depend on the same local administrative instruments as those of
old Korea.[12] In some cases the local officials and bureaucrats

[7] Furutani to Ishizuka, October 31, 1908, ibid., No. 284, pp. 44–45; The
Annual Report (1908–1909), pp. 47–49.

[8] Ibid., p. 49.

[9] Chōsenshi Gakkai, Chōsenshi Taikei: Kindaishi [An Outline of Korean
History: Modern Period], p. 136; Japan, Chōsen Chusatsu Kempei
Shireibu, Chōsen Shakai Kō [Analysis of Korean Society], pp. 6–8.

[10] The Annual Report (1908–1909), p. 53; see also "Tax Collection in
Korea," The Korea Review, VI (1906), 366–376; "The Korean Prefecture," ibid., pp. 378–382.

[11] Kuzū, I, 200.

[12] "Tax Collection in Korea," The Korea Review, VI (1906), 366–376.

in the existing administrative machinery opposed change and proved noncooperative.[13] Above all, the peculiar framework of the local administration in traditional Korea made it difficult to gain cooperation from local bureaucrats through legal sanction, for they (the *ajŏn* level and below) were neither appointed nor paid by the central government. They took their share from the taxes which they collected; and sometimes their positions in the villages were honorary.

In May 1908 Song Pyŏng-jun, leader of the *Ilchinhoe*, was given the portfolio of the Ministry of Home Affairs, and the resident-general and the Korean government summoned conferences of provincial governors and provincial secretaries at Seoul in May and June. Most of the governors, according to a report, "expressed their desire to recover the power of taxation and police and to obtain greater administrative discretion." [14] In compliance with their request, or more likely because of administrative expediency, the centralization of local administration was in some degree relaxed. The governor was restored the power to recommend "candidates for the post of District Magistrate, from among those residing within his jurisdictional province," and to appoint, promote, or dismiss *chusa*, or subordinate officials, "with the exception of Japanese appointed in that capacity." The police function was also partially restored to the governor and the provincial police department, though usually a Japanese police inspector was attached to the governor.[15]

As the relaxation of central control of local administration was taking place, seven out of thirteen governors were replaced and the remainder were transferred to other places "according to their special qualifications." [16] Also, out of a total of 133 county

[13] "Kankoku Chihō Seikyō" [Local Political Situation in Korea], Itō to Hayashi, June 22, 1907, *Japanese Foreign Office* (microfilms), MT 1.5.3.11, 122–138; Ishizuka to Ishii, December 28, 1908, *ibid.*, 193–200; also "Kankoku Genji ni okeru Chihō Jinshin no Jōkyō" [The Political Attitude of the Local Populace at present in Korea], printed on November 1, 1909, *JA (Korea)*, No. 305, pp. 24–26; for the same report from the Kunsan Residency, see *ibid.*, No. 318, pp. 5–8, 26–27, 32; from the Inch'ŏn Residency, see *ibid.*, No. 316, pp. 30–31, 43–45, 56–57.

[14] The *Annual Report* (1908–1909), p. 49.
[15] *Ibid.*, p. 52.   [16] *Ibid.*

magistrates, 44 were newly appointed, 49 dismissed, and 27 transferred to other places "during six months from July 1, 1908."[17] The policy of appointing "a competent Japanese" as a subordinate official in each magistracy was initiated in 1909.

On the whole, it can be said that there was less effort exerted in producing a replica of the Japanese government in Korea at the local level than at the national; and the rate of change among local personnel was accelerated but was not as great as among officials in Seoul. Japanese control at the local level was maintained indirectly through the Japanese-controlled police force and gendarmerie and by the manipulation of the pro-Japanese *Ilchinhoe*.

With the appointment of Japanese vice-ministers, judges, police chiefs, and so forth to replace the Japanese advisers, Korea's loss of its independence was virtually complete. However, Japan had made little progress in winning the acquiescence of the Korean people to the alien rule. Itō correctly foresaw popular uprisings of much more formidable nature than those prior to July 1907, and decided to reinforce the Japanese forces in Korea by an additional brigade and to disband the Korean army.

The infantry brigade arrived in Korea on July 27 in response to Itō's repeated requests and immediately took over garrison duties at various provincial centers, while the Japanese division that had been stationed in scattered locations in Korea was now concentrated in Seoul. Four Japanese destroyers also arrived at Inch'ŏn on July 29.[18]

During the night of July 31, 1907, Itō, as agreed beforehand, had the Korean emperor issue a decree disbanding the Korean army and requesting use of Japanese troops to suppress any violent opposition to the disbandment. Early in the morning of August 1, some of the superior officers of the Korean army in Seoul, already deprived of their arms, were summoned by the commander of the Japanese garrison force, and the imperial rescript ordering their disbandment was read to them by the

[17] *Ibid.*, p. 54.

[18] See a series of reports from the Japanese army headquarters in Korea to the army chief of staff, Tokyo, in *Japanese Foreign Office* (microfilms), MT 2.4.1.9., 937–938, 946–947, 956, 963.

Korean minister of the army: "Our existing army, which is composed of mercenaries, is unfit for the purposes of national defence," and disbandment was needed to make way "for the eventual formation of an efficient army." [19] The officers were told to assemble their men in the Seoul Central Drill Field without arms and dismiss them after paying gratuities. Their weapons would be seized in their absence. Some of the more promising commissioned and noncommissioned officers were to serve with the infantry palace bodyguard of one battalion strength. Some were to be sent to the cadet school and still others were to be incorporated in the Japanese army. [20]

One officer, "commander of the smartest and best of the Korean battalions," committed suicide in anger and desperate protest. [21] His men rose in mutiny, and another battalion followed suit. They secured weapons and cartridges by breaking into the ammunition room, nearly killing their Japanese military instructors, and started firing at the Japanese. Companies of Japanese infantry were dispatched hurriedly to the scene, and for three and one-half hours the Korean soldiers defended themselves. When the mutiny was put down, there were among the Koreans 12 officers and 56 others dead, 5 officers and 54 others wounded, and 516 captured. On the other hand, the injury inflicted upon the Japanese forces was one officer and two noncommissioned officers dead and 40 others dead or wounded. [22] Meanwhile the disbandment ceremony was conducted speedily in the presence of four Japanese companies. [23]

[19] Cited from McKenzie, *Tragedy of Korea*, p. 161; see also Japan, Chōsen Chūsatsugun Shireibu, *Chōsen Bōto Tōbatsu Shi* [Records on the Subjugation of Korean Rebels] (Ryūzan, 1913), pp. 33–34.

[20] "Kankoku Guntai Kaisan no Junjo[oyobi] Guntai Kaisan no Hōhō" [The Korean Army Disbandment Procedure and Its Methods], July 1907, *JA (Korea)*, No. 328, pp. 3–7; see also "Guntai Kaisan Shimatsu" [Summary Report on Korean Army Disbandment], Itō to Saionji, August 1, 1907, *Japanese Foreign Office* (microfilms), MT 2.4.1.9, 608–609.

[21] McKenzie, *Tragedy of Korea*, p. 161; see also U.S. Dept of Commerce and Labor, *Commercial Korea in 1904*, p. 2456.

[22] "Report on the mutiny" [prepared by] Maruyama, August 2, 1907, *Japanese Foreign Office* (microfilms), MT 2.4.1.9, 982–983.

[23] McKenzie, *Tragedy of Korea*, p. 161.

The rest of the Korean army distributed throughout the country was disbanded separately between August 3 and September 3, 1907. The Kanghwa detachment of the Suwŏn regiment rose in mutiny against the disbandment order but was quickly suppressed by the Japanese garrison force. The Wŏnsan regiment prior to disbandment stole weapons and escaped. All the others were reported as having peacefully followed the order.[24] Many disbanded and unemployed Korean soldiers dispersed throughout the peninsula and joined the Korean rebels known as *uibyŏng* (the Righteous Army) who had been sporadically fighting against the Japanese forces since the conclusion of the Protectorate Treaty. The control of rebellious soldiers, however, required measures different from those used to nullify opposition among the anti-Japanese elite. To this we will turn later.

To counteract organizational agitations Japan utilized the *Ilchinhoe*, which Song Pyŏng-jun, a leader of the *Tonghak* Rebellion, helped organize with the explicit objective of promoting Japanese annexation of Korea.[25] Included in its leadership were some of the *Tonghak* and the former Independence Club leaders. The followers were mostly recruited from the *Tonghak* believers, those who worked for pay for the Japanese military in Korea during the Russo-Japanese War, and those who were poor and jobless and sought the protection of the local Japanese in order to maintain their livelihood.[26] The acquiescence of many local

[24] Chōsenshi Gakkai, *Chōsenshi Taikei: Kindaishi* [An Outline of Modern Korean History: Modern Period], p. 218. See also Hasegawa to Itō, September 7, 1907, *JA (Korea)*, No. 274, pp. 46–48. The *Japanese Foreign Office* (microfilms), MT 2.4.1.9, sects. 3–5, have an extensive — almost daily — reporting on the Korean army disbandment process and on the subjugation of rebels. Much of this military report — probably more systematically and in detail — has been reproduced in the *Chōsen Bōto Tōbatsu Shi* [Records on the Subjugation of Korean Rebels], published by Japan, Chōsen Chūsatsugun Shireibu in 1913.

[25] Komatsu Midori, *Meiji Gaikō Hiwa* [Hidden Story of Meiji Diplomacy], (Tokyo, 1936), p. 401.

[26] Kuzū, I, 18–19; see also "Kankoku Genji ni okeru Chihō Jinshin no Jōkyō" [The Present Condition of the Public Opinion of the Local Populace in Korea], printed on November 1, 1909, *JA (Korea)*, No. 305, pp. 39–41; "Kankoku Chihō Seikyō" [Local Political Situation in Korea], Ishi-

Korean officials to this pro-Japanese group was apparently to avoid the stigma of being regarded as anti-Japanese. Though Itō sought to engineer mass acceptance of Japanese rule in Korea, it is not clear to what extent he purposely promoted the *Ilchinhoe* at the outset. Itō wanted it as a genuine Korean movement. In fact, however, *Ilchinhoe* was assisted by Uchida, a leader of the Amur Society (or the Black Dragon Society) and a close ally of the Yamagata faction in Japan.[27] Initially, the Japanese military in Korea made financial contributions to the *Ilchinhoe* and sought its assistance. Later, the Residency-General decided, in January 1907, to give it a monthly subsidy of 2,000 yen.[28]

Above all, Japan controlled the dissident Korean elements through her command of the instruments of violence and the exercise of police power as broadly interpreted from the stipulation in Article IV of the protocol between Japan and Korea signed on February 23, 1904. The Japanese officials at both the national and local levels used their political and administrative discretion widely; and the tendency to oppress the Koreans was more conspicuous outside the capital, where Japanese activities were less liable to public and foreign criticism.[29]

Some of these discretional practices were formalized later. The so-called Peace Preservation Law was promulgated on July 24, 1907. This law "authorized the Minister of Home Affairs to dissolve any association if he deemed such a step necessary for the maintenance of peace and order in the country." The police authorities were given power "to limit, suspend, or dissolve any assembly, meeting or gathering of crowds, in case of necessity for such a step in maintaining peace and order."[30] A new political organization could not be formed without approval by the proper police authority. On August 26, 1908, the imperial ordinance regarding educational associations was promulgated along with

zuka to Ishii, December 28, 1908, *Japanese Foreign Office* (microfilms), MT 1.51.311, 183–193.

[27] Kuzū, I, 40, 562–565.

[28] *Ibid.*, pp. 159–171, 240; see also *JA (Korea)*, No. 346, pp. 40–41; and No. 316, p. 3.

[29] "Editorial Comment," *The Korea Review*, VI (1906), 392.

[30] The *Annual Report* (1910–1911), pp. 85–86.

the private school ordinance, which required their registration and license;[31] and the solicitation of any contribution required permission from the minister of Home Affairs (cabinet ordinance No. 2 issued in February 1909).[32] (These were eventually followed by an order on August 23, 1910, by the Police Affairs Department which stated, "The holding of public meetings in connection with political affairs or the gathering of crowds out of doors [either for the purpose of religious worship or for education], was prohibited.")[33]

The Japanese also made great efforts to control the symbol manipulators in Korea. In a strict sense, there were no mass media of communication in Korea then, because the only existing mass medium, the newspaper, had a limited circulation due to the prevalence of illiteracy, the isolation of many communities, and the lack of purchasing power in the general public. Even so, the press, supplemented by verbal communication of its content between those who had direct access to it and those who did not, did serve to relay information on certain issues and events. This combination occurred in the situation where, under the quickened pace of important events, the news was eagerly awaited.

An observer of the events in Korea at the time summed up the influence of the press in the following manner: "The Korean's idea of the daily press is still somewhat crude, and is illustrated by the fact that when some statement is denied he is very likely to say, 'It must be true. The Paper say so.' "[34] Or, according to a Japanese official statement: "In a country like Korea, where public knowledge is yet backward and where insurrection and assassination are often provoked by seditious literature, proper measures of newspaper control and censorship are essential to the maintenance of peace and order."[35]

Most of the Korean publications (some daily, some weekly,

[31] The *Annual Report* (1908–1909), pp. 172–173.

[32] The *Annual Report* (1910–1911), p. 88; Maruyama to Sone, January 10, 1908, *JA (Korea)*, No. 369, pp. 56–57.

[33] The *Annual Report* (1910–1911), p. 88.

[34] Homer B. Hulbert, *The Passing of Korea* (New York: Doubleday, Page & Co., 1906), p. 340.

[35] The *Annual Report* (1910–1911), p. 86.

and some monthly) were issued by religious and political organizations of some standing but with limited circulations. The rest
did not show any organizational affiliation. On the whole, however, all of them exhibited strong political propensities.

According to a Japanese official report, there were in 1909
eight monthly journals published in Korea, of which two (the
Monthly Journal for Education and the *Youth*) were circulated
nationwide. The circulation of the rest was local and provincial.
There were seven daily newspapers. The *Taehan Maeil Sinbo*,
owned by an English journalist named E. T. Bethell, was most
widely circulated — about "ten times more than any others." The
lowest circulation numbers were reported for the *Kungmin Sinbo*,
the official paper of the *Ilchinhoe*, and the *Taehan Sinmun*, which
was owned by a Japanese.[36]

The Japanese authorities began exercising control over the
Korean press immediately after the conclusion of the Protectorate
Treaty.[37] When the Advisory Police Board was established in
1906, it was entrusted with the control of the press published by
Koreans and "had power to examine the draft of each paper or
to prohibit the publication of the same if facts were misrepresented or comments made injurious to public peace."[38]

A general law concerning the press was promulgated on
July 24, 1907. According to this law, "the publisher of a newspaper is required to receive from the Minister of Home Affairs
permission to publish, his application being made through the
Police Inspector-General in Seoul, or through a Provincial Governor in the provinces; and 300 *yen* is to be furnished as a
guarantee fund by the publisher but in the case of a newspaper
engaging in religious or literary work this guarantee fund is not
required." Also the minister of Home Affairs was empowered to
prohibit the sale or distribution of the newspaper, to confiscate it,
and to suspend or prohibit its publication if he deems it "injurious

[36] "Kankoku Genji ni okeru Chihō Jinshin no Jōkyō" [The Present
Condition of the Public Opinion of the Local Populace in Korea], printed
on November 1, 1909, *JA (Korea)*, No. 305, pp. 42–45. The report does
not include the *Mansebo*, the Ch'ŏndogyo official paper.
[37] See *JA (Korea)*, No. 194, p. 164.
[38] The *Annual Report* (1908–1909), p. 85.

to public order or good morals." The publisher or editor of such a newspaper was made liable to imprisonment or a fine.[39]

Freedom of the press having been severely restricted, some Korean agitators resorted to the secret circulation of political pamphlets.[40] Some books were also published in Korean and circulated, among which the most popular were *A History of the Fall of Vietnam, A History of the Fall of Poland, A History of American Independence, A History of Independence of Sweden, A History of Italian Independence, An Outline of History of Eastern Countries,* and *Requisite Readings for the Minor.*[41]

These printed works were, however, controlled later by the law concerning publication, No. 6, issued in February 1909, which was effective beginning in March. According to the provisions of this law, "a person desirous of publishing a book or picture must apply to the minister of Home Affairs through the local authority for permission to publish, the signature and seal of the publisher being conjoined, and a copy of the manuscript submitted."[42] Any person publishing a book or a picture without an official permit was subject to penalties. The sale or distribution of books and printed matter already published could be prohibited when deemed "injurious to peace and order or to public morals," and the minister of Home Affairs was authorized to confiscate the printing blocks.[43]

Papers printed in the Korean alphabet were published at Vladivostok, San Francisco, and Hawaii and distributed in Korea. In addition there were some Korean newspapers published by foreigners in Korea; of particular importance were those of Bethell. On April 20, 1908, the press law was amended and expanded to include the above cases. By a further amendment on April 30, 1908, the Japanese newspapers published by the Japanese in Korea were included in the law, as they were sometimes aggres-

[39] *Ibid.*

[40] Itō to Sone, October 21, 1908, *JA (Korea)*, No. 297, pp. 65–66.

[41] "Kankoku Genji ni okeru Chihō Jinshin no Jōkyō" [The Present Condition of the Public Opinion of the Local Populace in Korea], No. 305, pp. 39–41.

[42] The *Annual Report* (1909–1910), p. 47.

[43] *Ibid.*, p. 48.

sive in their antiforeign and anti-Korean sentiment and critical of Japan's Korean policy. Some of the regulations in the law as they stood by April 30, 1908, forbade a newspaper from inserting the following matters:

1. Anything calculated to impair the dignity of the Imperial Households of Japan and Korea;
2. Matters detrimental to peace and order, or subversive of established custom;
3. Official documents not made public;
4. Matters concerning the preliminary hearing of major or minor criminal offenses before public trial, etc.;
5. [In addition], the resident, if he deems it necessary, may forbid a newspaper to insert matter concerning military and diplomatic affairs or other topics requiring secrecy.[44]

In 1909 the distribution of newspapers published in Japan was also brought under official control, and the local resident was authorized to suspend or confiscate them, if he deemed it necessary.

In 1909 most of the newspapers confiscated in Korea had been published in Japan. This may imply an extensive circulation by 1910 of Japanese newspapers that were critical of and aggressive toward Japan's Korean policy. In 1908 and 1909, all the Korean language newspapers confiscated, except the *Taehan Maeil Sinbo*, were published by Koreans abroad and smuggled into the peninsula.[45] The native-owned newspapers in the country were subjected to unreserved control by the authorities, so that no confiscation was necessary for them. The *Taehan Maeil Sinbo*, owned by Bethell, presented a difficult problem to the Japanese authorities, even though the press law of July 24, 1907, was amended in April 1908 in order to extend official control to this English-owned paper.

In seeking to consolidate her position, Japan was working in a hostile environment. Despite inducements and persuasion, Koreans remained unreconciled to Japanese control. The memory of

[44] The *Annual Report* (1908–1909), p. 87.
[45] The *Annual Report* (1908–1909), p. 86; the *Annual Report* (1909–1910), p. 49; the *Annual Report* (1910–1911), p. 87.

the past Japanese invasions was certainly a factor, but the over-bearing and aggressive behavior of the Japanese residents further intensified Korean resentment.

For instance, Japanese rule meant the stationing of a large garrison force in strategic areas through the country (in the name of peace and order), mostly at the expense of the Korean farmer. The compensation that Japanese authorities paid for the land was far below the market price.[46] The plight of the farm population worsened with the expansion of Japanese activities. Japanese construction of railways involved the employment of cheap or sometimes free labor and seizure of farm lands, some of which were subsequently turned over to new groups of Japanese immigrants.[47]

Many reforms were introduced. However, the traditional Korean psychology and the attitude of the people toward the foreign intruder were such that the execution of many Japanese policies and reform measures was interpreted by the general populace as further diminution of their interests. The centralization of the powers and functions vested traditionally in local officials meant constant meddling with local autonomy by a Japanese agent of the central government; and the local Korean officials, now defunct and powerless to squeeze the villagers, were also without incentives to cooperate with agents of the central government. Moreover, the Japanese introduced the system of verification and registration of landownership. Many Korean landowners did not understand this novel requirement and ignored it, only to lose their titles to lands that had been theirs for generations. Judicial reform meant complication of the bureaucratic procedure for the populace, making it impossible for the common people to bring their complaints before the court.[48] Regarding Japan's currency reform, the editor of the Korea Review stated,

[46] Miura to Komura, May 24, 1902, *Japanese Foreign Office* (microfilms), MT 5.1.4.22, 4–5, 84–90.

[47] "Korean Force Labor," *The Korea Review*, V (1905), 346–348.

[48] "Kankoku Genji ni okeru Chihō Jinshin no Jōkyō" [The Present Condition of the Public Opinion of the Local Populace in Korea], reported by the Kunsan Residency for October-December, 1909, *JA* (Korea), No. 318, pp. 3–5.

"We have never for a moment believed that Japan would be guilty of the monstrous injustice of entirely casting out the counterfeit nickels and leaving thousands of innocent Koreans bankrupt."[49] Japanese commercial influence meant a rise in prices in some areas and a gradual breakdown of a self-sufficient mode of life in the villages.[50]

There are many more examples. One might add in particular some of the financial burdens the Japanese administration forced on the Koreans. New taxes, as on liquor and tobacco, were imposed despite much local opposition; and the tax levies on the land were not reduced although new revenue-raising taxes were imposed.[51] Sometimes, the Japanese tax collectors were merciless in demanding the stipulated sums from the people.[52]

All in all, the Japanese domination of Korean life did not prove advantageous to the people. Quick action was necessary to justify its rule in the eyes of the people, but the fruits of reform were naturally slow in maturing.[53] The effort to buy the allegiance of the people was futile. Yet, the political and social structure of the country was such that the lower stratum of society could not and did not voluntarily mobilize itself against the alien rule.

In an effort to secure the peaceful assimilation of the peninsular nation into the Japanese empire, Japan tried with little success to utilize the prestige of the Korean emperor. At each important step in the annexation process, Japan obtained new treaties and agreements sanctioned by the Korean sovereign. Between 1905 and 1910 the outward integrity of the emperor and his court was preserved. This maintenance of the outward status quo in the central structure of the government was designed to minimize

---

[49] "Editorial Comment," *The Korea Review*, V (1905), 228–230. See also Yuasa Mitsuru, "Kindai Nicchō Kankei no Ichi Kōsatsu" [A Study on Modern Political Relations Between Japan and Korea], *Chōsen Gakuhō*, No. 24 (July 1962), p. 174.

[50] "Kankoku Genji ni okeru Chihō Jinshin no Jōkyō" [The Present Condition of the Public Opinion of the Local Populace in Korea], report, printed on November 1, 1909, No. 305, pp. 41–42.

[51] For various forms of Korean opposition to the new taxes, see a report from the Kunsan Residency, *ibid.*, No. 318, p. 32.

[52] *Ibid.*, pp. 5–7.

[53] *Ibid.*, No. 395, pp. 19–62.

popular antipathy to Japanese rule and to obtain the collaboration of the ruling oligarchy in the Japanese consolidation of
their position.

In the traditional Korean political process, the people in time
of difficulty would presumably voice their discontent by appealing
to the emperor. Thus it was the *Ilchinhoe* that urged upon the
emperor the utility of a Japanese protectorate over Korea before
the Protectorate Treaty was eventually imposed on her. The
Japanese cabinet's annexation plan was adopted on July 6, 1909,
more than a year before the event actually took place.[54] Again,
it was the *Ilchinhoe*, in connivance with some Japanese political
leaders, that presented a petition to the emperor in December
1909 to come to an agreement with Japan over annexation. At
the same time the Japanese authorities refused to permit the
Korean court to accept counterpetitions.[55]

In traditional Korea the emperor sent out secret agents —
"censors" — to investigate malpractices of local officials when he
had reason to suspect them. Furthermore, an imperial pacifier
was dispatched when there was a political disturbance (in addition to the issuance of an imperial edict or proclamation). The
Japanese authorities also used these methods in a desperate effort
to pacify the rebels and to seek cooperation of the general populace in the process.

An imperial edict was issued on July 19, 1907, to stop disturbances in Seoul.[56] As the influence of the rebels, or the Righteous
Army, became stronger in the interior, the authorities urged the
new emperor to cooperate with the Japanese force in the pacification effort.[57] An imperial rescript was issued on September 18,
1907, in which the emperor "earnestly advised the insurgents to
return to peaceful avocations, pointing out the foolishness of

[54] Komatsu, *Meiji Gaikō* [Hidden Story of Meiji Diplomacy], p. 405;
"Kankoku Heigō ni Kansuru Ken" [Matters concerning the Korean Annex-
ation], *Gaikō Nenpyō*, I, 315–317.

[55] Sammons to Wright, July 20, 1907, enclosed in Sammons to Assistant
Secretary of State, July 22, 1907, *J.D.* XCOV, case No. 1166; Terauchi
to Sone, December 3, 1909, *JA (Korea)*, No. 346, pp. 1–2; Dec. 4, *ibid.*,
p. 4; Katsura to Sone, Dec. 8, 1909, *ibid.*, pp. 29–32.

[56] The Imperial Edict cited in Shakuo, pp. 361–362.

[57] Hasegawa to Itō, September 7, 1907, *JA (Korea)*, No. 274, pp. 46–48.

continuing an unlawful opposition to the new regime which had been adopted as the national policy." [58] At the same time, four Korean officials were dispatched to the insurgent areas with the imperial order "to lay down their arms and return to lawful life." [59] On December 13, 1907, another imperial edict was issued and fresh messengers were sent out to convey "His Majesty's decision to pardon all insurgents who had already surrendered or who should surrender to the authorities." [60] Because the Japanese forces were still unsuccessful in exterminating the insurgent elements in the interior, "His Majesty" in the edict of September 1, 1908, expressed "regret that peace in the country was being restored so slowly, in spite of the fact that many measures had been adopted to pacify the insurgents." He also gave notice that "the surrender of repentant insurgents would be accepted only till the end of October . . . and that any insurgent captured after that date would be dealt with as a criminal." [61]

In some cases, it was reported that these messengers from the emperor were beaten or killed by the rebels and their supporters. It is not certain how effective this use of the imperial authority was in the effort to subdue the insurgents. It was reported, however, that "this measure was so effective that 1,229 insurgents made acts of surrender in one month after the promulgation of the Edict." [62]

In order to counteract the rumor that the new emperor and the imperial family were captives in the palace, Japan made efforts to bring their seclusion to "an abrupt end." [63] The new emperor proceeded to the Ancestors' Temple on November 18, 1907, to proclaim the policy of reform. He called for order and cooperation in the pursuit of national policies and an emphasis on practical rather than theoretical education. [64] The new and ex-emperors both drove about the city of Seoul in open carriages — a

[58] See the *Annual Report* (1908–1909).

[59] *Ibid.*   [61] *Ibid.*

[60] *Ibid.*   [62] *Ibid.*

[63] Sammons to O'Brien, November 18, 1907, enclosed in Sammons to Assistant Secretary of State, November 19, 1907, *J.D.* CXLVI, case No. 1166.

[64] Cited from the *Annual Report* (1908–1909), p. 3.

precedent-breaking policy. The empress herself appeared in an open carriage with her face uncovered. If Itō's policy was to urge a closer contact between the people and the imperial family for the purpose of reasserting the prestige and power of the emperor and his court, the people as a whole seemed to be dismayed and unbelieving. There was undoubtedly in the minds of Koreans the notion that the sudden change was directed by the Japanese.

On January 4, 1909, an imperial mandate was issued announcing an imperial tour throughout the country, guided and escorted by the resident-general.[65] Accordingly, two extensive tours were conducted in January and February of 1909 to the south and north of the peninsula. These were the coldest months of the year in Korea. The selection of the time for the tour was mystifying, even if it was taken for granted that the tour was for the purpose of quieting the insurrectionary elements by permitting the emperor to convey personally the message that he wished the people to obey his mandate and the established rule. The purposes of the imperial journeys, as declared in the rescript, were to inspect personally the conditions prevailing among the people to acquire intimate knowledge of the situation, and at the same time to announce a new era under competent guidance of reform and progress.

The Japanese officials and their Korean collaboraters made a great occasion of the tour. Preparations for the reception of the imperial party were directed by the central government authorities. The raising of both the Japanese and Korean flags, fireworks, the public school children's parade, and the exhibition of various kinds of produce were the major items in the reception celebration.[66]

The emperor himself and his court officials accompanying the tour were reported as greatly impressed — particularly by the

[65] Translation of "the Imperial Mandate of January 4, 3rd year of Yung Hui," *Official Gazette*, January 5, 1909, enclosed in Sammons to O'Brien, January 5, 1909, enclosed in Sammons to Assistant Secretary of State, January 5, 1909, *J.D.*, CXLVI, case No. 1166.

[66] "Hōgei Shidaisho" [Instruction concerning Reception Procedure], January, n.d., 1909, *JA (Korea)*, No. 296, pp. 34, 35, 42; Satake to Koto, January 9, 1909, *ibid.*, No. 303, pp. 38–39.

Japanese navy stationed at Masampo and Pusan in the south. Also, the resident-general had the opportunity to make eight speeches to the crowds gathered to welcome the emperor and his entourage. "Among much important advice, suggestion and information given in these speeches," an official report stated, "the Resident-General particularly announced the object of undertaking the Imperial Journey and often pointed out his duty of guiding the Korean Emperor and his Government toward enlightened administration, which is of vital importance not only for the welfare of the Korean people but also for the preservation of peace in the East and thus ultimately for the peace of the world at large." [67]

After the tour both in the north and south, the emperor personally visited the official mansion of the resident-general to convey his "heartfelt thanks for the eminent services you have rendered us" by going along on the tours and giving the people "valuable information and counsel." [68]

The Japanese authorities also announced that the trip was "one of the revelations to the people of the changed order now prevailing in Korea. . . ." This announcement went on to say that the speeches made by the resident-general "undoubtedly produced a deep impression upon a certain class of people who were ignorant or misinformed as to the new regime undertaken by the Emperor and the Government of Korea under the protectorate of Japan." [69]

During the imperial journey, there were reported such incidents as the refusal of some local Korean officials to cooperate with the Japanese authorities in urging the people to raise the Japanese flag in addition to the Korean, and the utterance of some discourteous remarks by people among the reception crowds. [70] In this connection, according to the American consul general, the Korean people were rather alarmed by the unprecedented

[67] The *Annual Report* (1908–1909), pp. 25–26.

[68] Cited in the *Annual Report* (1908–1909), p. 26.

[69] *Ibid.*, p. 25.

[70] Matsumoto to Fukagawa, February, n.d., 1909, *JA (Korea)*, No. 301, pp. 128–132; Kuzū, I, 49.

action and speculated that "it was just the forerunner of removing the Emperor to Japan."[71]

The unprecedented imperial journey may have induced some Koreans to approve the new progressive way of life, if not the Japanese overlordship and the total loss of Korean independence.[72] It may also be suggested that the general impact of the tour was an increased sense of nationalism among the people. No change was recorded in the attitude of the insurgents toward the established authorities and in the noncooperative attitude of the native Christians toward the Japanese.

One of the outcomes of the Japanese-inspired political transition in Korea was an upsurge of popular interest in modern education. Generally, the modern type of education with a variety of academic disciplines was first introduced in Korea by Christian missionaries. The Methodist missionaries, as a part of their policy of breaking down the psychological inhibitions of the Koreans toward a Western religion, seemed to have started their mission work with philanthropic enterprises such as building hospitals and dispensaries in the capital as well as initiating the first separate high schools for boys and girls.[73] Thus, in 1887, both the *Paejae Haktang* for men (Hall for Rearing Useful Men, so named by the emperor) and the *Ihwa Haktang* for women were organized by American Methodist missionaries — the former with six students in attendance for the purpose of learning English, and the latter with one student but increased to a student-body of 18 the next year.[74] As the Christian activities progressed, each mission and native church established Sunday schools and various educational institutions. A marked increase of students was especially noted in the church schools following the Sino-Japanese war, and after 1905 a rapid increase of rural schools was reported.[75]

[71] Sammons to O'Brien, January 5, 1909, enclosed in Sammons to Assistant Secretary of State, January 5, 1909, *J.D.*, CXLVI, case No. 1166.

[72] Kikuchi, (The P'yŏng'yang Resident), to Itō, February 7, 1909, *JA (Korea)*, No. 301, pp. 115–120.

[73] George L. Paik, *The History of Protestant Missions in Korea (1882–1910)* (P'yŏng'yang: Union Christian College Press, 1920), p. 150.

[74] *Ibid.*, p. 121; "Women's Work in Korea," *Korean Repository*, III (January 1896), 3–4.

[75] The *Annual Report* (1908–1909), p. 170.

Japan promoted its own supervised education. On August 27, 1906, general regulations for common schools were issued in the form of an imperial edict and a decree of the minister of education. By this regulation, the central government was authorized to direct the elementary school system with prescribed courses and textbooks with "emphasis on moral and Japanese language teaching."[76] After 1907, regulation over even private schools became extensive.

For the normal school (there was only one), an official report (1907) stated, "the course of study is nearly the same as that of the normal school in Japan, except that the Japanese language constitutes one of the most important subjects in the Korean normal school." And no private normal school was to be permitted.[77]

The same regulation also provided for one Korean high school, one peers school called the *Suhakwŏn* for the children of the imperial family and the nobility, and a few foreign language schools. Later on in this period, the government provided a girls' high school in 1908, and the regulations concerning industrial schools were promulgated in 1909. Meanwhile, other professional schools were established; and the Japanese authorities sent a small number of Korean students to Japan for education. Altogether 52 students had been sent by the end of 1909, including seven sent by the imperial household.[78]

The ordinance for private schools was promulgated on August 26, 1908, by which the government was authorized to license private schools and impose government-approved textbooks.[79] The principals of private schools were required to submit detailed

[76] The *Annual Report* (1907), pp. 96–97.

[77] *Ibid.*, p. 97.

[78] The *Annual Report* (1909–1910), p. 156. "Of these 52 students, 13 were studying law, political science, and economics; 9 pedagogy and literature; 21 technical courses in such sciences as commerce, agriculture or industry." "In addition there were 25 students receiving government aid."

[79] "The Private School Ordinance," the *Annual Report* (1908–1909), Appendix, pp. 203–205. By the end of December 1909, the following private schools had received government recognition: 2 high schools, 3 industrial schools, 829 mission schools and 1,353 schools of miscellaneous nature. See the *Annual Report* (1909–1910), p. 153.

annual reports to the minister of education revealing their enroll-
ment, courses of study, and financial status.

Article X of the private school ordinance stated in part, "A
school may be closed by the order of the Minister of Education
in case of violating laws or ordinances or injuring peace or order."
Article VII had to do with the selection of teachers in private
schools from among those who had the moral and educational
qualifications.

Also regulated were the textbooks for schools. The regulations
promulgated in August 1908 stated, "Text-books to be used in
a school shall be sent to the Minister of Education for official
approval." These regulations were to prevent the distribution of
"a large number of text-books compiled by private individuals
which are incompatible with the conditions now existing in the
peninsula." More particularly, these regulations were aimed at
"certain foolish native authors, taking advantage of the unsettled
state of minds of the Koreans, [who] compiled text-books of a
seditious nature referring to the independence of the country,
inculcating anti-Japanese insurrection or using dangerous words
to excite students."

The criteria for official approval were as follows:

A. Concerning political matters;
   1. Whether it injures or criticises the relations and friendship
     between Korea and Japan.
   2. Whether it contains words or opinions opposed to the na-
     tional policy, injuring the peace and order of the country, or
     disregarding the interests of the people and the State.
   3. Whether it contains matter contrary to traditional customs.
   4. Whether it fosters senseless or mistaken patriotism.
   5. Whether it contains words or matter stirring up ideas against
     Japan or ill feeling on the part of Koreans against Japanese
     or other foreigners.
   6. Whether it contains opinions with reference to current
     political questions.
B. Concerning social matters;
   1. Whether it contains words or descriptions of an indecent
     nature or other matter violating good morals.
   2. Whether it contains references to extreme socialism or mat-
     ter injurious to social peace.

3. Whether it contains matter relating to meaningless and foolish superstitions.
C. Concerning educational matters;
  1. Whether it contains mistaken or incorrect matter.
  2. Whether the grade, volume, or materials used in it are suited to the purpose of the proposed textbook.
  3. Whether the method of compiling is proper.[80]

The textbook regulations came into force on September 1, 1908. Meanwhile, the government textbooks were sold and distributed free of charge in all the schools in Korea.

Stultifying restrictions placed on Korean education were one more example of the ever-intensifying Japanese control over the Korean people. During these years of Japanese "protection," Japan had steadily whittled down sovereign rights until Korea became hardly distinguishable from a colony. To prevent any adverse reaction from foreign quarters, Japan proceeded with caution, allowing ample time for foreign observers to acquiesce before a further step on the road to annexation was taken. The Japanese tactic of obtaining Korea's "consent" to legitimize each step was not the quickest way to expand Japanese control, but it was the safest in that it provided least provocation to interested foreign powers.

Japan's effort to win acquiescence from the people was far less successful. Either for genuinely patriotic reasons or for more selfish considerations relating to employment opportunities, social status, or economic well-being, most Koreans remained hostile to the Japanese. Some of the Japanese-sponsored innovations had little or no political significance, such as the introduction of modern medical and sanitation facilities and the construction of highways and railroads; but they failed to convince the Koreans of the beneficence of Japanese rule. The violent resistance movement, particularly after 1907, was a testimony to Japan's failure.

[80] The *Annual Report* (1908–1909), pp. 175–176.

11.

The Korean Court, the Press,
and Foreign Friends

Itō's "gradualism" meant the preservation of the status quo in the structure of the Korean ruling oligarchy. In order to show that the enforcement of the protectorate over Korea did not presuppose a revolutionary change in the government, Itō did not attempt to disturb the traditional veneration of the emperor. Itō also kept all the old cabinet members who had signed the Protectorate Treaty, save Han Kyu-sŏl, who refused to work with the resident-general because of his determined opposition to the protectorate. Min Yŏng-gi, who had also opposed the treaty to the last and refused to sign, was retained in his old position as minister of the treasury. With the establishment of the Residency-General, the only organizational change brought about within the Korean cabinet was the dissolution of the Ministry of Foreign Affairs. The former minister of foreign affairs was transferred to the position of prime minister, which had been vacated by the resignation of Han Kyu-sŏl. Itō apparently sought the cooperation of the ruling oligarchy in Korea by preserving its personal interests and by maintaining an outward appearance of governmental stability, although politically intelligent Koreans knew it was a farce. Itō's gradualism, however, soon ran into difficulties.

The ruling oligarchy surrounding the emperor, kept intact by Itō, was from the outset the strongest opponent of Japanese rule; the emperor led this opposition. The Hague mission of 1907 has already been discussed. The Emperor was adept at feeding the stream of discontent, but failed to support those followers whose actions stemmed from his own secret instructions and the suggestions of foreign sympathizers.

The first incident in defiance of the Japanese overlordship was the circulation in 1905 of a letter of appeal to the foreign governments which had had treaty relationships with Korea. Homer B. Hulbert, an American Protestant missionary and teacher for almost 20 years and a close friend of the Korean court, presented the letter to the American government in person; but he was refused an appointment with President Theodore Roosevelt. He had intended to demonstrate to the president that Korea was being treated "unjustly and oppressively" by Japan and to urge that the United States should endeavor to bring about a just settlement under the terms of the Korean-American Treaty of 1882.[1] President Roosevelt "completely ignored the appeal."[2] Then, the *Korean Daily News* and the *Taehan Maeil Sinbo* printed a letter with the emperor's signature in their issue of January 20, 1906, which claimed that the emperor had not signed or agreed to the protectorate treaty, and denied the legality of Japanese interference in internal affairs and the appointment of a resident-general.[3] The letter included an invitation to "the Great Powers to exercise a joint protectorate" for a maximum of five years.

The editor of the papers explained that the letter was a duplicate of the original conveyed to President Roosevelt by Hulbert; but when the Japanese inquired, the emperor emphatically denied the authenticity of the letter.[4] After this incident, the Residency-General placed the imperial treasury under tighter control for the

[1] Morgan to Root, October 19, 1905, *K.D.*, XXII.

[2] Paul H. Clyde, *A History of the Modern and Contemporary Far East* (New York: Prentice-Hall, 1937), p. 436.

[3] Watanabe to Maruyama, August 21, 1906, *JA (Korea)*, No. 336, pp. 1–7. *Korean Daily News*, January 20, 1906 (?), *ibid.*, No. 330, pp. 5–6. For Hulbert's own statement in this connection, see the *New York Herald*, July 22, 1907. The clipping of this statement in *Japanese Foreign Office* (microfilms), MT 2.4.1.9, 700–701. See also an article by Douglas Story on Korea in the September 4 issue of the *London Tribune* which was reproduced in H. B. Hulbert, ed., *The Japanese in Korea: Extracts from "The Korea Review"* (Seoul, 1907), pp. 76–79.

[4] Komatsu Midori, *Chōsen Heigō no Rimen* [Background of the Japanese Annexation of Korea] (Tokyo, 1920), pp. 24–25, and chap. 8.

purpose of denying any fund to the emperor for this type of anti-Japanese activity.

One can deplore these "intrigues" — as the Japanese referred to them — with as much justification in 1904–1905 as the similar clandestine diplomatic moves of the previous decades, especially 1885–1886 or 1895–1896. One must not, however, ignore the presence of a watchful and overbearing foreign influence in Seoul at each of these times that made it difficult, if not impossible, for the Koreans to seek external aid to restrain the aggressive foreign power, be it China or Japan. Prior to 1904, Korean diplomatic intrigues had some chance of success because of the relatively favorable international circumstances, particularly following the Treaty of Shimonoseki. In 1904–1905 no foreign country was sufficiently powerful and interested in Korea to check Japan; the Korean pleas were pitifully unsuccessful.

In December 1905 another special agent for Korea, Min Yŏng-ch'an, the Korean minister to France, arrived in Washington to make a plea for American support in annulling the Protectorate Treaty. He had an interview with Secretary of State Elihu Root, but, as could have been anticipated, he received no more encouraging a response than Hulbert. Roosevelt's policy of turning his back on Korea's pleas for help at the time of national crisis is open to criticism from the standpoint of international morality;[5] however, the critic must also raise the question of how and with what prospect of success the United States could have intervened. It may be difficult to approve the American policy, but it certainly is not difficult to understand the reasons for it.[6]

The Korean court made equally futile appeals to other foreign powers. In March 1905 a Japanese consular agent in Shanghai reported to Tokyo that a confidential letter from the Korean emperor had been delivered to the former Russian minister to Korea, Pavlov, now in Shanghai. The letter allegedly requested Russian assistance to expel the Japanese. Pavlov allegedly wrote

[5] For examples of such criticism see McKenzie, *Korea's Fight for Freedom*, p. 101; Homer B. Hulbert, *The Passing of Korea* (New York: Doubleday, Page and Co., 1906), pp. 222–224.

[6] See Tyler Dennett, *Roosevelt and the Russo-Japanese War* (Gloucester, Mass.: Peter Smith, 1925), pp. 305–306.

a reply in April 1905 promising early Russian help to rescue the Korean emperor from the oppressive Japanese hands; but it is not certain whether the reply eluded the vigilance of the Japanese authorities and reached the Korean capital.[7] The Japanese army also seized a letter written by a relative of the Korean emperor, Yi Chae-hyŏn, requesting that the former Korean minister Yi Pŏm-jin, go to Russia to acquaint the Russian government with the plight of the nation under Japanese occupation.[8] In October, at about the time of Hulbert's departure for America, a former secretary of the Korean legation in London, Yi Ki-hyŏn, attempted to board a steamer for China; he was arrested by the Japanese gendarmes on suspicion that he was headed for England to solicit British sympathy through his British acquaintances.[9] Although it is difficult to verify these clandestine moves allegedly made by the Korean court because the Japanese authorities appear to have been extremely suspicious and prone to exaggeration, none of these can be refuted either by contrary evidence or by logical deduction based on our understanding of circumstantial factors.

Korea stood alone in November 1905, with her capital virtually under Japanese martial law.[10] Outside the capital, because of slow communications and probably because of the absence of strong political awareness among the rural population, there was no significant *immediate* popular reaction to the protectorate agreement. It was only sometime after the disturbance in Seoul following the signing of the Protectorate Treaty that local opposition began to grow in strength. A number of organizations emerged ostensibly for the purpose of religious, educational, or social activities; many of them, however, disappeared within a short while. One of the most unique was an organization which urged smokers to quit smoking and save the money to repay

[7] Matsuoka (acting consul at Shanghai) to Komura, March 29 and April 17, 1905, *NGB*, XXXVIII, Part I, 640–642, 649–650.

[8] Hagiwara (in Seoul) to Komura, May 1, 1905, *ibid.*, pp. 651–652.

[9] Hagiwara to Komura, October 22, 23, and 27, *ibid.*, pp. 662–665.

[10] The last American minister to Korea, E. V. Morgan, wrote in November 1905 that the Korean government "cannot be considered to have acted entirely as free agents." Even D. W. Stevens made a similar admission in January 1906. See Harrington, p. 333, n. 28.

Korea's debt to Japan totaling 13 million yen. Within a little over a month after it had started in March 1907, this association, called the National Foreign Debt Reimbursement Association, collected over 160,000 yen from those who felt that indebtedness was incompatible with national independence.[11]

Where there is no popular basis for politics, political groups tend to be factional in their organization and manifestation of purpose. Such was the case in Korea. There were no political parties in Korea as we understand them today, but various factional political groups did exist. And there is some correlation between a growing sense of crisis among the elites within Korean society and the rise of various kinds of factional political groups.

Because these types of political groups are issue or crisis oriented, their durability also corresponds with the life span of the issue or crisis. When the crisis subsides or the issue loses its meaning within the context of time and place, these groups are in a sense alienated from their initial purpose, and they eventually disappear from the political scene. Some groups maintain the same outward appearance and retain the same initial members despite social and political flux. Yet, absence of these visible changes does not necessarily mean that these organizations remain unchanged. They acquire different objectives.

Between 1905 and 1910, there was one consistent issue in Korean politics: cooperation or noncooperation with Japanese rule. Inasmuch as this issue was national in character, the nontraditional organizational elites appealed for mass support. Such mass organizations, if not mass parties, were the *Ilchinhoe* and the *Taehan Hyŏp'hoe* (Great Han Association). In 1909 the Japanese authorities listed 13 other provincial and local organizations; some were academic societies and others were professional and labor organizations, but all were engaged to some extent in propagandizing activities.[12] When in August 1910 these

[11] See a lengthy report on Korean political situation sent by Itō to Foreign Minister Hayashi Tadasu, June 4 and 22, 1907, in *NGB*, XXXX, Part I, 556–561, 566–568.

[12] "Kankoku Genji ni okeru Chihō Jinshin no Jōkyō" [The Condition of the Public Opinion of the Local Populace in Korea], printed on November 1, 1909, *JA (Korea)*, No. 305.

organizations were ordered to dissolve,[13] membership as listed in the *Annual Report* varied from 140,175 for the *Ilchinhoe* to a mere 73 for the Literati Association. Only four of the organizations achieved more than a few hundred members, and the Great Han Association was second only to the *Ilchinhoe* despite the fact that it had a membership of only 7,379.[14]

Nothing was said about the basic determinants of the membership in the above-mentioned official list, and its reliability is of a dubious nature. A correspondent of the *Yomiuri Shimbun*, in his report on August 4, 1910, about three weeks before the date of the official list, gives different figures on the membership of these same organizations: the *Ilchinhoe*, 91,896 members with 100 subsidiary organizations; the Great Han Association, 20,289 with 55 subsidiary organizations; and the North and West Educational Association, 18,025 with 15 subsidiary organizations.[15] All the other organizations had much smaller memberships. There was much instability within political organizations.

Many of these organizations were established in 1910 when the question of annexation was publicized by the *Ilchinhoe*. The Nationalism Agitation Society and the National Great Speech Association were organized in July and December 1909, respectively. (They were merged into the Political Friends' Association in April 1910). And, except for the *Ilchinhoe*, the Great Han Association, and the North and West Educational Association, all others were organized in 1910. Most of the organizations which existed prior to 1910 disappeared from the political scene, changed their names by amalgamating other elements, were ordered to dissolve before 1910, or were too insignificant to come under the order of wholesale dissolution in August 1910.

The *Ilchinhoe* dated from August 1904. In addition, in 1905 there were such political organizations as the *Poanhoe*, the *Hyŏpdonghoe*, the *Taedong* Club, the *Kongjinhoe*, and the *Tae-*

[13] Cf. The *Yomiuri Shimbun*, August 4, 1910, in *Meiji Shimbun Shūsei*, XIV, 284.

[14] The *Annual Report* (1910–1911), p. 86.

[15] The *Yomiuri Shimbun*, August 4, 1910, in *Meiji Shimbun Shūsei*, XIV, 284.

han Chakanghoe (a residue of the *Tonghaktang*).[16] In 1907 only a few of these were still active, and new groups emerged. Thus, the organizations listed in 1907 included the *Ilchinhoe*, the *Taehan Chakanghoe*, the *Suryuhakhoe**, the *Hambuk Hŭnghakhoe**, the *Tongyuhoe**, the *Taedong* Club, and other Christian organizations.[17] The list is by no means complete, but it should be sufficient to indicate the ephemeral nature of these organizations.[18]

A few newspapers adopted openly anti-Japanese editorial policies. The *Hwangsŏng Sinmun*, for example, attacked the protectorate agreement by asking in its editorial if it was worthwhile "for any of us to live any longer."[19] E. T. Bethell's English-language paper, the *Korean Daily News*, and its sister paper in Korean, the *Taehan Maeil Sinbo*, were particularly outspoken in criticizing the Japanese administration of Korea. The problem of Bethell and his papers, which were the most widely circulated among the Koreans, was very annoying to the Japanese authorities. As a citizen of a Japanese ally, Great Britain, he enjoyed extraterritorial rights in Korea. The press law, which had been promulgated with special reference to newspapers published by foreigners, did not prove to be effective in Bethell's case: "There was no means of examining the contents of these publications until they had been printed and actually delivered to their subscribers, so that offending copies had nearly always reached the public before it was possible for the authorities to issue orders forbidding their sale and distribution."[20] The Japanese authorities kept track of the regular subscribers of Bethell's papers — more easily in the country than in the city. But despite these measures, the number of readers and their influence did not decline.

The Koreans regarded Bethell's papers as the only mouthpiece

[16] *Hoe* means "association"; *Tang*, "party."
[17]* Those not mentioned in 1905.
[18] The list is compiled from Shakuo's work; Chōsenshi Gakkai, *Chōsenshi Taikei: Kinseishi* [An Outline of Korean History: Modern Period].
[19] Quoted from McKenzie, *Tragedy of Korea*, p. 140.
[20] The *Annual Report* (1908–1909), p. 89. "Taehan Maeil Sinbo [Bethell] Shobatsu ni taisuru Chihō Minshin no Jōkyō" [Local Public Attitude in Regard to Japanese Legal Action on Mr. Bethell of the *Taehan Maeil Sinbo*] (1908), *JA (Korea)*, No. 306, pp. 130–133.

through which they could voice their complaints.[21] Some insurgent leaders who were captured and imprisoned claimed they took up arms against the Japanese because they became indignant about Japanese rule after reading Bethell's papers. Some used the papers to demonstrate the righteousness of their cause.[22] The Japanese authorities also charged that Bethell's alleged irresponsible statements were the cause of riots and bloodshed following the abdication of the Korean emperor.

Even though his papers did not prove to be intentionally biased, the dissemination of the news unfavorable to Japanese rule and the critical attitude toward foreign management of Korean affairs were regarded by Japan as damaging to its prestige and administration. Consequently, "some attempts were made to win him over and secure his silence, but as it failed, the Japanese authority resolved to crush him," reported Frederick A. McKenzie, who was in Korea at that time. He continued, "The Japanese were making his life as uncomfortable as they possibly could, and were doing everything to obstruct his work. His mails were constantly tampered with; his servants were threatened or arrested on various excuses, and his household was subjected to the closest espionage." [23]

The Japanese administration started its own official papers to counteract Bethell's influence. The *Seoul Times* became the official English newspaper under the editorship of Mr. Zumoto, an able Japanese journalist who had once been the editor of the *Japan Times*. The Japanese authorities also started the *Keijō Nippō* in Seoul, in both Japanese and Korean. There were other Japanese-owned Korean newspapers in Seoul, but almost all of them, in financial difficulty, gave way to this official paper.[24]

The following excerpts from the editorial in the September 6, 1907, issue of the *Keijō Nippō* may indicate the pattern of Japa-

21 McKenzie, *Tragedy of Korea*, pp. 214–215.

22 Matsui to Nabeshima, July 4, 1908, *JA (Korea)*, No. 327, pp. 21–28.

23 McKenzie, *Tragedy of Korea*, p. 213; see also "Editorial," the *Korean Daily News*, December [n.d.], 1906, cited in *ibid.*, p. 217.

24 McKenzie, *Tragedy of Korea*, p. 214; the *Tokyo Asahi*, August 15, 1906, *Meiji Shimbun Shūsei*, XIII, 129.

nese propaganda used to undermine the influence of the *Taehan Maeil Sinbo*. "Is it wise for the Korean people to give their confidence to men of another race, and to alienate men of their own race? . . . The Japanese have great interests here. If our people trust their own government they will support them. If, however, our people follow the guiding of the Englishman Bethell's crooked pen we cannot tell what will happen to them . . . Asia for the Asiatics and Europe for the Europeans is the law of nature." [25]

There are two clear themes in the above passage, "Asia for the Asiatics" and the common interests between Japan and Korea based on geographical and racial proximity and friendship. These seem to reflect the opinions held by the Japanese government and the Japanese authorities in Korea, but it is not certain how receptive the Korean newspaper audience was to these themes. If there was any reaction, it seems to have been negative since Bethell's papers continued to thrive.

Failing in all the other attempts to suppress Bethell's papers, Japan in desperation took the matter up with the British ambassador in Tokyo and the British government. During the summer of 1906, the Japanese authorities had several articles from the *Taehan Maeil Sinbo* translated and sent to the British government.[26] They repeatedly insisted that the British government do something about Bethell.[27]

The dominant influence of Bethell's papers in the minds of the Korean newspaper public was beyond dispute; and considering the disturbances in the interior, especially after July 1907, the British government had to act somehow. The Japanese authorities wanted to silence all the factual news.[28] Bethell was at last sub-

[25] Cited in McKenzie, *Tragedy of Korea*, pp. 215–316. According to McKenzie, the above is from the *Tai Kan Nippo*, but it ceased its Korean language edition on October 14, 1906. See The *Kokumin Shimbun*, October 23, 1906, *Meiji Shimbun Shūsei*, XIII, 158.

[26] Director General in the office of the Resident-General to Vice-Minister of Foreign Affairs, July 2, 1906, *JA (Korea)*, No. 336, pp. 129–196. For the translated articles, see *ibid.*, appendix 1–28.

[27] Tsuruhara to Itō, January 18, 1907, *ibid.*, No. 269, pp. 55–56; Itō to Hayashi, October 13, 1907, *ibid.*, No. 344, pp. 80–156.

[28] For the articles, see *ibid.*, No. 336, appendix 1–28 and Itō to Hayashi, *ibid.*; McKenzie, *Tragedy of Korea*, pp. 224–240.

jected to the "China and Corea order in Council" of 1904, which was amended in February 1907, in regard to the activity of British journalists in the Far East.

Henry Cockburn, the British consul-general in Seoul, visited Tokyo to confer with the British legation there in September 1907. Upon his return he summoned Bethell to appear before a specially appointed court to answer the charge of "adopting a course of action likely to cause a breach of the peace." Bethell, without his attorney, stood before the court held in the consular buildings, with Mr. Cockburn acting as judge.

The charge was based on eight articles, some of which had appeared in the *Korea Daily News*, some in the *Taehan Maeil Sinbo*, and some in both papers. Six articles were descriptions of the fighting between the Righteous Army and the Japanese forces in the interior, one was about the proposed visit of the crown prince of Japan to Korea, and one in Korean urged the Koreans to value and cherish their independence.

Bethell was convicted and ordered to enter into recognizance of £ 300 to be of good behavior for six months. The *Korea Daily News* itself commented on the court decision: "The effect of the judgment is that for a period of six months this newspaper will be gagged, and therefore no further reports of Japanese reverses can be published in our columns." [29] The Japanese also made note of this with satisfaction and stated that "after Bethell's case the articles of the *Taehan Maeil Sinbo* changed their outlook." [30]

The case of Bethell was yet to be finished. According to Itō, in 1908 Bethell again became vindictive, "instigating disturbances, encouraging treasons, and inducing assassination." [31] A Japanese official report stated that as soon as the six-month term of good behavior expired, Bethell's papers again showed seditious activity.[32]

[29] Cited in McKenzie, *ibid.*, p. 224.
[30] Maruyama to Itō, November 6, 1907, *JA (Korea)*, No. 344, p. 2.
[31] Itō to Hayashi, May 1, 1908, *ibid.*, No. 289, pp. 4–8; see also the *Annual Report* (1908–1909), p. 88.

Bethell was again brought into court on June 15, 1908, to answer a complaint laid before the British consular court. This time the defendant was represented by counsel, and the proceedings were presided over by Judge Bourne of Shanghai. Counsel for the defendant applied to have the case heard before a jury, but the application was refused. After several days' deliberation, during which Yang Ki-t'aek, Bethell's Korean subeditor, testified for Bethell, Bethell was sentenced to imprisonment for three weeks and required subsequently "to give security for good behaviour during six months or to be deported." He was immediately sent to Shanghai to serve his sentence, and his papers were entrusted to his colleague, Marnham.[33]

What amounted to the finishing touch for Bethell's cause came a little later. Bethell with his Korean subeditor was charged with embezzlement of the public funds of the National Foreign Debt Reimbursement.[34] The *Taehan Maeil Sinbo* and other Korean papers took care of the publicity and advertisement[35] for the fundraising project, and for those contributions sent to the *Taehan Maeil Sinbo*, Yang was named as general secretary.[36]

The newspapers in Korea were not a profitable enterprise. The natural question was then: How did he operate the papers financially? Maruyama, the police inspector general, reported to General Baron Hasegawa during Itō's absence on January 18, 1907, that the papers by Bethell were branch organizations of a Russian newspaper in Harbin and that both were financed by the Russian government. The same report also revealed the Korean emperor was secretly making a monthly contribution of 500 yen

[32] *Ibid.*

[33] McKenzie, *Tragedy of Korea*, p. 120.

[34] "Kankoku Chihō Seikyō" [Local Political Situation in Korea], Itō to Hayashi, *Japanese Foreign Office* (microfilms), MT 1.5.3.11, 122–138.

[35] Shakuo, p. 441. For a good English description of its history, see "The Recent Seoul Trial," *North China Daily News* (Shanghai), October 3, 1908, *JA (Korea)*, No. 336, pp. 73–74.

[36] "Kenki" [Gendarmerie Secret Report], July 27, 1908, *ibid.*, No. 355, pp. 66–67; "Kankoku Chihō Seikyō" [Local Political Situation in Korea], *ibid.*, pp. 122–138.

to the papers, plus occasional bonus contributions for their continued publication.[37]

Yang was arrested and detained in prison for interrogation. The British consul general in Seoul, Cockburn, complained to the Japanese authorities on behalf of Marnham, the new employer of Yang.

Maruyama explained that he was acting in compliance with the order from the Korean minister of home affairs to investigate the accounting of the fund, and the Japanese authorities stated that Yang's arrest did not have anything to do with the second Bethell trial.[38] Thus, there developed an interesting episode that highlighted a dilemma in Japan's Korea policy.

Itō was then in Tokyo, leaving his office in the care of the vice-resident-general. Before he left Seoul, Itō instructed Maruyama not to relate the accounting of the fund at the second Bethell trial, but to require *all* the collectors to submit their books for careful examination.[39]

However, only the criminal proceedings against Yang were reported by Cockburn to the British government. The British ambassador in Tokyo, acting on instructions from London, referred Cockburn's report to the Japanese foreign minister. Itō sent a telegram to the Residency-General in Seoul, asking if Maruyama was acting according to his instructions. In reply Maruyama produced three Koreans as the complainers who asked for an investigation by the Korean minister for home affairs, for whom Maruyama was ordered to act.[40] Meanwhile, Yang had been detained in prison since July 12, and the few visitors he had been permitted were not allowed privacy.

Marnham, after having visited Yang, told Cockburn: "Yang . . . is ill, worn to a skeleton, and on the verge of collapse. . . . He is confined day and night together with nineteen others in a room twelve feet by fourteen, making twenty people

[37] Maruyama to Hasegawa, January 18, 1907, *ibid.*, No. 336, pp. 187–188; Watanabe to Maruyama, August 21, 1908, *ibid.*, pp. 1–7.

[38] Maruyama to Nabeshima, July 25, 1908, *ibid.*, pp. 66–67.

[39] Itō to Sone, July 22, 1908, *ibid.*, pp. 89–91.

[40] Maruyama to Nabeshima, July 25, 1908, *ibid.*, pp. 66–67.

in that small space in the great summer heat." [41] Cockburn sent a written message to Miura, the Japanese resident in Seoul, declaring that Yang must have better care if he were to survive the ordeal. Miura, however, showed indifference to the request, arguing that whatever treatment he was receiving was better than the treatment under the Korean government, and no partial favor should be given to Yang over the others who were likewise awaiting trial.[42] When informed of this message, Itō was displeased with the pretention of impartiality on Miura's part and instructed that better treatment be granted Yang.[43] Itō further ordered that Yang be sent to a hospital.

The nurses, somehow having mistaken the order from the police department, released Yang the next day, and he found security in Marnham's residence which was protected by extra-territoriality. As he was resting at Marnham's residence, a British doctor diagnosed Yang's condition as "dangerously ill"; and Marnham, in cooperation with Cockburn, insisted that Yang be kept there until his recovery.[44] The original date of the hearings for Yang's case was set on August 15, but with Yang in the custody of Marnham it was postponed until August 31.

Meanwhile, Bethell had completed his prison sentence and returned to Seoul, where he testified by affidavit at a staff meeting of the National Foreign Debt Reimbursement Association on July 30. Bethell stated that the only unauthorized private use of the fund was 5,000 yen to assist in his house construction since September 1907. The Japanese authorities could not produce any evidence to make a criminal charge against Yang, and there followed "the complete collapse" of Yang's prosecution.[45] Itō was very much disturbed by this fiasco.

[41] MacDonald to Itō, August 5, 1908, related to Sone, *ibid.*, No. 306, pp. 63–68.

[42] Sone to Itō, August 2, 1908, *ibid.*, No. 390, pp. 2–3.

[43] Itō to Sone, August 2, 1908, *ibid.*, No. 306, pp. 61–62; the same to the same, August 10, 1908, *ibid.*, No. 206, pp. 76–77; Itō to MacDonald, August 8, 1908, *ibid.*, pp. 69–71.

[44] Sone to Itō, August 14, 1908, *ibid.*, No. 290, pp. 28–31.

[45] "The Recent Seoul Trial," *North China Daily News* (Shanghai), October 3, 1908, in *ibid.*, No. 356, pp. 73–74. See also Kim Chŏng-myŏng, VIII, 49–55.

It is difficult to estimate how much decline in popularity Bethell's papers suffered during and after the trials, but some pro-Japanese Korean organizations were exploiting the opportunity by urging a boycott of the papers.[46] The public attitude concerning the trials was not uniform in its sympathy toward Bethell. On the whole the proceedings testified as to the authoritative position of Japan in Korea, if not Japanese justice.[47] They are also indicative of a divided house in Japan's administration of Korean affairs; for even within his Residency-General, Itō often had to cope with unwilling subordinate officers.

Bethell permanently left Seoul shortly afterward, still being watched by the Japanese secret service. Maruyama was relieved of his position.[48]

As the Japanese resented the British newspaperman, so were they suspicious of the influence of foreign missionaries as their activities increased in Korea. The Korean court did not openly encourage Christianity but had been at least favorably disposed toward the missionaries. The missionaries, particularly American ones, were often invited to give counsel on various problems. "When Korea was in danger," wrote one of the American missionaries, "the emperor turned to the missionaries for succor." Or, "when the Emperor found his own property insecure, he asked a missionary to take charge of his private investments." [49] The Korean court hoped that it could "discover a new improved method of soliciting and procuring 'help' from so-called Christian nations," through its contact with the missionaries.[50]

The years from 1897 to 1906 saw the rise of Christianity in Korea. This growth came at a time of rapid political change,

[46] *Ibid.*

[47] *"Taehan Maeil Sinbo* 'Bethell' Sobatsu ni taisuru Chihō Minshin no Jokyō" [Local Public Attitude in regard to Japanese Legal Action on Mr. Bethell of the *Taehan Maeil Sinbo*], 1908, *ibid.*, No. 306, pp. 130–133.

[48] Ishizuka to Tsuruhara, August 27, 1908, *ibid.*, No. 290, p. 76; Wakabashi to Nabeshima, December 4, 1908, *ibid.*, No. 352, p. 182. This telegram was about the death of Mr. Bethell on May 1, 1909.

[49] L. H. Underwood, *Underwood of Korea* (New York: F. H. Revell Co., 1918), p. 204.

[50] Ladd, p. 402.

which was characterized by the ascendency of Japanese influence; and the historical tie of Protestantism with liberalism and with nationalist movements proved to be a sore obstacle to Japanese political control.

In 1904 there were 174 missionaries of 14 denominations in Korea.[51] This number increased to 205 in 1909.[52] Of the 174 in 1904, 148 or 85 percent were Protestant missionaries; and of the 205 in 1909, the 157 Protestant missionaries represented 77 percent. Furthermore, almost all of the Protestant missionaries in both 1904 and 1909 were American.

Detailed and systematic analyses which are available on the Presbyterian missionaries in Korea, who were the most active, show that (1) the most rapid increase in the number of Presbyterian missionaries in Korea occurred from 1904 to 1909; (2) the number of Korean pastors increased rapidly after 1904; and (3) the number of churches in Korea showed a distinct increase after 1894 but the increase was particularly marked during the period 1904–1909.[53]

It is undoubtedly true that some missionaries and native ministers intentionally appealed to the symbols of anti-Japanese feeling and Korean patriotism to seek followers. Anti-Japanese opposition seemed to be more prevalent within the Presbyterian mission than any other missions in Korea. On the whole, however, the accepted policy of the missionaries toward political matters was that of neutrality.[54] According to George L. Paik, "As far as we can discover in the private letters of the missionaries, a large number favored and cooperated with the Japanese and made an effort to quiet the restlessness of the Christians."[55] Some of the

[51] *The Missionary Review of the World*, XVII (March 1904), frontispiece.

[52] "Chōsen Kitokukyō Bukyō Ichiranpyō" [Tables of Christianity Propagation in Korea] (1909), *JA (Korea)*, No. 357, pp. 137–138.

[53] Paik, chaps. v and vi.

[54] Arthur J. Brown, *Report on a Second Visit to China, Japan, and Korea (1909)* (New York: Board of Foreign Missions of the Presbyterian Church, U.S.A., 1910[?]), p. 6.

[55] Paik, p. 401.

ordained Korean pastors even attempted to carry their evangelist activities to the rebels and sought an end to armed resistance to Japanese rule.[56] The so-called Epworth League within the church was disbanded in 1906 on the ground that "the League had in many places changed the purpose of the church, and became a political organization.[57]

The policy of neutrality that was advocated by the missionaries was a difficult one to maintain on many occasions. For "the problem of the missionaries was to win the confidence of the Japanese and at the same time to hold the faith and trust of the Koreans who declared the Japanese to be their enemies." [58] When Japanese forces landed in Korea in 1904, the missionaries welcomed them, as they believed that "the Japanese would help to better things." When Itō became resident-general, "the prevailing sentiment was that it would be better for the people to submit and to make the best of existing conditions." [59] Itō himself sought the cooperation of the missionaries in maintaining peace and order.

Itō explained the essence of his policy in this connection in the following manner: "In the early years of Japan's reformation, the senior statesmen were opposed to religious toleration, especially because of distrust of Christianity. But I fought vehemently for freedom of belief and religious propaganda, and finally triumphed. My reasoning was this: civilization depends on morality and the highest morality upon religion. Therefore religion must be tolerated and encouraged." [60] Itō sent a message of welcome with a gift of 10,000 yen to the World's Christian Student Federation held in Tokyo in April 1907. In addition to this, the Residency-General heavily subsidized the Young Men's Christian Association in Seoul "in recognition of its service for the good of

[56] Sammons to O'Brien, April 4, 1908, enclosed in Sammons to Assistant Secretary of State, April 4, 1908, *J.D.* DCCXLIII, case No. 13438.

[57] Methodist Episcopal Church, Board of the Missionary Society, *Annual Report* (1906), p. 322. Hereafter cited as M.E. North Report.

[58] Paik, p. 340.

[59] McKenzie, *Korea's Fight for Freedom*, p. 218.

[60] Cited in McKenzie, *ibid.*, p. 211; see also Ladd, p. 396; M. E. North Report for 1907, p. 29.

the Koreans."[61] And Song, the Korean home minister, was reprimanded by Itō when he made a statement on February 16, 1909, which discredited American missionaries.[62]

Despite Itō's policy of cooperation with the missionaries and their policy of political neutrality, much ill-feeling was created in the minds of missionaries by the ill-treatment of Koreans by Japanese immigrants and police forces. On occasion some missionaries openly expressed their disapproval.

The Korean converts turned to the missionaries for advice and assistance. The missionaries were often regarded as "apostles of Justice and Righteousness." [63] Their sense of ethics and human rights and the trust placed in them by the Korean converts caused some missionaries to clash directly with the Japanese authorities. The missionary was understandably incensed when church buildings and land were seized by the Japanese with little or no compensation to the congregation.[64] The Japanese military rule resulted also in violence, such as that reported by Rev. Elmer M. Cable to his mission: "Our church at Annai was burned to the ground by the Japanese soldiers, and at Sajackhoe three of the Christians were seized and tied to a stake and ordered to be shot. Two of them were killed, but one escaped and his almost miraculous deliverance made a deep impression on the people." [65] As a result of clashes between Korean students in mission schools and the Japanese garrison force, school buildings were destroyed in reprisal.[66] These strong-handed methods used against native Christians greatly embarrassed the Japanese civilian authorities in Korea.[67] It seems that most of the Japanese activities toward the missionaries and their followers were on the whole predicated

[61] Ladd, p. 396.

[62] "Prince Itō vindicates Missionaries," *Japan Advertiser*, March 3, 1909, enclosed in O'Brien to Bacon, March 3, 1909, *J.D.*, CXLVI, No. 1166; see also O'Brien to Itō, February 26, 1909, *JA (Korea)*, No. 372, appendix 1–2.

[63] Paik, p. 338.

[64] *Korea Mission Field* (January 1906), p. 57.

[65] *M.E. North Report for 1908*, pp. 41–42.

[66] Sammons to Assistant Secretary of State, July 11, 1908, *J.D.*, CXLVI, case No. 1166.

[67] Okabe to Tsuruhara, May 21, 1908, *JA (Korea)*, No. 293, pp. 34–35.

on the belief that this largest nongovernmental Christian organization was a threat to Japanese rule and a source of anti-Japanese
sentiment.[68]

With all her control mechanisms, Japan was slow in inculcating
her values in the minds of the Korean people and promoting willing acceptance of her authority. In contrast the growth of Christianity in Korea was phenomenal. After a rather slow and painful
beginning following the Sino-Japanese War, Korea became such
a fertile soil for Christian missions that their success has been
called "one of the marvels of modern history." [69] Especially, the
growth of missionary activity in Korea during the period 1905–
1910 was viewed by the Japanese with a sense of uneasiness, as
Christianity constituted the only remaining potentially powerful element in Korea not under Japanese control.

In 1904 there was a reported total of 95,495 native Christians
of communicants and noncommunicants and of all the denominations, and by 1909 the number had increased to 153,124. The
sources of the above figures are different, and their statistical
bases might not have been the same. Yet, there is a clear indication of a great increase in church membership between 1904 and
1909.[70] Undoubtedly, intensive missionary effort was a factor in
the rapid growth in the number of Korean Christians, but there
were various other reasons as well.

The Japanese seemed to impugn the motives of the Korean
converts. A Japanese editor in Seoul charged that Koreans joined
the Christian churches merely for material gain, for social reasons, or to gain protection from various persecutors.[71] The Japanese authorities emphasized, above all, that the church members
were primarily interested in obtaining tax relief.[72]

A psychological explanation was given by Professor Ladd who

[68] Sammons to Assistant Secretary of State, July 11, 1908, *J.D.*, CXLVI,
case No. 1166.

[69] "Report of Commission I," *World Missionary Conference* (1910),
p. 71.

[70] See *The Missionary Review of the World*, XVII (March 1904),
frontispiece; "Chōsen Kitokukyō Bukyō Ichirampyō" [Table of Christianity
in Korea] (1909)," *JA (Korea)*, No. 357, pp. 137–138.

[71] "News Calendar" *The Korea Review*, I (June 1901), 267.

[72] *The Annual Report* (1910–1911), p. 38.

visited Korea upon Itō's invitation; he credited the "uplifting" nature of the protectorate regime with providing the impetus for Koreans to join "a modern and improved form of religion. . . ." He went on to emphasize the need for "the firm, strong hand of the civil power of the Japanese authorities in Korea to purify Korea," for "the larger the number of the converts, the more need of discretion and diligence for the process of improving their quality. . . ." [73]

Some missionaries offered their opinions on the motives of the converts. According to Hulbert, the Korean temperament was receptive to Christianity, a "combination of rationality and idealism." [74] Rev. C. E. Sharp divided the motives of Korean Christians into three categories: (1) uniting for mutual help, (2) seeking Western learning and culture, and (3) "a work of God's spirit in the hearts of many." [75]

Summarizing the missionary point of view, Paik stated that, in addition to genuine conversion, many Koreans became Christians for the following reasons:

1. Dissatisfaction due to political oppression and maladministration and general poverty;
2. Admiration of Western civilization;
3. The religiousness of the people;
4. Replacement of their powerlessness with the protection of the church;
5. Attraction of fellowship among the converts;
6. The Korean family and village power structure; i.e., when the influential individuals in the village and one's family were converted the rest in the community followed suit, and the missionaries, particularly those of the Presbyterian Church, tried to cultivate a sympathetic feeling toward them among these informal elites in the Korean society. [76]

Furthermore, Korean Christians at the time were predominantly from the lower and uneducated classes of the people, and except

[73] Ladd, pp. 391–395.
[74] Hulbert, *The Passing of Korea*, p. 126.
[75] C. E. Sharp, "Motives for Seeking Christ," *Korean Mission Field*, II (August 1906), 182.
[76] Paik, pp. 248–249, 384.

at the beginning of the Presbyterian mission, proselytizing activities were primarily aimed at the "working" classes.[77]

Even though Paik states, "Strange as it may seem, few converts were actuated by political motives," [78] this statement is more applicable to the earlier converts than to those converted between 1904 and 1910. In the latter period, many Koreans became Christians for political reasons, but their motivation was not so much to organize the Korean Christians against Japanese rule as merely to seek their own political asylum.[79] The general anti-Japanese feelings among the native Christians seem to have been caused among other things by their general perception of group strength and of the Western concepts of political rights and freedom.

In order to prevent the politicization of the organized Christian churches, Japan sought the collaboration of the missionaries. At the same time, the Japanese treated leniently the other faiths competing with Christianity in Korea. The activities of the native religious groups, including the residues of the earlier *Tonghak* movement, which were "more political than religious in nature" received tacit Japanese approval.[80] Buddhism, which had been suppressed throughout the history of the Yi dynasty, had been revived as a part of the first reform programs as early as 1895 by the importation of Japanese Buddhist missionary monks.[81] The number of Japanese Buddhist bishops in Korea showed an increase between 1906 and 1910. Their number together with that of Japanese Christian missionaries for the Japanese residents in Korea amounted to 52 in 1906. This number gradually increased to 56, 87, 105, and 137 in 1907, 1908, 1909, and 1910, respectively. As the Japanese Christian missionaries could never have

[77] *Ibid.*, p. 205.
[78] *Ibid.*, p. 155.
[79] "Kenki" [Gendarmerie Secret Report] (November 27, 1909), *JA (Korea)*, No. 357, pp. 273–274.
[80] "Kankoku Genji ni okeru Chihō Jinshin no Jōkyō" [The Present Condition of the Public Opinion of the Local Populace in Korea], report, printed on November 1, 1909, *ibid.*, No. 305, pp. 34–36; see also the *Yomiuri Shimbun*, August 4, 1910, *Meiji Shimbun Shūsei*, XIV, 384.
[81] For the mention of "several schools under Buddhist Missionaries from Japan," see the *Annual Report* (1907), p. 95.

been numerous, these figures reflect the increasing number of Buddhist priests. Some Buddhist priests were to serve the Japanese Buddhist residents in Korea, but others came to propagandize among the Koreans.[82] But its influence as a counterbalance to Christianity was limited, if such influence existed at all.[83]

In summary, we have seen the process whereby Japan was gradually eliminating the last desperate resistance against her rule from the upper strata of Korean society. Japan indeed had to cope with the various social and political strata differently, as each commanded a different instrument of resistance. And, she used persuasion where she could and force where needed. There was no serious threat to Japan's position of authority in Korea; but in this tug-of-war between the means of persuasion and violence, the Japanese decision-makers were by no means united and the chain of her command showed occasional disruptions. In the end, however, the use of force played an important part in the management of Korea before the annexation, as will be shown in the following chapter.

[82] *The Missionary Review of the World*, IX (January 1895), 63.

[83] "Kankoku Genji ni okeru Chihō Jinshin no Jōkyō" [The Present Condition of the Public Opinion of the Local Populace in Korea], report, printed on November 1, 1909, *JA (Korea)*, No. 305, pp. 34–36.

12.

The Insurgents: The Righteous Army

The farming population living in the villages constituted the masses of traditional Korean society. For centuries these people lived in a society where one's role was rigidly determined by birth in accordance with a status-oriented political philosophy. They were unaware of their potential collective power, and the traditional inculcation of the virtue of obedience to superiors had produced a mentality which was politically inert and retiring. In the last years of the Yi dynasty this politically malleable docility of the Korean masses was all the more apparent.

Korean villagers, "diligent, simple, patient, and superstitious," were closely attached to the land, living in small communities of their own, pretty much self-sufficient and often isolated from the rest of the world. They had a good deal of autonomy in local affairs, and they organized their various guilds for mutual service and other purposes. This way of life generated a strong provincialism among the people, which was naturally intensified by their ignorance. National consciousness had not developed among them until as late as 1905–1910,[1] if at all.

It has also been pointed out that in the last years of the Yi dynasty the people were increasingly subjected to various forms of official and unofficial squeeze. If not in open rebellion, there were complaints, murmuring, and utter distrust of the ruling class. Their long pent-up feelings readily disposed them to wel-

[1] "Kankoku Genji ni okeru Chihō Jinshin no Jōkyō" [The Present Condition of the Public Opinion of the Local Populace in Korea], report printed November 1, 1909, *JA (Korea)*, No. 303, pp. 22–23.

come change.[2] However, the masses were not willing to make the sacrifice needed to produce change, nor did they have knowledge of how to go about it. This inability to make a collective effort for change in the existing society did not necessarily mean that they were unconcerned with their own welfare. The Japanese tried to win the support of the masses, but their efforts remained largely ineffective.

In the process of rebel subjugation, the Japanese sought to buy the allegiance of the people by reviving the imperial myths. Contrary to Japanese expectations, however, this policy engendered national consciousness among the masses. To make it worse, this consciousness was intensified by the long interval of political uncertainty in the transition period and by anti-Japanese agitation conducted by the various Korean elite elements.

Also, in their efforts to subjugate the rebels, the Japanese authorities made relentless use of force. In so doing, they made little attempt to separate the rebels from the masses. A genuine mass disturbance in Korea between 1905 and 1910 occurred only in Seoul. At the outset the core of rebel strength did not include farmers — who made up the largest occupational group in Korea at the time, accounting for 85 percent of the total population. However, the rebel movement against the Japanese authorities after 1907 became almost a mass movement, certainly due to the indiscriminate method of rebel subjugation and the gradual awakening of national consciousness.

The fact that the mass disturbances over the signing of the Protectorate Treaty were confined to Seoul was an indication of the geographical limitations of political awareness within the populace and of the degree of allegiance to the ruling oligarchy. After the conclusion of the Protectorate Treaty, there were locally organized opposition movements in the southern provinces. In most cases they were sporadic and lacked centralized direction; they were often occasioned by the ill-treatment of Koreans by Japanese settlers and by the *Ilchinhoe*.[3]

[2] *Ibid.*, pp. 28–39.

[3] Paddock (American consul general in Seoul) to Wright, July 7, 1906, enclosed in Paddock to Assistant Secretary of State, July 10, 1906, *J.D.*, CXLI, case No. 1166.

Of the three locally organized opposition groups, two were led by former high government officials and the third by a minor government official. The two former high officials were Min Chongsik in Hongju, south Ch'ungch'ŏng province, and Ch'oe Ik-hyŏn in Sunch'ang, north Chŏlla province. They were subsequently captured and their forces of about 500 men and 450 men, respectively, were dispersed. The third group in north Kyŏngsang province with a strength of about 1,000 men led by Sin Ŭl-sŏk was not dispersed until 1907.[4] Hence by 1907 all active local opposition movements were suppressed, temporarily at least. However, in the wake of the forced abdication of the emperor and the disbandment of the army in July 1907, more serious armed resistance movements erupted in different parts of Korea.

The Japanese authorities, perhaps in anticipation of such disturbances, had ordered the confiscation of all firearms in the possession of Koreans and imposed a rigid control over the manufacture of arms.[5] Furthermore, all ways of smuggling them were cut off by the port authority and the Japanese offshore police.[6]

The bases of operation of the so-called *Uibyŏng* (the Righteous Army) were scattered in the mountainous areas. Many insurgents in the villages disguised themselves as farmers and attacked Japanese passers-by, settlements, and small units of Japanese troops.[7] They would quickly appear in numbers of 100, 200, 500, or 1,000 men, attack their prey, and retreat into the mountains before a Japanese force of adequate strength could be called to the scene.[8]

[4] Chōsen Chūsatsugun Shireibu, *Chōsen Bōto Tōbatsu Shi* [Records on the Subjugation of Korean Rebels], p. 10; for the identification of Sin Ul-sŏk, see "Chomei naru Kankoku Bōto no Shuryō Chōsa" [The Survey of Chief Rebel Leaders in Korea], *Japanese Foreign Office* (microfilms), MT 2.4.1.9, 1787–1792.

[5] The *Annual Report* (1908–1909), pp. 81–82.

[6] *Ibid.*, pp. 90–91; "Kenki" [Gendarmerie Secret Report], Dec. 7, 1907, *JA (Korea)*, No. 357, pp. 281–282; the same, November 24, 1909, *ibid.*, No. 357, p. 270; Sone to Itō, January 16, 1908, *ibid.*, No. 288, pp. 1–5.

[7] Benta to Tsuruhara, September 10, 1907, *ibid.*, No. 274, pp. 106–107; see also, Chōsen Chūsatsugun Shireibu, *Chōsen Bōto Tōbatsu Shi* [Records on the Subjugation of Korean Rebels], p. 13; McKenzie, *Tragedy of Korea*, p. 169.

[8] Chōsen Chūsatsugun Shireibu, p. 9; see also Tsuruhara to Chinda,

These guerrilla-type attacks were at times so frequent and widely scattered that the Japanese army commanders were unable to respond.[9] As precautionary measures, small Japanese settlements in the interior of the peninsula were moved to the cities and Japanese travelers were asked to stay home.[10] Many of the Japanese gendarmerie and police units already stationed at strategic locations were in fact immobilized because they could be moved in response to the reports of attacks only at the risk of leaving these places defenseless during their absence. The major task of pacification, therefore, fell on the shoulders of the Japanese garrison force other than the gendarmerie.[11]

The real strength of these guerrilla fighters is very difficult to estimate. It was reported that it numbered approximately 50,000 at the end of 1907, 70,000 in 1908, 28,000 in 1909 and 19,000 in 1910.[12] Other than being a general indication of the trend in numerical strength, these figures do not seem to be reliable. The difficulty lies in determining where and how often the insurgents came into contact with the Japanese troops.

Concerning the rebel leaders, information is meager. An official report gives the names of the 65 *significant* leaders as of 1908 and their places of birth, previous occupations, and the location of their forces.[13] However, this interesting collection of data is not too meaningful, because for many of the leaders neither occupation nor birthplace were known. Many former Korean soldiers seem to have played a more active leadership role than in the period prior to 1907. Also, Confucian scholars seem to have played an important role. North and South Ch'ungch'ŏng provinces, often regarded as the *yangban* provinces in traditional Korea, were the birthplaces of only two out of the

December 13, 1907, Japanese Foreign Office (microfilm), MT 2.4.1.9, 1309.

[9] Benta to Tsuruhara, *JA (Korea)*, No. 274, pp. 106–107.

[10] Shakuo, pp. 423–424.

[11] Tsuruhara to Itō, September 10, 1907, *JA (Korea)*, No. 275, pp. 88–89.

[12] Shakuo, p. 427.

[13] "Chomei naru Kankoku Bōto no Shuryō Chōsa" [The Survey of Chief Rebel Leaders in Korea].

known 28 leaders. North Kyŏngsang province, which was also included in the ruling class region, provided nine leaders; whereas Kyŏnggi province, which was regarded as the ruling oligarchy region together with Seoul, produced only five. Among those who were known as former Confucian scholars, two were born in south Hamgyŏng province, two in north Kyŏngsang province, one each in Kyŏnggi and Kangwŏn provinces. Similarly, for former officials and soldiers, birthplaces can be classified in the following manner: military — two in Kangwŏn province, one in south or north P'yŏngan province, and five unknown; civilian officials — four in north Kyŏngsang, one in Kyŏnggi, and one unknown. On the whole, this analysis of rebel leaders on the basis of the available data does not correlate with the regional characteristics of the ruling class in traditional Korea. (See Chapter 1.)

There are no systematic data to determine the general composition of all the rebel forces. But still, since the new upsurge came after the abdication of the emperor and, more particularly, after the disbandment of the Korean army, it seems probable that a great number of former army officers and soldiers constituted the core of the new resistance. The rest of the rebellious elements as enumerated by the Japanese authorities included:

1. The local Confucian scholars and *yangban*, who resisted the changes brought about by the Japanese reform and who fought for the old ways;
2. Those who were politically ambitious and trying to exploit the opportune moment of the disturbances;
3. The traditional Korean bandits, the *hwajŏk* (the armed robbers);
4. Some who joined the rebels due to the abuse of political favoritism locally given to the *Ilchinhoe* by the Japanese officials, and some who volunteered for the rebel cause, having been influenced by the doctrines of the missionaries.[14]

This was the most thorough and conclusive enumeration of the

[14] Chōsen Chūsatsugun Shireibu, pp. 7–8.

rebellious elements. If they mentioned them at all, most Japanese official reports and other publications merely called these elements, "rebels," "insurgents," "law-breakers," "bands," or "dissatisfied, unemployed, and anti-Japanese Koreans." [15] Whatever was missed in the Japanese enumeration was supplied by Western observers and their additions included: (1) merely adventurous natives who joined the rebels to obtain food from the more thrifty; (2) some who were jobless as "a result of the destruction of their villages"; [16] (3) others seeking compensation for the ill-treatment by Japanese settlers; [17] and (4) some young men in the villages who were forced into the insurgent ranks.[18] In this connection, also, the influence of Bethell's papers has already been discussed. On the whole, what is definitely not reported concerning the insurgent ranks is the active and voluntary participation in the cause of the Righteous Army by the populace as a whole and particularly the two largest occupational groups in Korea, the farmers and the merchants.

The Righteous Army existed in name only by July 1907, due to successful Japanese suppression, but it was revived through the addition of new recruits from among the recently disbanded, unemployed soldiers. In some cases these disbanded soldiers became drill-masters in schools in various localities.[19]

In 1904 it was reported that the Korean standing army contained about 17,000 men trained in "European methods." [20] Within the next year, Japan forced Korea to reduce the army

[15] See the annual reports and the other publications cited throughout this work.

[16] (1) and (2) are from a statement by the Rev. Miller in Sammons to Dodge, September 10, 1907, enclosed in the same to Assistant Secretary of State, September 10, 1907, *J.D.*, CXLV, case No. 116.

[17] (3) is from Paddock to Wright, July 7, 1907, enclosed in Paddock to Assistant Secretary of State, July 10, 1907, *ibid.*

[18] "Chu Mon-soh Chōshusho" [Chu Mon-soh Interrogation Papers], Taguma (in Kando) to Akashi, related to Sone, September 25, 1908, *JA (Korea)*, No. 359, pp. 42–52.

[19] Paik, p. 317.

[20] U.S. Dept of Commerce and Labor, *Commercial Korea in 1904*, p. 2456.

sharply; at the time of its disbandment, the Korean army had about 9,000 men with 311 officers.[21]

Despite their low social and political prestige compared with civilian officials, these 311 officers have been classified as the members of the ruling class in Korea since they were definitely recruited from the *yangban* class. The common soldiers, without prestige and often underpaid and mistreated, were recruited from among the commoners — from the landless peasants, the men in the peddlers' guilds, and the mountain tiger hunters skilled in the use of firearms. Some were forced into being soldiers. Those who were not compelled to join the army voluntarily joined to find an outlet for their social and political, if not their personal, frustrations. By joining the military service, they did not become members of the ruling class, but they had a better opportunity to obtain official recognition and to share the values of the ruling class and the elites of the country.

They were untrained and unequipped. One of the first reform efforts of the Korean government was to modernize the army, and even as late as 1905 the government expenditure for the Ministry of the Army amounted to 2,466,447 yen out of a total of 7,123,815.[22] Nevertheless, at the time of disbandment the American consul general in Seoul observed that Korean troops were of "an uncertain quality, unreliable, and apt to join with a mob in a crisis." [23] But they were soldiers by profession who in the past had exhibited courage and skill in fighting.

By suddenly disbanding the army, the Japanese eliminated any possibility of organized resistance by the Korean military; but the same act provided a good source for recruiting rebels, and many of the demobilized men eventually joined the Righteous Army. Having allied themselves with the rebel force for their livelihood, if not strictly for their anti-Japanese feelings, they could

[21] Chōsenshi Gakkai, *Chōsen Taikei: Kinseishi*, p. 216; "First General Report of Korean Finances, October, 1904–1905," enclosed Morgan to Root, November 27, 1905, *K.D.*, XXII.

[22] See Japan, The Residency General in Korea, *Kankoku Zaisei Shisetsu Kōyō* [The Essential Aspects of Japanese Financial Administration in Korea] (Keijō, 1910 [?]), pp. 17–18, 32–44.

[23] Sammons to Assistant Secretary of State, August 1, 1907, *J.D.* CXLV, No. 1166.

honorably live on the dole of Korean sympathizers. Indeed, there was no place besides the Righteous Army where the disbanded Korean soldiers could easily employ their professional skills without incurring a sense of shame or guilt.

To subjugate the rebels the Japanese gendarmerie sought the collaboration of the local Koreans under an order of the minister of home affairs issued on November 9, 1907, which organized the so-called Self Defense League in each *kun* with the *kunsu* (the master of county) as head. It was then composed only of the members of the *Ilchinhoe* that actively participated. Otherwise, the order remained almost a dead letter.[24] The uselessness of this association for distinguishing the rebels from others in the locality was admitted by the Japanese themselves. An official report stated, "As a whole, their work . . . did not prove satisfactory except under the closest supervision, and most of them failed to carry out even a part of their intended functions."[25] When the league forced the people to secure passports which would differentiate them from the rebels, the system backfired, for some rebels obtained passports and passed themselves off as peaceful villagers when necessary.[26]

Indeed, the primary instrument used by Japan to pacify the rebels was the application of force. This was in part unavoidable as most of them were in organized bands, and other means of control and persuasion seemed to be ineffective. The Japanese authorities acted on the assumption that the Koreans as a whole were sympathetically disposed to the rebels, if not actively participating in the rebellion. General Hasegawa complained to Itō that, although the rebels were harming peaceful people, the Koreans were generally inclined to be sympathetic to these lawbreakers.[27] Hasegawa, therefore, issued a proclamation in Itō's absence, promising pardon for those insurgents who repented and rewards for informers; and at the same time he also threatened to punish whole villages in reprisal for any aid given to the insurgents. As a result, many villages were burned for having

[24] Kuzū, I, 369, 374–375.
[25] The *Annual Report* (1908–1909), pp. 82–83.
[26] Akashi to Sone, January 28, 1908, *JA (Korea)*, No. 288, pp. 16–26.
[27] Hasegawa to Itō, September 7, 1907, *ibid.*, No. 274, pp. 46–48.

harbored and cooperated with the rebels.[28] Schools and churches were destroyed by the Japanese forces when uprisings were caused by students and by members of the churches.[29]

The villagers were caught in the middle, for if they helped the Japanese they were labeled pro-Japanese and became the target of rebel reprisals, and vice versa. Neutrality was indeed difficult for the helpless populace. And, no doubt, some atrocities were committed by the guerrillas against the peaceful villagers.

The news of the strong-handed methods utilized by the Japanese in the suppression of the rebels leaked abroad. Hayashi, the Japanese minister for foreign affairs, telegraphed to Itō: "I am informed of the fact that the British Government is investigating the validity of the reports of frequent atrocities to Koreans by the Japanese force." The telegram continued, "The reports seemed to indicate that in connection with the suppression of the rebels the Japanese force burned many villages which harbored the rebels and exposed the peaceful villagers mercilessly to cold and hunger. . . ."[30] In reply, Itō stated, "During my absence, an atrocious military order had been issued for the purpose of suppressing the rebels, and I ordered the Commander of the Japanese garrison force to modify the uncivil practice." In the same reply, however, Itō rationalized the use of strong-handed methods by saying that whatever atrocities had been committed by the Japanese force were due to the fact that Japan had to meet incessant rebel uprisings with the limited strength available. Furthermore, he suspected that the Christian missionaries in Korea sent exaggerated reports abroad.[31]

Between July 1907 and December 1908, approximately 6,880 houses were burned, most of them Korean-owned. During the

[28] Cited from Robert T. Oliver, Korea, Forgotten Nation (Washington, D.C.: Public Affairs Press, 1944), pp. 40–42; and McKenzie, Korea's Fight for Freedom, pp. 135–136.

[29] McKenzie, Tragedy of Korea, chaps. 16 and 18; Chōsen Chūsatsugun Shireibu, Chōsen Bōto Tōbatsu Shi [Records on the Subjugation of Korean Rebels], p. 13.

[30] Hayashi to Itō, November 29, 1907, JA (Korea), No. 330, pp. 9–10.

[31] Itō to Hayashi, November 20, 1907, ibid., pp. 11–12. Also for the same see Japanese Foreign Office (microfilms) MT 2.4.1.9, pp. 1286–1287.

same period, approximately 120 Japanese civilians and 1,250 Korean civilians were killed. In the years from 1906 through 1910, the record shows a total of 136 Japanese killed and 277 wounded. During the same period, there were 17,779 Koreans killed and 3,706 wounded.[32] On the whole the figures are indicative of heavy Korean casualties and material damage for their opposition to Japanese rule. Furthermore, the comparatively small number of rebels captured reflects the Japanese military policy of not taking prisoners, especially after 1907.[33]

The brutal suppression caused hundreds of peacefully inclined families to sympathize with the rebels. Their numerical strength increased in 1908, the second year of new rebel movements. Furthermore, as the result of repressive measures the rebel center shifted from the mountainous areas and the military post areas, where disturbances were reported at the time of the disbandment of the Korean army, to the more densely populated and agricultural areas in the southwestern part of the peninsula.[34] It was also during the months when farmers were economically hard-pressed, from March to June in both 1908 and 1909, that the rebel attacks became most rampant.[35] (See Appendix, Table VII.)

One should be cautious in making generalizations from these facts due to the nature of the Japanese expeditions sent to subdue the insurgents. The Japanese garrison force was mobile, literally seeking out the rebel elements through many and extensive campaigns. Because of the climate, this force apparently relaxed its activities during the winter. These modifications cast doubt on the validity of some of the aggregate figures in this reference, but do not detract from the observation that more frequent contact between Japanese forces and rebels and an increase in the number of rebel bands occurred during the spring months. The observation also holds true in the case of rebel contacts with the Japanese police and gendarmerie forces more or less stationed on the spot.

[32] Chōsen Chūsatsugun Shireibu, Appendix, Table 2.
[33] Sammons to O'Brien, June 12, 1908, enclosed in Sammons to Assistant Secretary of State, June 12, 1908, *J.D.* CXLVI, case No. 1166.
[34] See Chōsen Chūsatsugun Shireibu, Part 3 and Appendix Table 2.
[35] *Ibid.,* tables 9a and 9b.

In the end, the efficiency of well-planned and extensive Japanese policing efforts at the expense of everything else succeeded partly in silencing the people, but the relentless use of force sowed a crop of bitter hatred against the new ruler of the peninsular kingdom; and the sullen, powerless people came to harbor a strong resentment of the Japanese.

13.

The Rise of Japanese Militarism

As early as 1907, the Japanese government had regarded annexation as "a natural consequence" of Article II of the Portsmouth Treaty that recognized Japan's "predominant" interests in Korea and provided for Japan's "direction, protection, and supervision" of Korean affairs. Even Itō, an advocate of a moderate and cautious policy, admitted the eventuality of annexation. Japan's elder statesmen and the cabinet that deliberated on Japan's new demands on Korea following the Hague incident of 1907 decided to annex Korea if the government should be unwilling to sign a new agreement. It is clear, therefore, that annexation had become by the end of 1907, if not earlier, a matter of timing and method.

Advocates of an early annexation were not lacking in either country. At the height of the political crisis over the Hague incident, a group of six Japanese chauvinists, including the well-known Tōyama Mitsuru, submitted a memorandum to the Japanese government proposing immediate annexation as the better of the two alternative policies for Japan. (The second alternative was to exercise the sovereign powers in Korea as a mandate from the Korean throne, presumably without eliminating Korea as a sovereign entity.)[1] Uchida Ryōhei, Tōyama's disciple and the

[1] This memorandum dated July 14, 1907, is one of several examples of extremists' views that appear appended to Prime Minister Saionji's instructions to Foreign Minister Hayashi, then in Korea; Saionji stated that Japanese public opinion was "unexpectedly strong [insistent on drastic measures]." See *NGB*, XXXX, Part I, 461. See also Conroy, pp. 385–387.

adviser to the *Ilchinhoe*, accused Itō of not having gone far enough in settling the Hague incident. Uchida was a vociferous advocate of annexation at the earliest possible time. It was probably on his initiative that Song Pyŏng-jun and another *Ilchinhoe* leader, Yi Yong-gu, began serious discussions with him in the summer of 1908 concerning the methods and procedures for a merger of Japan and Korea. He had come to consider early in 1908 that Itō was unfriendly to the *Ilchinhoe* and that the resident-general should resign so that the annexation might go through. As a means of forcing Itō to resign, Uchida attempted to create a crisis in the Korean cabinet by inducing Song Pyŏng-jun to quit. Itō weathered the Uchida-*Ilchinhoe* intrigue, and Song stayed on when the influential post of home minister was offered. Nevertheless, by the fall of 1908, there was an irreparable cleavage between Itō and Prime Minister Yi Wan-yong on the one hand and Uchida and the *Ilchinhoe* on the other.

Itō's decision to resign his Korean post probably was not because of pressures from Uchida and his group. Itō perhaps knew when to quit. He also had come to feel that he should not be bogged down any further in the quagmire of administration in Korea but should return to the center of Japanese politics from which he had been absent for some time.[2] He had prepared for his resignation by installing Viscount Sone Arasuke, former minister of finance of Japan, as vice-resident-general in September 1907. In June 1909 Itō was succeeded in his Seoul post by Sone and became the president of the Privy Council. In July Itō made his last trip to Korea, ostensibly in order to take leave of the Korean emperor, and obtained another agreement from the Korean government by which Japan took complete charge of the administration of justice and prisons.[3]

By coincidence or design, while Itō was on this farewell trip to

[2] It is said that Katsura Tarō, who became prime minister for the second time in July 1908, did not want Itō to return to Tokyo for fear that the latter would lead the *Seiyūkai* against his administration. See Kuzū, I, 610–611.

[3] See the text of the Memorandum of July 12, 1909, in *NGB*, XXXXII, Part I, 182. It was signed by Yi Wan-Yong and Sone, but Itō was its real originator. See Komatsu, pp. 59–60.

Korea, the Japanese government reached a definitive decision on the question of annexation. Meeting on July 6, 1909, the cabinet approved a policy proposal that had been prepared in the previous March by Foreign Minister Komura Jutarō and which had received the approval of Prime Minister Katsura and Itō. Katsura and Komura had anticipated that Itō would raise difficulties about the proposal; but when they unfolded the plan on April 10, 1909, Itō readily expressed his complete agreement.[4] As approved by the cabinet in July, Japan was to carry out the annexation at a suitable time, thus bringing Korea under Japan's rule in name as well as in fact.[5]

Following this momentous decision by the cabinet, more detailed plans were formulated by the Japanese Foreign Office. They stipulated that, at the time of annexation, an imperial decree should be promulgated setting forth the reasons for the action and also guaranteeing full protection of foreign interests in Korea; that the imperial family of Korea should be accorded honor and pension in a manner similar to the members of the Japanese imperial clan; etc. The cabinet approved these details in late July.[6] Subsequently, Itō also gave his assent.[7]

Itō left Japan on October 16, 1909, to tour the Kwantung Leased Territory and Harbin for three or four weeks. The official explanation was that it was to be a private tour with no official mission. Although there is no way of determining Itō's real purpose, a plausible explanation states that he intended to confer with Russian officials on the Korean question.[8] In 1907 Itō had urged the obtaining of Russia's acquiescence in the annexation of Korea. In 1910 Japan informally notified Russia of the impending annexation and sought Russian "understanding." [9] Therefore, it may be assumed that Itō had intended to test Russian

[4] *Ibid.*, pp. 8–17; *Komura Diplomacy*, II, 376–379. See also Conroy, pp. 374–378.

[5] The text of the cabinet decision of July 6, 1909, appears in *NGB*, XXXXII, Part I, 179–180.

[6] *Komura Diplomacy*, II, 382–385.

[7] Komatsu, p. 17; Conroy, p. 377.

[8] Shakuo, pp. 481–482.

[9] See Motono (St. Petersburg) to Komura, April 20, 1910, *NGB*, XXXXIII, Part I, 118.

reaction to the recent Japanese decision when he went to Harbin
to meet the Russian finance minister.[10] An Chung-gŭn, the Korean who assassinated Itō as he emerged from a conference with
this Russian official, is said to have believed that Itō's talks were
to be of a nature "injurious to the interest of Korea." [11] Itō's
sudden death did not have any serious effect on either Japanese
public opinion or on the policy of the government. The incident
was treated as an isolated case of tragedy that should not influence
policy.[12]

In Korea, however, there was fear that Japan might retaliate for
the assassination of one of her most illustrious statesmen by a
Korean.[13] During this uneasy period, the *Ilchinhoe* submitted
a memorial to the Korean throne and petitions to the prime minister and the resident-general proposing the absorption of Korea
by Japan, for the welfare of the Korean nation and for peace in
the Far East. These documents were hardly Korean in origin.
They had been drafted by Uchida and his Japanese friends in
early November 1909. Unaware that their government had already decided to annex Korea, these Japanese extremists had also
organized an "Association of Comrades on the Korean Question"
in November 1909, presumably to exert pressure on the Japanese
and Korean authorities. The memorial and the petitions of the
Ilchinhoe were first shown to Prime Minister Katsura, Marshal
Yamagata, and General Terauchi, the minister of war. These
three men represented the military faction in the governing circles of Japan and had shown varying degrees of interest in the
activities of Uchida and his company. Uchida was particularly
solicitous of support from War Minister Terauchi to whom he
explained that the submission of the *Ilchinhoe* proposal would be
carried out as though no Japanese had any knowledge of it. What
Uchida had in mind was to use his Korean stooges to stir up the

[10] For an official account of Itō's activities at Harbin, see Kawakami
(consul-general at Harbin) to Komura, October 26, 1909, *NGB*, XXXII,
Part I, 196–197.

[11] Quoted from the *Annual Report* (1909–1910), p. 46.

[12] Kuzū, II, 182; *Komura Diplomacy*, II, 385–386.

[13] Shakuo, pp. 503–507. Representatives from the imperial family, the
government, and various organizations of Korea attended the state funeral
for Itō held in Tokyo in November, 1909. *Ibid.*, p. 481.

Korean political scene and provide an excuse for the use of Japanese force to settle the Korean question once and for all. Apparently Terauchi and his patron, Marshal Yamagata, approved Uchida's conspiracy with a warning that nothing be done that might put the Japanese government in an embarrassing position.[14]

The *Ilchinhoe* documents exploded like a bombshell. With a few minor exceptions, the great majority of the various political, religious, and social organizations came out with strong denunciations against "the traitors." Prime Minister Yi Wan-yong, who had recently rid the cabinet of Song Pyŏng-jun, the militant leader of the *Ilchinhoe*, had long regarded this association as his political foe. Basically Yi Wan-yong and the *Ilchinhoe* were rivals for Japanese favors for their own selfish political ends. The fact that the Residency-General and the Japanese military authorities did not see eye to eye on all occasions aggravated the rivalry. Yi Wan-yong played up to Sone, while the *Ilchinhoe*, which from its inception had been the servant of the Japanese military, continued to look toward the Japanese generals in Korea for support. In a way, therefore, the feud between Yi Wan-yong and the *Ilchinhoe* reflected the competitive and often antagonistic relationship between the Japanese civilian and military authorities in Korea. Even with Itō's prestige and skills, the Residency-General had discovered that the military was not always pliable. Sone, apparently lacking any solid base of support in the Japanese political scene, found the military in Korea more difficult to handle than had Itō. At any rate, Yi Wan-yong opposed the annexation proposal — according to the apologist for the *Ilchinhoe* — because he himself wanted credit for the annexation when it came.[15] The prime minister of Korea, therefore, induced all

[14] Kuzū, II, 197–256. The *Ilchinhoe* petition to Sone also emphasized the ethnic and cultural affinity between Japan and Korea. See the full texts of the memorial and the two petitions in *ibid.*, pp. 221–256. The fact that Yamagata and Terauchi endorsed these petitions for annexation is also stated in Tokutomi, III, 751–752. Tokutomi cites a letter from Terauchi to Yamagata, Dec. 13, 1909, in which Terauchi expressed his annoyance at Resident-General Sone who was displeased by the petitions.

[15] Kuzū, II, 184. The *Ilchinhoe* supplied the coolie service to the Japanese army during the war of 1904–1905, received substantial subsidies from the funds set aside for the intelligence operations of the Japanese army,

opponents of the *Ilchinhoe*, including some of his recent foes, to close their ranks and crush the *Ilchinhoe*'s design.

The day following the submission of the petitions by the *Ilchinhoe*, a mass rally took place in Seoul, allegedly on Yi Wan-yong's instigation, where "thousands" of agitated Koreans listened to speeches attacking the *Ilchinhoe*. This meeting, attended by a few elder statesmen of Korea including Kim Yun-sik, resolved to submit its own petition against the annexation proposal. Within the Korean cabinet, voices were raised to punish the leaders of the *Ilchinhoe*. Resident-General Sone's reaction to the petition was also extremely unfriendly. He apparently viewed the *Ilchinhoe*'s agitation as an unnecessary, potentially harmful stunt perpetrated by selfish glory seekers.[16] Sone was above all concerned with the commotion that threatened to disturb peace in the capital. He, therefore, ordered a strict ban on all political meetings in the city. Sone's attempt to order Uchida out of Korea, however, was foiled, temporarily at least, by the Japanese military authorities in Korea. On direct orders from General Terauchi, the military provided armed escorts of Japanese gendarmes to protect Yi Yong-gu, Uchida, and other annexationists.[17] The Uchida-*Ilchinhoe* group, faced with opposition from the Korean cabinet and Sone, took the matter to the Toyko government by submitting a petition for annexation to Prime Minister Katsura. At the same time, Uchida and his Japanese comrades began urging the Japanese cabinet to dismiss Sone.[18]

Prime Minister Katsura apparently was intent on playing his own cautious game. On the one hand, he decided that the petition from the *Ilchinhoe* had failed, in view of the significant reactions

and collaborated with the Japanese forces fighting the Righteous Army. See *ibid.*, I, 159–171, 240–241.

[16] For details on anti-*Ilchinhoe* agitations among the Koreans, see Shakuo, pp. 525–528. According to Kuzū, Sone took it as a personal affront that the *Ilchinhoe* had started its agitations for annexation without consulting him in advance. See Kuzū, II, 297. Sone issued a public warning against any organization that disturbed the peace and declared that there had not been any change in Japan's official policy toward Korea. *Komura Diplomacy*, II, 386.

[17] Kuzū, II, 265–267, 408–411.

[18] *Ibid.*, pp. 466–467.

against annexation and the cold attitude shown to the *Ilchinhoe* by Japanese in both countries. Katsura had to free himself from the *Ilchinhoe*'s conspiracy which he had had prior knowledge of but had not opposed. In early February, Katsura let it be known that the decision on annexation would be exclusively a concern for the Japanese government and that no Korean meddling in the matter would be tolerated. On the other hand, Katsura resolved to get rid of Sone, whose cold reception of the petition from the *Ilchinhoe* lent, perhaps unwittingly, support to the anti-Japanese sentiment in Korea. Sone was recalled to Japan in January 1910, and Katsura pointedly ignored him. In May the frustrated resident-general, who probably had not understood the intricacy of Japanese high politics, resigned pleading illness.[19]

On May 30, 1910, General Terauchi received the additional post of resident-general of Korea. The appointment of the powerful war minister to the Korean post was in itself an indication of Japan's determination to push through the annexation by force if necessary. Japan had already informally notified the Russian and British governments that the incorporation of Korea into the Japanese empire was imminent. On June 3 the cabinet adopted an outline for future Japanese rule. Korea was to be ruled by a governor-general who would be responsible directly to the Japanese throne and would be authorized to rule by fiat, because the Japanese Constitution was not to apply to Korea "for the time being."[20] Drafts of a treaty of annexation, of imperial edicts to be promulgated at the time of annexation, and of public announcements were prepared and adopted by the cabinet on July 8.[21] On the same date the cabinet also approved the texts of various ordinances to be issued immediately following the annexa-

[19] See Katsura's memorandum, February 2, 1910, to Sugiyama who acted as the intermediary between Katsura and Uchida, and Sugiyama's letter to the *Ilchinhoe* based on Katsura's memorandum in Kuzū, II, 501–503. On Sone's recall and resignation see *ibid.*, pp. 466, 616–651. For descriptions of the unenthusiastic reaction among Japanese journalists in Japan and in Korea to the *Ilchinhoe* proposal, see *Komura Diplomacy*, II, 386–387; Shakuo, pp. 528–536.

[20] The text of the cabinet decision of June 3, 1910, appears in *NGB*, XLIII, Part I, 660.

[21] *Komura Diplomacy*, II, 387.

tion. They had been prepared by a committee of officials from the Foreign Office and the Residency-General and dealt among other things with the new name for Korea, the legal status of Koreans under Japanese rule, the treatment of foreign residents, new rules for foreign trade, the treatment of the imperial family, and the establishment of a Government-General to rule Korea.[22]

Terauchi's greatest concern, however, was the prevention of any serious uprising or other violent opposition to the annexation. In mid-June, prior to his departure for Korea, Terauchi gave orders to the Japanese military and civilian authorities in Korea to obtain a complete transfer of police powers from the Korean government and to unify all the law enforcement agencies — the Korean police, the "Residency Police" and the gendarmerie — under the direction of the commander of the gendarmerie. By the end of June, over ten thousand policemen and gendarmes were placed under the direct command of a major-general in the Japanese army; officers in the gendarmerie headed the provincial police forces.

A reign of terror descended upon Korea. All political discussion and assembly was banned; all newspapers, whether under Japanese or Korean management, that criticized the Residency-General or carried any story on the annexation were suspended; individuals suspected of being dangerous to the Japanese regime were arrested; all Korean organizations were placed under constant police surveillance; streets in Seoul were patrolled by gendarmes and policemen. In effect, unproclaimed martial law prevailed.[23]

When Terauchi arrived in the capital amidst an impressive display of Japan's armed might, the city resembled an army camp. It took only a week after the formal presentation of the Japanese draft to conclude the treaty of annexation. The entire process of negotiation and deliberation in the councils of both governments had been conducted in absolute secrecy and deliberate haste, because of the fear that the longer the negotiations the greater would be the possibility of an information leak with its attendant danger of violent reactions from the Koreans.

[22] For more details see Komatsu, pp. 87–106.
[23] *Ibid.*, pp. 543–547.

The Korean-Japanese Treaty of August 22, 1910, contained eight brief articles in which the Japanese emperor accepted the Korean emperor's cession of all rights of sovereignty; appropriate honor and maintenance were to be provided for members of the imperial court and other Koreans who had given meritorious service; and the entire government and administration was assumed by the government of Japan, with the promise to employ in public service those Koreans who proved duly qualified and loyal to the new regime.[24] The promulgation of the treaty had been originally scheduled for August 26, three or four days being enough to acquaint the foreign powers that had treaty relationships with Korea. Since August 27 was the anniversary of the Korean emperor's coronation ceremony in 1907, the Korean government requested a three-day delay in announcing the treaty, and Japan consented.[25]

The treaty was formally made public on August 29, 1910, followed by a barrage of imperial edicts and official proclamations on both sides of the Korean Strait. The Japanese emperor declared that the annexation was inevitable "in order to maintain public order and security and to advance the happiness and well-being of the people" of Korea. The Korean emperor spoke of "the long-standing weakness and deep rooted evils" in the nation that could not be rectified except by "entrust[ing] Our great task to abler hands than Ours."[26] Foreign powers were notified that (1) all treaties concluded with Korea were null and void and Japan's existing treaties with them would apply to Korea; (2) foreigners in Korea were to enjoy the same rights as the foreign residents in Japan and become subject to Japanese jurisdiction; (3) the existing rates of export and import duties and tonnage dues for Korea's foreign trade were to remain in force, applicable to both Japanese and foreign nationals, for a period of ten years; (4) foreign vessels would be permitted to engage in coastal trade between the open ports of Korea and between those ports and

[24] For an English translation of the treaty, see NGB, XLIII, Part I, 681–682. For a Japanese text, see ibid., p. 679–680.

[25] Terauchi to Komura, August 22, 1910, ibid., p. 686.

[26] See English translations of the Korean and the Japanese imperial rescripts, August 29, 1910, in Tewksbury, pp. 39–41.

any open ports of Japan for a period of ten years; and (5) the
existing open ports of Korea would remain open except for Masan
(where the Japanese naval base had been established), while
Sinuiju at the mouth of the Yalu would be opened for the first
time.[27]

Foreign powers, particularly Great Britain, had shown concern lest the annexation might jeopardize the rights and interests
of their nationals; as a matter of fact, these were the only problems that foreign governments had raised in connection with the
annexation. Japan accommodated the wishes of these foreign
powers, except for the termination of extraterritorial rights for
foreigners in Korea.[28]

On the day the treaty was announced, Terauchi was appointed
the first governor-general in Korea; he issued a lengthy proclamation addressed to the Korean people promising "the benefit of a
judicious and benevolent rule" coupled with a warning to "be
careful not to go astray." Terauchi also dealt with many specific
problems, economic development in particular. Interesting was
his promise of honor and monetary aid to various classes in
Korea — the imperial family, officialdom, the *yangban* or the
Confucian class, and "the dutiful sons and daughters, virtuous
wives" and others who epitomized traditional morality. Terauchi
promised exoneration for those local officials who might have
misappropriated part of the tax receipts and amnesty to some
deserving inmates of prison. More important, perhaps, were the
waiver of farmers' unpaid land taxes prior to 1908 and their un-
repaid grain loan from the public granary prior to 1910, and the
reduction of the land tax due in the fall of 1910 by one-fifth.[29]
Clearly it was an attempt to purchase the goodwill of practically
every social class.

The immediate reaction of the man in the street to the final
collapse of the Yi dynasty and the loss of national independence
was not as violent in outward expression as it had been after the

[27] See the Japanese proclamation dated August 22, 1910, *ibid.*, pp. 37–38.
[28] See, for example, Komura to Katō (London), August 11, 1910, *NGB*,
XLIII, Part I, 674.
[29] See an English translation of the full text of Terauchi's proclamation
in Tewksbury, pp. 41–44.

protectorate agreement of 1905 or after the imperial abdication of 1907. This was largely because of the relentless and thorough security precautions taken by the police. The pedestrians in Seoul read the official bulletins posted throughout the city without much sign of emotion and departed silently — feeling the gaze of Japanese gendarmes on their backs. The superficially calm reception may have also been due to a sense of resignation: for the past five years the people had seen Japan gradually turning their country into a Japanese territory; desperate appeals to foreign powers, mass demonstrations, scathing journalistic attacks, the Righteous Army, and political assassinations — all had failed to stop the Japanese.

Koreans of all classes felt frustrated and powerless. There were a few cases of attempted and actual suicide in the privileged classes and some refused to accept the Japanese peerage proffered to them; however, most felt completely helpless under the harsh and effective military rule and attempted to make the best out of the nation's tragedy. Japan offered titles of nobility, from marquis to baron, carrying various annual stipends, to 76 Koreans, most of whom were former high officials; and 70 of them accepted the offer.[30] Perhaps a great majority of those who accepted did not welcome Japan's rule but were willing to accept the compensation offered for their acquiescence. A message sent to Terauchi by the Korean emperor a few hours after the signing of the treaty of annexation may serve as an illustration; the message read in part as follows:

> We trust that Prime Minister Yi will have concluded all necessary matters of business [working] directly with the Resident-General. That being so, We shall henceforth have nothing to do with the affairs of state; it suffices to regulate the affairs of Our family and to perpetuate the ceremonies and sacrificial offerings of Our Imperial Family. A matter that requires the special consideration of the Resident-General is that We shall be at a loss . . . if the existing Imperial Household . . . should be drastically modified and suffer a sharp reduction in the number of its personnel. . . . We trust that the kindness of the Imperial Family of your country toward Us shall not change in the future. We hear that the same amount of

[30] See a complete list of 76 names in Shakuo, pp. 607–608.

money as in the past shall be granted . . . We are deeply grateful for this. . . .[31]

Immediately after he had approved the transfer of sovereignty to Japan, the Korean emperor was no longer concerned with the future of the nation and the people he had just handed over to the alien ruler. Rather, he was beseeching the alien viceroy not to reduce the number of his household servants and giving thanks for the promised annual allowance. It was an ignominious end for the Yi dynasty and many members of its ruling class; it was a tragic end for Korean independence.

[31] Translated from *ibid.*, pp. 565–566.

Conclusion

During the three decades prior to the Japanese annexation, Korea had changed from a nation isolated in a virtually forgotten corner of Northeast Asia to one of the critical areas in the international struggle for power. This change was not Korea's own choice; international circumstances beyond its control were largely responsible. The extension of a powerful Western civilization to Asia, the rise of modern Japan, and the decline of China were the external forces that shook the peninsular kingdom loose from its long-accustomed position within a China-centered sphere and opened Korea, first to Japan and then to the United States and other Western nations.

The growth of Japanese influence in Korea in the first half of the 1880s caused China to assert its role as the suzerain nation of Korea with unprecedented vigor and determination. For ten years following the Treaty of Tientsin of 1885, Japan had to acquiesce to China's domination. The Sino-Japanese War, however, reversed the balance of power in Korea, enabling Japan to enjoy a position of supremacy in the peninsula for two years. The withdrawal of China also marked the end of the polemics on the legal status of Korea that had baffled, if not annoyed, the Western governments as well as Japan. Thus, China's claim that Korea was autonomous but dependent on China was replaced by a formal recognition of the complete and full independence of Korea.

The brief period of Japanese predominance in the neighboring kingdom was abruptly terminated early in 1896, when Korea turned to Russia for protection. Russia's position as the most influential foreign power in Korea was a temporary windfall, which lasted only as long as the Russian agents in Korea acted with prudence and unobtrusiveness. After two years, Russia's position disintegrated — although not completely — as suddenly as it had been established. There ensued a period of six years when Korea enjoyed the maximum freedom of action since the opening of the country. But when the unstable balance of power between Russia and Japan finally gave way in the war of 1904–1905, Japan quickly recovered its position of supremacy in the peninsula and, with the acquiescence of the major powers, expanded it into a protectorate. In the years between 1905 and 1910, Japan proceeded with caution, keeping one eye on foreign reactions and another on those of the Koreans, to incorporate Korea into the Japanese empire.

Closely intertwined with these international developments affecting the position of Korea was her own inability to bring about transformations in society to meet the changing needs. The "paternalistically authoritarian government without any well-defined mechanism for centralization" was nominally under the personal rule of a monarch who displayed, throughout the period under study, only weak and ineffective leadership. Surrounding him were the ruling oligarchs and their rivals who competed in currying his favor. Politics at the national level, therefore, degenerated into court politics. Factional strife at the court had plagued the Yi dynasty for at least three centuries and it did not abate when difficult questions of foreign relations confronted the government.

A faction was bound less by a common ideology than by an intricate network of personal loyalty, obligation, and expectation. These peculiarities made the partisan strife vicious and complex. In a sense such labels as "pro-China" or "conservative," and the like have limited application to these factions, because they designate political or ideological orientation of a certain faction only under a given set of circumstances at a given time. As the circumstances changed the same faction came to embrace an entirely different ideology. The key to deciphering the seemingly illogical behavior of a faction that contradicts its ideological professions of an earlier time is to ask this simple question: Against whom is this action directed?

The injection of foreign influences, as guided by the amoral dictates of realpolitik, into the domestic power struggle added another dimension of complexity. China, Japan, and Russia threw their support to whichever faction best suited their political schemes, while the Korean factions, with equal ease, moved from one foreign patron to another.

Only about 3 percent of the population concentrated in the Seoul region and the southern provinces of Ch'ungch'ŏng (north and south) and Kyŏngsang (north) were the actual or potential participants in the decision-making process at the national and provincial level. The remaining 97 percent, especially the peasants, suffered from misgovernment, heavy taxation, illegal levies, and capricious administration of justice; and the rigid stratification of the society reinforced by the orthodox Confucianism allowed little opportunity for them to seek redress. Common people were abused and forgotten.

Political crises in the 1880s and 1890s did produce a few individuals who attempted in vain to reform and revitalize the moribund society. But no new class emerged to meet the challenge of a new era and to present effective opposition to the conservative elements. Korea's political system lacked resilience and adaptability. The existence of strong traditionalism precluded the possibility of a revolution either from above or below.

The ruling faction sought a way out not in any internal reforms but in manipulation of external relations with foreign powers. The principle of *sadae* had been one of the cardinal rules of the Yi dynasty's foreign relations; it was the embodiment of the suzerain-dependent relationship that had characterized the traditional East Asian international system. Necessity had dictated Korea's adoption of this principle when her external relations were thought of largely in terms of maintaining her national existence by a show of submission and loyalty to a strong Chinese neighbor. In the course of centuries, *sadae* had become a mental fixation that discouraged national self-reliance. Confronted with the extraordinary problems of the late nineteenth and the early twentieth centuries, Korean response was almost axiomatic: she sought foreign protectors. Lacking knowledge and experience in the art of diplomacy in the modern world, Korea naïvely assumed that she could check one foreign power with another — a simple proposition that took no account of the complex and interacting factors that determined the behavior of a nation. The shifty search for protection proved to be worse than a mere failure; it nurtured the suspicion of foreign powers that Korea's government was not only unreliable but also incapable of maintaining independence by its own effort. Korea's own weakness tempted her neighbors to seek political hegemony in the peninsula. The Sino- and Russo-Japanese wars attested to the danger inherent in Korea's position.

Japan's victory in these wars eliminated the other two neighbors from the race to control the peninsula. The Japanese objective in 1905, if not earlier, was eventual annexation; but there was considerable ambivalence among the Japanese leaders as to the means and the timetable for achieving this end. The uncertainty was partly — and only partly — due to Japanese fear of foreign intervention on behalf of Korea; she proceeded with deliberate care not to invite any unfriendly reaction. Furthermore, within the Japanese oligarchy there apparently was a lack of understanding of Korean society. An examination of her records in Korea in 1905–1910 fails to show any systematic application of specific techniques in imposing her rule and gaining popular acceptance. In any case, to the gratification of Itō and his supporters of a gradualist policy, no foreign intervention ensued in the wake of the protectorate treaty.

Itō's scheme at first was to tighten the Japanese hold without incurring Korean antipathy. He maintained the status quo in the governing circle of Korea. He had advisers supervising the Korean administration. Itō was careful not to precipitate the final annexation. Soon, however, he was faced with an impasse in his double-barrelled setup, under which he had to contend on the one hand with the Korean government and on the other with the government of the Residency-General, both of which at times were successful in undermining his "safe-and-sane" policy.

The turning point in Japan's Korean policy was the fiasco of the secret Korean mission to the second Hague peace conference in 1907. This incident was not merely the very pretext that was needed for Itō's political enemies, as the *Japan Advertiser* put it, "for at least another substantial encroachment upon the farce of Korean autonomy"; it was also what the gradualist-minded Itō needed to administer annexation. After the secret mission incident, the Japanese hold was tightened by a quick succession of measures, including the replacing of advisers with vice-ministers and the disbanding of the Korean army.

In the process of suppressing the rebellious elements after 1907, the Japanese military and police used force and violence relentlessly and indiscriminately. These methods, however, drove many nonpolitical Koreans into the rebel camp; the rebel movement seemed to have become a mass movement. Nevertheless, by the time General Terauchi became the third and last resident-general in June 1910, the foundation for annexation had been completed. Korean insurgents, who once operated throughout the peninsula, had almost been exterminated. The widespread, forceful Korean opposition to the foreign overlordship patterned the subsequent Japanese rule. In 1910 the Residency-General was replaced by the Government-General, headed by a succession of military men.

Japan, a relative novice in the art of colonial management, could impose her will upon the reluctant Koreans through coercion, but she could not extinguish the nationalistic sentiments among the people. In this respect, the record of Japan's indirect control of Korea through the resident-generals repeated itself, *mutatis mutandis*, in the years 1910–1945. Japan won an empire with the force of arms; she ruled her colony through a military government; and the collapse of her military machine ended her empire.

After 35 years of Japanese rule, Korea regained national independence in 1945. It was a costly interlude in the history of the proud nation, a victim of the Machiavellian politics of imperialism and a victim of her age-long political malaise.

APPENDIX

TABLE I
POPULATION: GEOGRAPHICAL DISTRIBUTION [a]

		Domicile (May 1910)	Population (per square Li) [b]
Seoul		56,010	
	(301,073) [c]		(1,748)
Kyŏnggi		245,063	
Ch'ungch'ŏng	(347,147) [d]		
North		128,536	1,078
South		218,611	1,513
Kyŏngsang	(640,355)		
North		344,671	1,351
South		295,684	1,639
Chŏlla	(576,581)		
North		210,149	1,815
South		366,432	1,993
Kangwŏn		161,359	450
Hwanghae		221,600	870
Hamgyŏng	(275,535)		
South		194,768	494
North		80,767	247
P'yŏngan	(371,127)		
South		188,877	760
North		182,250	591
Total		2,894,777	916

[a] [Japan] Nihon Naikaku Tōkei Kyoku, *Dai Nihon Teikoku Tōkei Nenkan* [Japanese Statistical Yearbook] (Tokyo, 1910), p. 947; [Japan] Chōsen Sōtokufu, *Chōsen no Jinkō Genshō* [Population Phenomena of Korea] (Keijō, 1927), pp. 93–94. Hereafter cited as *Nihon Tōkei Nenkan* and *Chōsen Jinkō Genshō*, respectively.

[b] One *Li* is 3.3 miles.

[c] The figure in parenthesis for Kyŏnggi Do includes Seoul, the Capital.

[d] Figures in parentheses are tabulated on the basis of the original eight provinces of Korea before the reorganization making them thirteen.

TABLE II
RULING CLASS
(Based on the Figure of May 1910) [a]

	Govt. Employed (Domicile)	Unemployed (Domicile)	Confucian Scholars (Domicile)	Total (Domicile)
Seoul	2,095	1,189	188	3,472
Kyŏnggi	1,425	1,879	1,297	4,601
Ch'ungch'ŏng	(1,353)	(28,310)	(3,113)	(32,776)
North	472	5,829	1,251	7,552
South	881	22,481	1,862	25,224
Kyŏngsang	(2,679)	(14,422)	(3,817)	(20,918)
North	1,066	13,130	3,560	17,756
South	1,613	1,292	257	3,162
Chŏlla	(3,114)	(3,836)	(5,210)	(12,160)
North	1,292	2,113	1,752	5,157
South	1,822	1,723	3,458	7,003
Kangwŏn	903	1,790	1,097	3,790
Hwanghae	723	720	1,239	2,682
Hamgyŏng	(2,129)	(1,536)	(1,934)	(5,600)
South	1,705	865	1,568	4,138
North	424	671	367	1,462
P'yŏngan	(1,337)	(535)	(1,179)	(3,051)
South	556	177	730	1,473
North	771	358	449	1,578
Total	15,758	54,217	19,075	89,050

[a] *Nihon Tōkei Nenkan* (1910), p. 947; *Chōsen Jinkō Genshō*, p. 94.

TABLE III

OCCUPATIONAL AND GEOGRAPHICAL DISTRIBUTION OF THE COMMONERS
(Based on the Figure of May 1910)[a]

	Commerce	Agriculture	Fishery	Industry	Mining (Domicile)	Coolie	Others	Unemployed	Total
Seoul	13,672	8,643	87	3,310	60	9,825	4,055	12,886	52,538
	(29,286)[b]	(219,020)	(2,649)	(5,103)	(81)	(15,783)	(7,777)	(13,401)	(293,000)
Kyŏnggi	15,614	210,377	2,562	1,793	21	5,858	3,722	515	240,462
Ch'ungch'ŏng	(13,512)	(286,922)	(2,289)	(1,464)	(422)	(5,822)	(2,210)	(1,830)	(314,371)
North	4,882	112,117	5	684	153	2,072	463	608	120,984
South	8,630	174,805	2,284	780	269	3,750	1,747	1,122	193,387
Kyŏngsang	(37,345)	(548,294)	(6,317)	(5,980)	(141)	(13,148)	(4,609)	(3,603)	(619,437)
North	19,049	295,658	1,230	2,501	87	4,767	1,999	1,624	326,915
South	18,296	252,636	5,087	3,479	54	8,381	2,610	1,979	292,522
Chŏlla	(40,181)	(485,305)	(11,782)	(3,598)	(49)	(13,298)	(6,298)	(3,910)	(564,421)
North	18,857	174,881	812	2,061	48	4,923	2,031	1,379	204,922
South	21,324	310,424	10,970	1,537	1	8,375	4,267	2,531	359,429
Kangwŏn	7,600	142,855	2,874	345	167	2,194	825	209	157,569
Hwanghae	13,113	192,025	1,887	924	311	5,199	3,790	1,669	218,918
Hamgyŏng	(10,619)	(245,866)	(3,841)	(1,551)	(20)	(3,630)	(3,852)	(1,056)	(269,935)
South	8,214	171,019	3,039	1,199	18	3,058	3,130	953	190,630
North	2,405	74,847	802	352	2	572	222	103	79,305
P'yŏngan	(27,124)	(313,163)	(2,007)	(3,478)	(238)	(10,425)	(6,076)	(5,545)	(368,076)
South	18,397	151,948	1,011	1,599	91	5,309	5,023	4,026	187,404
North	8,727	161,215	996	1,879	147	5,116	1,073	1,519	180,672
Total	178,780	2,433,450	33,646	22,943	1,429	69,399	34,957	31,123	2,805,727

[a] *Nihon Tōkei Nenkan* (1910), p. 947; *Chōsen Jinkō Genshō*, p. 94.
[b] Seoul and Kyŏnggi figures combined.

TABLE IV
KOREAN TRADES TOTAL IMPORT AND EXPORT [a]
(Unit = Yen)

	Import and Export	Import over Export
1893	5,628,817	2,182,039
1894	8,327,644	3,520,348
1895	11,073,551	5,606,405
1896	11,536,600	1,802,624
1897	19,264,773	1,093,619
1898	17,734,519	6,108,073
1899	15,329,453	5,229,495
1900	20,638,129	1,500,593
1901	23,319,947	6,234,521
1902	22,161,345	5,224,339
1903	28,079,842	8,741,580
1904	34,933,306	19,871,876
1905	40,888,423	25,055,281
1906	39,207,031	21,402,013
1907	58,595,466	24,627,594
1908	55,138,833	26,912,213
1909	52,897,658	20,399,882
1910	59,696,599	19,868,913

[a] Compiled from [Japan] Kankoku Tōkanfu, *Kankoku Gaikoku Bōeki Nempyō* (Table of Annual Korean Foreign Trade and Shipping); [Japan] Chōsen Sōtokufu, *Chōsen Bōeki Nempyō* (Table of Annual Korean Trade and Shipping). See also, Shikata, "Chōsen ni okeru Kindai Shihonshugi no Seiritsu Katei" (The Rise of Modern Capitalism in Korea), 217.

TABLE V

KOREAN TRADE: IMPORT[a]

(Unit = Yen)

	Japan	China	Russia	Great Britain	United States	Others	Total
1893	1,949,043	1,905,698	25,414				3,880,155
1894	3,646,722	2,064,821	120,019				5,831,563
1895	5,838,739	2,119,641	129,833				8,088,213
1896	4,294,005	2,159,064	78,255				6,531,324
1897	6,432,060	3,535,918	99,536				10,067,514
1898	6,777,171	4,929,483	110,908				11,817,562
1899	6,658,200	3,471,313	97,827				10,227,340
1900	8,241,296	2,581,704	117,460				10,940,460
1901	9,051,881	5,617,741	26,848				14,696,470
1902	8,689,220	4,832,308	19,881				13,541,409
1903	11,554,969	5,358,600	126,972	780,265	398,377		18,219,183
1904	19,007,287	5,053,310	88,517	767,151	1,813,115	76,000	26,805,380
1905	23,561,899	5,945,312	101,649	363,897	1,978,812	8,013	31,959,582
1906	22,914,154	4,105,036	37,549	33,059	2,557,511	7,109	29,654,418
1907	27,363,872	4,465,696	—	5,517,596	3,295,558	793,527	41,436,249
1908	24,040,465	4,882,246	45,234	6,781,715	4,194,529	1,081,334	41,025,523
1909	21,852,245	4,473,209	44,404	6,478,224	2,396,975	1,403,713	36,648,770
1910	25,348,085	3,845,274	17,970	6,226,524	3,204,668	1,140,235	39,782,756

[a] Compiled from the same sources as Table IV.

TABLE VI
KOREAN TRADE: EXPORT[a]
(Unit = Yen)

	Japan	China	Russia	Great Britain	United States	Others	Total
1893	1,543,114	134,085	20,917				
1894	2,050,910	161,752	98,553				
1895	2,366,427	91,683	23,698				
1896	4,396,346	263,941	68,413				
1897	8,090,039	736,317	147,539				
1898	4,522,963	1,129,970	56,556				
1899	4,205,382	685,459	107,004				
1900	7,232,416	1,968,650	238,801				
1901	7,402,116	800,092	259,741				
1902	6,549,646	1,536,114	231,310				
1903	7,599,624	1,549,206	328,773				
1904	5,696,371	1,232,954	2,524	655			
1905	5,389,914	1,501,817	12,350	220			
1906	6,916,848	699,644	500,744	14,703	225	660	8,132,844
1907	12,649,267	3,179,845	657,629			11,715	16,498,456
1908	10,963,353	2,247,459	772,772	5,746	45,106	78,875	14,113,310
1909	12,081,738	3,203,461	784,528	50,126	68,978	60,057	16,248,888
1910	15,378,643	3,025,836	1,155,357	24,719	304,867	24,421	19,913,843

[a] Compiled from the same sources as Table IV.

KOREAN REBELS (1907–1911)
(Rebel Forces Contacted[a])

	Jan.	Feb.	Mar.	April	May	June	July	Aug.	Sept.	Oct.	Nov.	Dec.	Total
1907													
Garrison Forces								5,615	7,787	5,212	14,015	9,242	41,871
Gendarmerie								0	0	0	800	345	1,145
Police								400	200	0	300	200	1,100
Total								6,015	7,987	5,212	15,115	9,787	44,116
1908													
Garrison Forces	8,859	5,727	6,066	7,535	7,427	6,635	3,130	2,683	1,887	1,727	1,005	736	53,418
Gendarmerie	148	60	0	25	3,280	906	647	890	1,101	2,348	1,617	3,042	14,174
Police	0	147	400	20	687	153	156	106	153	30	188	197	2,237
Total	9,007	5,934	6,466	7,581	11,394	7,697	3,933	3,979	3,141	4,215	2,810	3,975	69,832
1909													
Garrison Forces	915	713	983	1,136	1,493	578	818	775	242	176	567	269	8,665
Gendarmerie	1,756	1,968	2,054	2,088	2,041	2,390	1,410	884	836	482	0	0	15,918
Police	180	660	134	62	48	49	47	0	0	0	0	0	1,180
Total	2,851	3,341	3,171	2,289	3,582	3,017	2,284	1,697	1,078	658	567	269	25,763
1910													
Garrison Forces	67	3	21	10	0	3	51	12	29	20	0	6	252
Gendarmerie	187	192	188	316	136	226	17	155	38	40	61	7	1,563
Police	33	0	4	0	0	0	8	23	4	0	4	0	76
Total	287	195	213	326	136	229	76	220	71	60	65	13	1,891
1911													
Garrison Forces	8	0	25	0	0	12							
Gendarmerie	49	42	21	25	26	5							
Police	0	0	3	0	0	0							
Total	57	42	49	25	26	17							

[a] [Japan], Chōsen Chūsatsugun Shireibu, *Chōsen Bōto Tōbatsu Shi* [Records on the Subjugation of Korean Rebels] (Ryūsan, 1913), Appendix Table 3.

REFERENCES

Bibliographical Listings

Cordier, Henri. *Bibliotheca sinica: Dictionnaire bibliographique des ouvrages relatifs à l'empire chinois.* 2d ed., rev., cor., et considérablement augm. 4 vols. and supplment. Paris: E. Guilmotoe, 1904–1924. Vol. IV.

Courant, Maurice. *Bibliographie coréene.* Paris: Imprimerie Nationale, E. Leroux, 1901.

Elore, J. McRee (comp.) *An Index to English Language Periodical Literature Published in Korea, 1850–1940.* Unpublished master's thesis, Yonsei University, Seoul, Korea, 1960.

McCune, Shannon B. (comp.). *Bibliography of Western Language Materials on Korea.* New York: International Secretariat, Institute of Pacific Relations, 1950.

Nahm, Andrew C. (comp.). *Japanese Penetration of Korea, 1894–1910: A Checklist of Japanese Archives in the Hoover Institution.* Stanford University, California: The Hoover Institution on War, Revolution, and Peace, 1959.

United States, Library of Congress. *Korea: An Annotated Bibliography.* 3 vols. Washington, D.C., 1950. Vol. I: *Publications in Western Languages.* Vol. III: *Publications in Far Eastern Languages.*

University of California, Institute of East Asiatic Studies. *Korea Studies Guide.* Compiled by B. H. Hazard, Jr., and others. Edited by Richard Marcus. Berkeley and Los Angeles: University of California Press, 1954.

Uyehara, Cecil H. (comp.). *Checklist of Archives in the Japanese Ministry of Foreign Affairs, Tokyo, Japan, 1868–1945: Microfilmed for the Library of Congress.* Washington, D.C.: Photoduplication Service, Library of Congress, 1954.

Young, John (comp.). *Checklist of Microfilm Reproductions of Selected Archives of the Japanese Army, Navy, and Other Government Agencies, 1868–1945.* Washington, D.C.: Georgetown University Press, 1959.

Western Language Publications

Documents

Annual Report of the Board of Foreign Missions of the Presbyterian Church in the United States of America.

Annual Report of the Missionary Society of the Methodist Episcopal Church. Cited as *M. E. North Report.*

Carnegie Endowment for International Peace, Division of International Law. *Korea, Treaties and Agreements.* Washington, D.C., 1921.

China, Imperial Maritime Customs. *Treaties, Regulations, etc., Between Corea and Other Powers: 1876–1889.* Shanghai: Statistical Department of the Inspectorate General of Customs, 1891.

Chung, Henry (comp.). *Treaties and Conventions Between Corea and Other Powers.* New York: H. S. Nichols, 1919.

"First Steps of Russian Imperialism in Far East," from *Krasny Archiv,* reproduced in *Chinese Social and Political Science Review,* XVIII (1934–35), 236–81.

Great Britain. The Foreign Office. *British and Foreign State Papers.* London, 1841. Vols. LXXIII (1881–82) to CIII (1909–10).

———. *British Documents on the Origins of the War: 1898–1914.* Edited by G. P. Gooch and Harold Temperley. 11 vols. London: H. M. Stationery Office, 1926–1938. Vols. I, II, and IV.

Japan. Bureau of Customs. *Annual Return of Corean Trade of the Empire of Japan.* Series.

———. ———. *Report on the Foreign Trade.* (Published by China inspectorate general of customs, 1885—; by Japan Bureau of Customs). Title varies. *Annual Reports on the Trade in Foreign Vessels* (1885); *Annual Trade Reports and Returns* (1886–1907); *Report on the Trade of Korea and Abstract of Statistics* (1907); *Reports of the Foreign Trade and Shipping* (1908); *Report on the Foreign Trade* (1909).

———. Residency General in Korea. *Annual Report on Reforms and Progress in Korea.* 1907—. Seoul: H. I. J. M.'s Residency General, 1908. Cited as *Annual Report.*

———. *Recent Progress in Korea.* Keijō, n.d.

McCune, George M. and John A. Harrison (eds.). *Korean-American Relations: Documents Pertaining to the Far Eastern Diplomacy of the United States.* Vol. I, *The Initial Period, 1883–86.* Berkeley and Los Angeles: University of California Press, 1951.

"On the Eve of the Russo-Japanese War," from *Krasny Archiv,* reproduced in *Chinese Social and Political Science Review,* XVIII (1934–35), 572–594; XIX (1935–36), 125–139.

Palmer, Spencer J. (ed.). *Korean-American Relations: Documents Pertaining to the Far Eastern Diplomacy of the United States.* Vol. II, *The Period of Growing Influence, 1887–1895.* Berkeley and Los Angeles: University of California Press, 1963.

"Russian Documents Relating to Sino-Japanese War, 1894–1895," from *Krasny Archiv*, reproduced in *Chinese Social and Political Science Review*, XVII (1935–36), 125–139.

Tewksbury, D. G. (comp.). *Source Materials on Korean Politics and Ideologies*. New York: International Secretariat, Institute of Pacific Relations, 1950.

United States. Department of State. *Papers Relating to the Foreign Relations of the United States*. Washington, D.C.: Government Printing Office, 1865. For the years 1871–72, 1881–1910. Cited as *U.S. Foreign Relations*.

————. ————. *Records of the Department of State, National Archives. Japan: Dispatches.* Cited as *J.D.*

————. ————. *Ibid. Korea: Dispatches.* Cited as *K.D.*

————. Department of Commerce and Labor. *Report on Trade Conditions in Japan and Korea.* By Raymond F. Crist, transmitted to Congress in compliance with the act of February 3, 1905, authorizing investigations of trade conditions abroad. Washington, D.C., 1906.

————. ————. *Commercial Korea.* Washington, D.C., 1904.

Books

Allen, Horace N. *Korea: Fact and Fancy.* Seoul: Methodist Publishing House, 1904.

————. *Things Korean.* New York: Fleming H. Revell Co., 1908.

Akagi, Roy H. *Japan's Foreign Relations, 1542–1936.* Tokyo: The Hokuseidō Press, 1936.

Asakawa, K. *The Russo-Japanese Conflict.* Boston and New York: Houghton, Mifflin and Co., 1904.

Beale, Howard K. *Theodore Roosevelt and the Rise of America to World Power.* Baltimore: The Johns Hopkins Press, 1956.

Bishop, Isabella Bird. *Korea and Her Neighbors.* New York: Fleming H. Revell Co., 1898.

Brown, Arthur J. *The Mastery of the Far East.* New York: C. Scribner's Sons, 1919.

————. *Report on a Second Visit to China, Japan, and Korea (1909).* New York: Board of Foreign Missions of the Presbyterian Church, U.S.A., 1910[?].

Ch'en, Jerome. *Yuan Shih-k'ai: 1859–1916.* Stanford, California: Stanford University Press, 1961.

Chung, Henry. *The Case of Korea: A Collection of Evidence on the Japanese Domination of Korea, and on the Development of the Korean Independence Movement.* New York: F. H. Revell Co., 1921.

Clark, Charles Allen. *Religions of Old Korea.* New York: Fleming H. Revell Co., 1932.

Clyde, Paul H. *A History of the Modern and Contemporary Far East.* New York: Prentice-Hall, 1937.

Conroy, Hilary. *The Japanese Seizure of Korea: 1868–1910 — A Study of Realism and Idealism in International Relations.* Philadelphia: University of Pennsylvania Press, 1960.

Croly, Herbert. *Willard Straight.* New York: Macmillan, 1924.

Curzon (Hon.), George Nathaniel. *Problems of the Far East.* Rev. ed. Westminister: Constable & Co., 1896.

Dallet, Charles. *Histoire de l'église de Corée.* 2 vols. Paris: Victor Palmé, 1874.

Dennett, Tyler. *Americans in Eastern Asia.* New York: Barnes and Noble, Inc., 1941.

———. *Roosevelt and the Russo-Japanese War.* Gloucester, Mass.: Peter Smith, 1925.

Denny, Owen N. *China and Korea.* Shanghai: Kelly and Walsh, Ltd., 1888.

Dong, Chon. *Can Agression Be Justified and Imperialism Rationalized by "Realism"?: A Review of Hilary Conroy's "The Japanese Seizure of Korea, 1868–1910."* Seoul: The Korean Research Center, n.d.

Gale, James S. *Korea in Transition.* New York: The Board of Foreign Missions of the Presbyterian Church of the U.S.A., 1909.

Grajdanzev, Andrew J. *Modern Korea, Her Economic and Social Development Under the Japanese.* New York: Institute of Pacific Relations, 1944.

Griffis, William Elliot. *Corea, the Hermit Nation.* New York: C. Scribner's Sons, 1907.

Harrington, Fred Harvey. *God, Mammon, and the Japanese: Dr. Horace N. Allen and Korean-American Relations, 1884–1905.* Madison: The University of Wisconsin Press, 1944.

Hayashi, Tadasu (Count). *The Secret Memoirs of Count Tadasu Hayashi.* Ed. A. M. Pooley. New York: G. P. Putnam's Sons, 1915.

Herz, John H. *Political Realism and Political Idealism: A Study in Theories and Realities.* Chicago: University of Chicago Press, 1951.

Hulbert, Homer B. *The History of Korea.* 2 vols. Seoul: The Methodist Publishing House, 1905.

———. (Ed.). *The Japanese in Korea: Extracts from the Korea Review.* Seoul: The Korea Review, 1907.

———. *The Passing of Korea.* New York: Doubleday, Page & Co., 1906.

Jessup, Phillip C. *Elihu Root.* 2 vols. New York: Dodd, Mead and Co., 1938.

Kang, Younghill. *The Grass Roof.* New York: C. Scribner's Sons, 1931.

Kim, Helen Kiteuk. *Rural Education for the Regeneration of Korea.* New York: Columbia University, 1931.

Kuno, Yoshi S. *Japanese Expansion on the Asiatic Continent.* 2 vols. Berkeley: University of California Press, 1937.

Ladd, George Trumbuli. *In Korea with Marquis Ito.* New York: C. Scribner's Sons, 1908.

Langer, William L. *The Diplomacy of Imperialism, 1890–1902.* New York: Alfred A. Knopf, 1935.

Lee, Chong-sik. *The Politics of Korean Nationalism.* Berkeley and Los Angeles: University of California Press, 1963.

Lee, Hoon Koo. *Land Utilization and Rural Economy in Korea.* Chicago: The University of Chicago Press, 1936.

Longford, Joseph Henry. *The Story of Korea.* New York: C. Scribner's Sons, 1911.

Lowell, Percival. *Chosen: The Land of the Morning Calm — A Sketch of Korea.* Boston: Ticknor and Co., 1888.

Malozemoff, Andrew. *Russian Far Eastern Policy, 1881–1904.* Berkeley and Los Angeles: University of California Press, 1958.

McCune, George M. *Korea Today.* Cambridge: The Harvard University Press, 1950.

McCune, Shannon. *Korea's Heritage.* Tokyo and Rutland, Vt.: C. E. Tuttle Co., 1956.

McKenzie, Frederick Arthur. *The Colonial Policy of Japan in Korea.* Proceedings of the Central Asian Society, London, December 1906.

————. *Korea's Fight for Freedom.* New York: F. H. Revell Co., 1920.

————. *Tragedy of Korea.* London: Hodder & Stoughton, 1908.

McLaren, Walter W. *A Political History of Japan During the Meiji Era, 1867–1912.* New York: C. Scribner's Sons, 1916.

Moon, Parker Thomas. *Imperialism and World Politics.* New York: The MacMillan Co., 1930.

Moose, Robert J. *Village Life in Korea.* Nashville: The Publishing House of the M. E. Church, 1911.

Morse, Hosea B. *The International Relations of the Chinese Empire.* 3 vols. London, New York: Longmans, Green, and Co., 1910–1918.

Nelson, Melvin Frederick. *Korea and the Old Orders in Eastern Asia.* Baton Rouge: Louisiana State University Press, 1945.

Oliver, Robert T. *Korea, Forgotten Nation.* Washington, D.C.: Public Affairs Press, 1944.

Osgood, Cornelius. *The Koreans and Their Culture.* New York: Ronald Press, 1951.

Paik, L. George. *The History of Protestant Missions in Korea (1832–1910).* P'yŏng'yang: Union Christian College Press, 1920.

Paullin, Charles O. *Diplomatic Negotiations of American Naval Officers, 1778–1883.* Baltimore: The Johns Hopkins Press, 1912.

Price, Earnest Batson. *The Russo-Japanese Treaties of 1907–1916.* Baltimore: Johns Hopkins University Press, 1933.

Pringle, Henry F. *Theodore Roosevelt: A Biography.* New York: Harcourt, Brace and Co., 1931.

Rhodes, Harry A. (ed.). *History of the Korean Mission, Presbyterian*

Church U.S.A., 1884–1934. Seoul: Chosen Mission Presbyterian Church, U.S.A., 1934.

Rockhill, William Woodville. *China's Intercourse with Korea from the XVth Century to 1895.* London: Luzac & Co., 1905.

Sands, William F. *Undiplomatic Memories: The Far East, 1896–1904.* New York: Whittlesey House, 1930.

Scalapino, Robert A. *Democracy and the Party Movement in Prewar Japan.* Berkeley and Los Angeles: University of California Press, 1953.

Stead, Alfred (ed.). *Japan by the Japanese: A Survey by Its Highest Authorities.* 3rd impression. London: W. Heinemann, 1904.

Takeuchi, Tatsuji. *War and Diplomacy in the Japanese Empire.* New York: Doubleday, Page & Co., 1935.

Taylor, A. J. P. *The Struggle for Mastery in Europe, 1848–1918.* London: Oxford University Press, 1954.

Taylor, George E. *The Struggle for North China.* New York: Institute of Pacific Relations, 1940.

Treat, Payson J., *Diplomatic Relations Between the United States and Japan, 1853–1895.* 2 vols. Stanford: Stanford University Press, 1932.

———. *Diplomatic Relations Between the United States and Japan (1895–1905).* Stanford: Stanford University Press, 1938.

———. *The Far East: A Political and Diplomatic History.* New York: Harper & Brothers, 1928.

Underwood, Horace Grant. *The Religions of Eastern Asia.* New York: The MacMillan Co., 1910.

Underwood, Horace Horton. *Modern Education in Korea.* New York: International Press, 1926.

Underwood, (Mrs.) Lillie (Horton). *Underwood of Korea: Being an Intimate Record of the Life and Work of the Rev. H. G. Underwood, D. D., LL.D., for Thirty-one Years a Missionary of the Presbyterian Board in Korea.* New York: F. H. Revell Co., 1918.

Uyehara, G. E. *The Political Development of Japan, 1867–1909.* London: Constable & Co., 1910.

Vinacke, Harold M. *A History of the Far East in Modern Times.* 4th ed. New York: F. S. Crofts & Co., 1941.

Weber, Max. *The Religion of China.* Tr. and ed. by H. H. Gerth. Glencoe: The Free Press, 1951.

Weems, Benjamin B. *Reform, Rebellion, and the Heavenly Way.* The Association for Asian Studies: Monographs and Papers, No. XV. Tucson: University of Arizona Press, 1964.

Weems, Clarence N. (ed.) *Hulbert's History of Korea.* 2 vols. New York: Hillary House, 1962.

Whigham, Henry James. *Manchuria and Korea.* London: Isbister & Co., 1904.

Wilkinson, W. H. *The Corean Government: Constitutional Changes, July*

1894 to October 1895, with an Appendix on Subsequent Enactments to June 30th, 1895. Shanghai: The Statistical Department of Inspectorate-General of Customs, 1897.

Yanaga, Chitoshi. *Japan since Perry.* 1st ed. New York: McGraw-Hill, 149.

Articles

"Abdication, Acclamation, Assassination," an editorial, *Korean Repository*, V (1898), 342–349.

"The Attempt on the Life of Kim Hongyuk," an editorial, *Korean Repository*, V (1898), 107–109.

"Baron von Moellendorff," *Korea Review*, I (1901), 245–252.

Choi, Woonsang. "The Korean-Japanese Relations, 1870–1910," *Korean Affairs*, 1 (1962), 162–188, 300–318; 2 (1963), 51–60.

"Confessions of a Tong Hak Chief," *Korean Repository*, II (1895), 234–236.

Dennett, Tyler. "American Choices in the Far East in 1882," *American Historical Review*, XXX (1924), 82–103.

Denny, O. N. "China and Korea," *Congressional Record*, 50th Congress, 1st session (1888), 8135–8140.

"The Downfall and Departure of the Minister of Home Affairs," an editorial, *Korean Repository*, II (1895), 268–270.

"The Fallow Land," *Korea Review*, IV (1904), 344–350.

Feller, A. H. "Protectorate," *Encyclopedia of Social Science*, XII, 567.

Gale, James S. "Korea in War Time," *Outlook*, 77 (1904).

"The Korean Coolie," *Korean Repository*, II (1895), 475–481.

"The Korean Gentleman," *ibid.*, pp. 1–6.

Gifford, D. L. "Education in the Capital of Korea," *ibid.*, pp. 281–287, 304–311.

"Great Changes in the Korean Government," *ibid.*, pp. 111–118.

Griffis, W. E. "Japan's Absorption of Korea," *North American Review*, 192 (1910), 516–526.

Han, Woo-keum. "The Stratification of the Yi Dynasty Society and the Process of Its Change," tr. by Kweenam Jahng, *Korean Affairs*, 2 (1963), 38–43.

"He is a Farmer," *Korean Repository*, V (1898), 229–234.

Heard, Augustine. "China and Japan in Korea," *North American Review*, CLIX (July–December 1894), 300–320.

"His Majesty, the King of Korea," *Korea Repository*, III (1896), 423–430.

Hulbert, Homer B. "The Independence Club," *Korean Repository*, V (1898), 281–287.

———. "Korean Reforms," *ibid.*, II (1895), 1–9.

———. "The Rise of the Yangban," *ibid.*, pp. 471–474.

Ike, Nobutaka. "Triumph of the Peace Treaty in Japan in 1873," *Far Eastern Quarterly*, II (May 1943), 286–295.

"In the Finance Department," *Korean Repository*, IV (1897), 434–436.

"The Independence Club and Vice-President of the Privy Council," an editorial, *Korean Repository*, V (1898), 270–272.

Jaisohn, Philip. "Korean Finance," *ibid.*, III (1896), 166–168.

————. "What Korea Needs Most," *ibid.*, pp. 108–110.

"Japan in North-East Korea," *Korea Review*, VI (1906), 338–341.

"Japanese Immigration," *ibid.*, pp. 341–346.

"Japanese Industrial Projects in Korea," *ibid.*, IV (1904), 289–298.

Jones, G. H. "Historical Resume of the Youth's Primer," *Korean Repository*, II (1895), 134–139.

Junkin, William L. "The Tong Haks," *ibid.*, pp. 56–60.

Kim, C. I. Eugene. "Japanese Rule in Korea (1905–1910): A Case Study," *Proceedings of the American Philosophical Society*, CVI (February 1962), 53–59.

————. "A Problem in Japan's Control of the Press in Korea, 1906–1909," *The Pacific Historical Review*, Vol. XXI, No. 4 (November 1962), 393–402.

"Korea and Its People," *The Gospel in All Lands* (1894), p. 412.

"Korean Guilds and Other Associations," *Korean Repository*, II (1895), 41–48.

Langer, William S. "The Origins of the Russo-Japanese War." English original of article subsequently published in *Europaische Gesprache* (Hamburg), IV (1926), 56 pp.

Lin, T. C. "Li Hung-chang: His Korea Policies, 1870–1885," *Chinese Social and Political Science Review*, XIX (1935–36), 202–233.

"M. Kir Alexieff," an editorial, *Korean Repository*, V (1898), 33–34.

McCune, George M. "Exchange of Envoys Between Korea and Japan During the Tokugawa Period," *Far Eastern Quarterly*, V (May 1946), 308–325.

McCune, George M. and Edwin O. Reischauer. "The Romanization of the Korean Language Based upon its Phonetic Structure," *Transactions of the Korean Branch of the Royal Society of Great Britain and Ireland*, XXIX (1934), 1–55.

Noble, Harold J. "The United States and Sino-Korean Relations, 1885–87," *Pacific Historical Review*, II (1933), 292–304.

"Obstacles Encountered by Korean Christians," *Korean Repository*, II (1895), 145–151.

"Official Corruption," *ibid.*, IV (1897), 110–111.

Paullin, Charles O. "The Opening of Korea," *Political Science Quarterly*, XXV (1910), 470–499.

"The Peddlers' Guild," *Korea Review*, III (1903), 337–342.

"Reformation, Revision, Regulation," *Korean Repository*, IV (1897), 192–195.

"A Retrospect: 1894," *ibid.*, II (1895), 29–36.

"Retrospect of 1903," *Korea Review*, IV (1904), 13–20.

"Right About Face," an editorial, *Korean Repository*, V (1898), 113–117.

Sands, W. F. "Korea and the Korean Emperor," *Century*, LXIX (1905), 577–584.

Schweinitz, Brunner. "Rural Korea: A Preliminary Survey of Economic, Social and Religious Conditions," *The Jerusalem Meeting of the International Missionary Council, the Christian Mission in Relation to Rural Problems*, New York: International Missionary Council, 1938, pp. 84–172.

Sunoo, Hag-won. "A Study of the Development of the Technique of Japanese Imperialism in Korea (1904–1910)," *Korea Review*, I (1948), 27–51. This journal started publication in 1948 bearing the same title as the old *Korea Review* that had been published earlier in this century but later discontinued.

"Tax Collection in Korea," *Korea Review*, VI (1906), 366–376.

"The Torture of Koreans," an editorial comment, *ibid.*, pp. 303–313.

Totter, G. and others. "Japanese Imperialism and Aggression: Reconsiderations: Review Article," *Journal of Asian Studies*, 22 (August 1963), 469–472.

Treat, Payson J. "China and Korea, 1885–1894," *Political Science Quarterly*, XLIX (1934), 506–543.

"The Treaty of Peace," an editorial, *Korean Repository*, II (1895), 235.

Tsiang, T. F. "Sino-Japanese Diplomatic Relations, 1870–1894," *Chinese Social and Political Science Review*, XVII (April 1933), 1–106.

"The Village Guilds of Old Korea," *Transactions of the Korea Branch of the Royal Asiatic Society*, IV (1913), part II, 13–44.

Vinton, C. C. "Slavery and Feudalism in Korea," *Korean Repository*, II (1895), 366–372.

Wagner, Edward W. "The Recommendation Examination of 1519," *Chōsen Gakuhō* (or *Journal of the Academic Association of Koreanology in Japan*) (Nara, Japan), No. 15 (April 1960), 1–80 (of the English section).

Willoughby, W. W. "Japan and Korea," *The Unpartisan Review*, 113 (1920), 24–42.

Wright, Mary C. "The Adaptability of Ching Diplomacy: The Case of Korea," *Journal of Asian Studies*, XVII (May 1958), 363–381.

Yoo, Hyung-jin. "Private Educational Institution in Korea; A study on the Sowon System," *Korean Quarterly*, 3 (Summer, 1961), 126–159.

Yun, T. H. (Yun, Ch'i-ho). "Popular Movement in Korea," *Korean Repository*, V (1898), 465–469.

242   KOREA AND THE POLITICS OF IMPERIALISM

"The Youth's Primer," *ibid.*, II (1895), 96–102.
X.Y.Z. "The Attack on the Top Knot," *ibid.*, III (1896), 263–272.

Far Eastern Language Publications
Documents

Ch'ing-chi wai-chiao shih-liao. [Diplomatic Source Materials of the End of the Ch'ing Dynasty]. Compiled by Wang Yen-wei and edited by Wang Liang. 125 *ts'e*. Peking: Wai-chiao shih-liao pien-tsuan ch'u, 1932–1935.

Chōsen Shiryō Hensankai. *Chōsen Kindai Shiryō; Chōsen Sōtokufu Kankei Jūyō Bunsho Sensyū* [Source Materials of Recent History of Korea; Important Documents of Japanese Government-General in Korea]. 5 vols. Tokyo: Yūhō Kyōkai, 1961.

Hiratsuka, Atsushi (ed.). *Itō Hirobumi Hiroku* [Unpublished Papers of Itō]. Tokyo, 1929. Cited as *Itō Hiroku.*

Itō Hirobumi (ed.). *Chōsen Kōshō Shiryō* [Materials on Negotiations with Korea]. 3 vols. Tokyo: Hisho Ruisan Kankōkai, 1936.

Japan (in Korea). *The Japanese Archives in Korea.* The 1894–1910 series, photographed for the Hoover Institution, Stanford University. Cited as *J. A. (Korea).*

———. Chōsen Sōtokufu [Government-General in Korea]. *Chōsen Bōeki Nempyō* [Table of Annual Korean Foreign Trade and Shipping]. Cited as *Chōsen Bōeki Nempyō.*

———. ———. *Chōsen Sōtokufu Tōkei Nempō* [Annual Statistical Report of the Government-General in Korea]. Cited as *Sōtokufu Tōkei Nempō.*

———. Kankoku Tōkanfu [Residency-General in Korea]. *Kankoku Gaikoku Bōeki Nempyō* [Table of Annual Korean Trade and Shipping]. Cited as *Kankoku Bōeki Nempyō.*

———. ———. *Kankoku Tōkanfu Tōkei Nempō* [Annual Statistical Report of the Residency-General in Korea]. Cited as *Tōkanfu Tōkei Nempō.*

———. ———. *Kankoku Zaisei Shisetsu Kōyō* [The Essential Aspects of Japanese Financial Administration in Korea]. Keijō, 1910[?].

———. Ministry of Foreign Affairs. *Archives in the Japanese Ministry of Foreign Affairs, 1868–1945.* Microfilmed for the Library of Congress. Especially the Meiji Period in the Meiji-Taisho Documents series (MT). Cited as *Japanese Foreign Office* (microfilms).

———. ———. *Nihon Gaikō Bunsho* [Japanese Diplomatic Documents]. Tokyo: Nihon Kokusai Rengō Kyōkai, 1949 —. Vols. XVII–XLIII. Cited as *NGB.*

———. ———. *Ibid., Supplement on the Russo-Japanese War.* 5 vols. Tokyo: Nihon Kokusai Rengō Kyōkai, 1960.

———. ———. *Nihon Gaikō Nenpyō narabi Shuyō Bunsho* [The Annals of Japanese Foreign Affairs and Important Documents]. 2 vols. Tokyo, 1955. Cited as *Gaikō Nenpyō.*

————. Naikaku Insatsukyoku. *Shokuinroku* [List of Government Officials].

————. Naikaku Tōkeikyoku. *Nihon Teikoku Tōkei Nenkan* [Japanese Statistical Yearbook]. Cited as *Tōkei Nenkan.*

Kim, Chŏng-myŏng (ed.). *Nikkan Gaikō Shiryō Shūsei* [Collection of Sources of Diplomatic Relations Between Japan and Korea]. 6 vols. Tokyo, 1962–1966.

Kim Yun-sik. *Unyangjip* [Collected Writings of Kim Yun-sik]. Edited by Hwang Pyŏng-uk. 8 vols. 1913 [?].

Komatsu, Midori (ed.). *Itō Kō Zenshū* [Collected Works of Prince Itō]. 3 vols. Tokyo, 1928.

Li Hung-chang. *Li Wen-chung-kung ch'uan-chi* [The Collected Writings of Li Hung-chang]. Edited by Wu Ju-lin, 100 ts'e. Nanking, 1908.

Nakayama, Yasumasa (ed.). *Shimbun Shūsei Meiji Hennenshi* [History of the Meiji Era by Newspapers]. 15 vols. Tokyo: 1934–1936. Cited as *Meiji Shimbun Shūsei.*

T'ongmun'gwanji [Records of the Office of Interpreters]. Ed. Kim Kyŏng-mun, *ca.* 1900. 2 vols. Seoul: Photo-reproduced by the Government General in Korea, 1944.

Yamamoto, Shirō (ed.). *Miura Gorō Kankei Bunsho* [Documents related to Miura Gorō]. Mimeographed. Tokyo: Meiji Shiryō Kenkyū Renrakukai, 1960.

Books

Aoyagi, Tsunatarō. *Chōsen Shūkyōshi* [History of Religion in Korea]. Keijō: 1911.

————. *Sōtoku Seiji* [Administration of the Government-General]. Keijō, 1918.

Asami, Rintarō. *Chōsen Hōsei Shikō* [A History of Laws in Korea]. Tokyo, 1922.

Chang, To-bin. *Han'guk Malnyŏnsa* [History of the Last Years of Han'guk]. 3 vols. Seoul: Tŏkhŭng Sŏlim, 1935.

Cho, Yong-man. *Aegukja Min Ch'ungchŏngkong* [The Patriot Min Yŏng-hwan]. Seoul: Kukje Munhwa Hyŏp'hoe, 1947.

Ch'oe, Ho-jin. *Kindai Chōsen Keizaishi* [Modern Economic History of Korea]. Tokyo, 1942.

Chŏng, Kyo. *Han'guk Kye'nyŏnsa* [History of the Last Years of the Yi Dynasty]. 2 vols. Seoul: Kuksa P'yŏnch'an Wiwŏnhoe, 1957.

Chŏng, Yak-Yong. *Mongmin Simsŏ* [Personal Memoirs on the Reform of the Local Administration of the Yi dynasty]. Tr. from the Chinese into Korean by Wŏn, Ch'anggyu. Seoul, 1956.

Chōsenshi Gakkai. *Chōsenshi Taikei* [An Outline History of Korea]. 3 vols. Keijō, 1928.

Chosŏn Ch'ulp'an Hyŏp'hoe. *Chosŏn Sinsa Pogam* [Mirror of Korean Gentlemen]. Seoul, 1912.

Hatada, Takashi. *Chōsenshi* [Korean History]. Tokyo, 1951.

Hayashi, Taisuke. *Chōsen Tsūshi* [Outline of the History of Korea]. Tokyo, 1912.

Hosoi, Hajime. *Chōsen Tōchi Shinri no Konponteki Henkō ni kansuru Ikensho* [Paper concerning the basic Reorientation of the Concept of Japanese Administration in Korea]. Tokyo, 1924.

――――. *Sen-Man no Keiei: Chōsen Mondai no Kompon Kaiketsu* [Administration of Korea and Manchuria: A Basic Solution of the Korean Problems]. Tokyo, 1921.

Hwang, Hyŏn. *Maech'ŏn Yarok* [Unofficial Records of Hwang Hyŏn]. Seoul: Kuksa P'yŏnch'an Wiwŏnhoe, 1955.

Im, Kwang-ch'ŏl (Rin Kōtetsu). *Chōsen Rekishi Tokuhon* [The Reader in Korean History]. Tokyo: Hakuyōsha, 1949.

In, Chŏng-sik. *Chōsen no Nōgyō Kikō Bunseki* [An Analysis of Korean Agricultural Structure]. Tokyo, 1937.

Inoue, Kaoru-Kō Denki Hensankai (ed.). *Seigai Inoue-Kō Den* [Bibliography of Marquis Inoue Kaoru]. 5 vols. Tokyo: Naigai Shoseki Kabushiki Kaisha, 1934.

Itani, Zen'ichi. *Chōsen Keizaishi.* [Economic History of Korea]. Tokyo, 1928.

Japan. Chōsen Chūsatsu Kempeitai Shireibu. *Chōsen Shakaikō* [Analysis of Korean Society]. Keijō, 1912.

――――. Chōsen Chūsatsugun Shireibu. *Chōsen Bōto Tōbatsu Shi* [Records on the Subjugation of Korean Rebels]. Ryūzan, 1913.

――――. Chōsen Sōtokufu. *Chōsen Buraku Chōsa Hōkoku* [Reports on the Investigation of the Korean Village]. Prepared by Odanai, Michitoshi. Keijō, 1923.

――――. ――――. *Chōsen ni Okeru Naichijin* [The Japanese in Korea]. Keijō, 1923.

――――. ――――. *Chōsen ni Okeru Shuppanbutsu Gaiyō* [Survey of Publications in Korea]. Keijō, 1931.

――――. ――――. *Chōsen no Genron to Sesō* [The Public Opinion and World Outlook of Korea]. Keijō, 1927.

――――. ――――. *Chōsen no Hanzai to Kankyō* [Crime and Environment in Korea]. Keijō. 1928.

――――. ――――. *Chōsen no Jinkō Genshō* [Population Phenomena of Korea]. Prepared by Yoshio Eisuke. Keijō, 1929.

――――. ――――. *Chōsen no Kosaku Kanshū* [Korean Tenant Farming Practices]. Prepared by Yoshio Eisuke. Keijō, 1929.

――――. ――――. *Chōsen no Shūraku* [Korean Villages]. 3 vols. Keijō, 1933–1935.

――――. ――――. *Chōsen no Tochiseido oyobi Chizei Seido Chōsa Hōkuku*

Sho [Reports of the Survey of the land and land-tax systems in Korea]. n.p., n.d.

———. ———. *Chōsen Shisei no Hōshin oyobi Jisseki* [Policies and Results of the Administration of Korea]. Keijō, 1915.

———. ——— *Chōsen Tetsudō Shi: Sōshi Jidi* [History of Railways in Korea: Early Period]. Keijō, 1937.

———. ———. *Chōsen Tsūshin Jigyō Enkaku Shōshi* [A Brief History of the Development of the Korean Communications Industry]. Keijō, 1914.

———. ———. *Chōsenjin no Shisō to Seikaku* [The Idea and Personality of the Korean People]. Keijō, 1927.

———. ———. *Chōsenjin no Shōgyō* [Korean Commercial Practices]. Prepared by Yoshio Eisuke, Keijō, 1925.

———. ———. *Nō-San-Gyoson ni okeru Chigiri* [Mutual Aid Associations in Rural, Mountain, and Fishing Villages]. n.p., n.d.

———. ———. *Richō Jidai no Zaisei* (manuscript) [Financial Administration during the Yi Dynasty]. Keijō, 1936.

———. ———. *Yūryō-men Chōsa* [Survey of Excellent Townships]. Keijō, 1911.

———. The Ministry of Foreign Affairs. (ed.) *Komura Gaikōshi* [History of Komura Jutarō's Diplomacy]. 2 vols. Tokyo: Shinbun Gekkansha, 1953. Cited as *Komura Diplomacy.*

Kambe, Masao. *Chōsen Nōgyōimin Ron* [Treatise on Japanese Agricultural Immigration to Korea]. Tokyo, 1910.

Kaneko, Kentarō *et al. Itō Hirobumi Den* [Biography of Itō Hirobumi]. 3 vols. Tokyo: Shunpokō Tsuishōkai, 1940.

Keijō Teikoku Daigaku Hōbun Gakkai (ed.). *Chōsen Shakai Keizai Shi Kenkyū* [Korean Socio-economic Research]. Vol. 6. Tokyo, 1933.

———. *Chōsen Keizai no Kenkyū* [Korean Economic Research]. Vol. I. Tokyo, 1929.

Kemuyama, Sentarō. *Seikanron Jissō* [The Truth Concerning the Korean Expedition Dispute in Japan]. Tokyo, 1907.

Kida, Teikichi. *Kankoku no Heigō to Kokushi* [Japan's History and Her Annexation of Korea]. Tokyo, 1910.

Kikuchi, Kenjō. *Kindai Chōsenshi* [Modern Korean History]. 2 vols. Tokyo, 1940.

———. *Daiinkun Den. Fu: Ōhi no Isshō* [Life of Taewŏn'gun. Supplement: Life of the Queen]. Keijō, 1910.

Kikuda, Sadao [with] Satsuyo Akizuki. *Seikanron no Shinsō to Eikyō* [The Truth Concerning the Korean Expedition Dispute in Japan and Its Impact]. Tokyo, 1941.

Kim Chŏng-ju. *Ilbon-ui Han'guk Ch'im'yaksa* [History of Japanese Aggression in Korea]. Tokyo: Shinkan Gakujutsu Kenkyukai, 1955.

Kim, Sang-gi. *Tonghak kwa Tonghaknan* [The Tonghaks and the Tonghak Rebellion]. Seoul: Taesŏng Ch'ulp'ansa, 1947.

Kim, To-t'ae. *Sŏ Chae-p'il Paksa Chasŏjŏn* [Autobiography of Dr. Sŏ Chae-p'il]. Seoul: Susŏnsa, 1948.

Kim, Yŏng-gŭn. *Chosŏn Kaehwa Pidam* [Hidden Stories on Modernization of Korea]. Seoul: Chŏng'ŭmsa, 1947.

Ko, Kwŏn-sam. *Kindai Chōsen Seijishi* [Modern Korean Political History]. Tokyo, 1930.

Komatsu, Midori. *Meiji Gaikō Hiwa* [Hidden History of Meiji Diplomacy]. Tokyo, 1936.

————. *Chōsen Heigō no Rimen* [Background of the Japanese Annexation of Korea]. Tokyo, 1920.

Kuroda, Hashihiko. *Gensui Terauchi Hakushaku Den* [Biography of Count Terauchi]. Tokyo, 1920.

Kuzū, Yoshihisa. *Nikkan Gappō Hishi* [Secret History of the Merger of Japan and Korea]. 2 vols. Tokyo, 1930.

Min, T'ae-wŏn. *Kapsin Chŏngpyŏn kwa Kim Ok-kyun* [The Coup of 1884 and Kim Ok-kyun]. Seoul: Kukje Munhwa Hyŏp'hoe, 1947.

Mun, Chŏng-ch'ang. *Kŭnse Ilbon-ui Chosŏn Ch'imt'alsa* [A History of Modern Japan Aggression of Korea]. Seoul: Sŏul Tachakkyo Ch'ulp'anbu, 1964.

Murayama, Chijun. *Chōsen no Ruiji Shūkyō* [Quasi-Religions in Korea]. Keijō: The Government-General in Korea, 1935.

Mutsu, Munemitsu. *Kenkenroku* [Memoirs]. Tokyo: Iwanami Shoten, 1933.

Nakai, Kitarō. *Chōsen Kaikoroku* [Memories of Korea]. Tokyo: Tōgyō Kenkyūkai, 1915.

Nichibei Tsūshinsha (ed.). *Shinsei Nihon Gaikō Hyakunenshi* [Diplomatic History of the Newly Born Japan During One Hundred Years]. Tokyo: Nichibei Tsūshinsha, 1953.

O, Chi-yŏng. *Tonghaksa* [History of the Tonghaks]. Seoul: Yŏngch'ang Sŏ'gwan, 1940.

Okudaira, Takehiko. *Chōsen Kaikoku Kōshō Shimatsu* [Negotiations on the Opening of Korea from Beginning to End]. Tokyo: Tōkō Shoin, 1935.

Paek, Nam-un. *Chōsen Shakai Keizai Shi* [Socio-Economic History of Korea]. Tokyo, 1933.

Pak, Tong-sŏ (Bark, Dong-suh). *Han'guk Kwallyo Chedo ui Yŏksajŏk Chŏngae* [A Historical Development of the Bureaucracy in Korea]. The Korean Research Center, Korean Studies Series, Vol. XI. Seoul, 1961.

Pak, Un-shik. *Han'guk T'ongsa* [The Tragic History of Korea]. Trans. and ed. Pak No-Kyŏng. Taegu, Korea: Talsŏng Inshwae Hoesa, 1946.

Rekishigaku Kenkyūkai (ed.). *Rekishigaku Kenkyū: Chōsenshi no Shomondai* [Historical Research: Problems in Korean History]. Tokyo: Iwanami Shoten, 1953.

Sakurai, Yoshiyuki (ed.). *Meiji Nenkan Chōsen Kenkyū Bunken Shi* [Annotated Bibliography of Japanese Publications on Korea during the Meiji Period]. Keijō, 1941.

Shakuo, Shunjō. *Chōsen Heigōshi: Ichimei, Chōsen Saikinshi* [History of Korean Annexation: Modern Korean History]. Keijō, 1926.

Shidehara, Hiroshi. *Chōsen Kyōikuron* [Treatise on Education in Korea]. Tokyo, 1919.

Shidehara, Taira. *Kankoku Seisōshi* [Notes on Political Factionalism in Korea.] Tokyo, 1907.

Shikata, Hiroshi. *Richō Jinkō ni Kansuru Ichi Kenkyū* [A Study of the Population in Korea during the Yi Dynasty]. Reprint from *Keijō Teikoku Daigaku Hōgakkai Honshū*, 9 (n.d.), 259–368, appendix 19 pp.

Shinobu, Seisaburō. *Mutsu Gaikō: Nisshin Sensō no Gaikōshiteki Kenkyū* [Mutsu Diplomacy: A Study of Diplomatic History of the Sino-Japanese War]. Tokyo: Sōbunkaku, 1938.

Sŏng, Chun-Dŏk (ed.). *Han'guk Sinmunsa* [History of Korean Newspapers.] Seoul, 1955.

Suzuki, Eitarō. *Chōsen Nōsonshakai Tōsaki* [Survey of Korean Agricultural Society]. Tokyo, 1944.

Tabohashi, Kiyoshi. *Kindai Nissen Kankei no Kenkyū* [A Study of the Japanese-Korean Relationship in Recent Times.] 2 vols. Keijō: Chūsū-in, the Government-General in Korea, 1940.

Taedong Ki'nyŏn. [Korean Chronicles]. Shanghai: Meihua Shukuan, 1905.

Takahashi, Hamakichi. *Chōsen Kyōikushi* [History of Korean Education]. Keijō, 1927.

Tatsumi, Raijirō. *Nisshin Sen'eki Gaikōshi* [Diplomatic History of the Sino-Japanese War]. Tokyo: Senmon Gakkō Shuppanbu, 1902.

Toganō, Shigeo. *Chōsen Saikinshi: Fu Kankoku Heigōshi* [History of Korea with History of Korean Annexation]. Tokyo, 1912.

Tokunaga, Isami. *Kankoku Sōran* [Korean Survey]. Tokyo, 1907.

Tokutomi, Iichirō. *Kōshaku Katsura Tarō Den* [Biography of Prince Katsura Tarō]. 2 vols. Tokyo, 1917.

———. *Kōshaku Yamagata Aritomo Den* [Biography of Prince Yamagata Aritomo]. 3 vols. Tokyo, 1933.

Yamabe, Kentarō. *Nikkan Heigō Shōshi* [A Brief History of the Merger of Japan and Korea]. Tokyo: Iwanami Shoten, 1966.

Yi, Man-gap. *Han'guk Nongch'on ui Sahoe Kujo* [The Social Structure of the Korean Village, A Sociological Study on the Six Villages in Kyŏnggi Province]. The Research Center, Korean Studies Series, Vol. 5. Seoul, 1960.

Yi, Man-gyu. *Chosŏn Kyoyuk* [History of Korean Education]. 2 vols. Seoul, 1947.

Yi, Nŭng-hwa. *Chosŏn Kidokgyo kŭp Waegyosa* [History of Christianity and Foreign Relations of Korea]. Seoul: Chosŏn Kidokgyo Ch'angmunsa, 1925.

Yi, Pyŏng-dŏ. *Han'guk Kuksa Taegam* [An Outline History of Korea]. Seoul, 1960.

Yi, Sŏn-gŭn. *Chosŏn Ch'oegŭn Chŏngch'isa* [Political History of Korea in Modern Times]. Seoul: Chŏng'ŭmsa, 1950.

————. *Han'guksa* [Korean History.] *Ch'oegŭnse P'yŏn* [Volume on Recent History]. Seoul: Ullyu Munhwasa, 1961.

————. *Han'guk Tongnip Undongsa* [History of Korean Independence Movement]. Seoul: Sangmunwŏn, 1956.

Yuge, Kotarō. *Chōsen no Kyōiku* [Education in Korea]. Tokyo, 1923.

Yun, Hyo-jŏng. *P'ung'un Hanmal Pirok* [Secret Records of the Turbulent Last Years of Korea]. Seoul: Yadamsa, 1937.

Yun, Paek-nam. *Chosŏn Hyŏngjŏngsa* [History of Korean Administration of Criminal Laws]. Seoul, 1948.

Articles

Asō, Takeki. "Gunseishi: fu Keisatsu Seido Shi" [History of the Military Organization: Supplement; History of the Police System], *Chōsenshi Kōza*, Series no. 1, (n.p., n.d.), pp. 1–224.

Chang, Mun-sŏn. "Choson Kŭnsesa Sigi Kubun e Kwanhayŏ" [On Periodization of Recent History of Korea], *Yŏksa Kwahak* [Historical Science]. (P'yong'yang: Choson Minju Chui Inmin Konghwaguk Kwahakwŏn Yŏksa Yŏnkuso), VI (1957), 67–72.

Ch'oe, Chun. "Kun'guk Ilbon-ui Taehan Ŏllon Chŏngch'aek" [The Policy of the Militarist Japan on the Korean Press], *Journal of Asiatic Studies*, IV (June 1961), 239–286. English summary, 287–290.

Kang, Chae-ŏn. "Chōsen ni okeru Hōkentaisei no Kaitai to Nōmin Sensō" [The Dissolution of the Feudal System and the Peasant War in Korea], *Rekishigaku Kenkyū* (Tokyo), No. 7 (July 1954), pp. 1–15; No 11 (November 1954), pp. 12–25.

Nohara, Shirō. "Kinsei Shina Chōsen o meguru Nichiro no Kankei" [Russo-Japanese Relations with Regard to China and Korea in the Recent Period], in *Sekai Rekishi Taikei* [An Outline of World History]. 25 vols. Tokyo: Heibonsha, 1934, IX, 351–407.

Ōuchi, Takeji. "Richō Makki no Nōson" [Agricultural Villages in the Last Years of the Yi Dynasty], *in* Keijō Teikoku Daigaku Hōbun Gakkai (ed.), *Chōsen Shakai Keizai Kenkyū* [Korean Socio-Economic Research], VI (1933), 227–296.

Paek, Sun-jae. "Tongnip Hyŏp'hoe Wŏlbo wa Kajŏng Chapji" [The Independence Association Monthly and Home Magazines], *Sasangge* (September 1965), pp. 270–274.

Shikata, Hiroshi. "Chōsen ni okeru Kindai Shihonshugi no Seiritsu Katei" [The Rise of Modern Capitalism in Korea], in Keijō Teikoku Daigaku

Hōbun Gakkai (ed.), *Chōsen Shakai Keizaishi Kenkyū* [Korean Socio-Economic Research], VI (1933), 1–226.

––––––. "Ichiba o tsūjite mitaru Chōsen no Keizai" [Korean Economy seen through the Market], in Keijō Teikoku Daigaku Hōbun Gakkai (ed.), *Chōsen Keizai no Kenkyū* (Korean Economic Research], vol. 1 (1929).

Tsumagari, Kuranoshō. "Chōsen ni okeru Kosaku Mondai no Hatten Katei" [The Developmental Stages of Tenant Problems in Korea], *ibid.*, 227–296.

Yamabe, Kentarō. "Kōshin Nichiroku no Kenkyū" [A Study on the "Daily Records of 1884"], *Chōsen Gakuhō*, No. 17 (October 1960), pp. 117–142.

Yuasa, Mitsuru. "Kendai Nicchō Kankei no Ichi Kōsatsu" [A Study on Modern Political Relations Between Japan and Korea], *Chōsen Gakuhō*, No. 24 (July 1962), pp. 160–182.

Unpublished Dissertations

Arnold, Dean Alexander. "American Economic Enterprises in Korea: 1895–1939." Unpublished Ph.D. dissertation, University of Chicago, 1954.

Ford, Harold Perry. "Russian Far Eastern Diplomacy, Count Witte, and the Penetration of China, 1895–1904." Unpublished Ph.D. dissertation, University of Chicago, 1950.

Karl, Hongkee. "A Critical Evaluation at Modern Social Trends in Korea." Unpublished Ph.D. dissertation, University of Chicago, 1934.

Kim, Chong-ik. "Japan in Korea (1905–1910): The Techniques of Political Power." Unpublished Ph.D. dissertation, Stanford University, 1959.

Kim, Han Kyo. "The Opening of Korea." Unpublished master's dissertation, University of Chicago, 1957.

––––––. "The Demise of the Kingdom of Korea: 1882–1910." Unpublished Ph.D. dissertation, University of Chicago, 1962.

Merrill, John Espy. "American Official Reactions to the Domestic Policies of Japan in Korea (1905–1910)." Unpublished Ph.D. dissertation, Stanford University, 1957.

Weems, Clarence N., Jr. "The Korean Reform and Independence Movement: 1881–1898." Unpublished Ph.D. dissertation, Columbia University, 1954.

GLOSSARY OF ORIENTAL PROPER NAMES AND TERMS USED IN THE TEXT
WITH THEIR CORRESPONDING
CHINESE CHARACTERS

Ajŏn* 아전 (衙前)
An Chung-gŭn 安重根
Aoki Shuzō 青木周藏
Asan 牙山

Ch'angdŏk (Palace) 昌德(宮)
Cheguk Sinmun 帝國新聞
Cheju-do 濟州島
Chemulpo 濟物浦
Ch'en Shu-t'ang 陳樹棠
Cheng Tsao-ju 鄭藻如
Chinda Sutemi 珍田捨己
Ch'ing 清
Ch'inil Tang 親日黨
Cho Pyŏng-se 趙東世
Cho Pyŏng-sik 趙東式
Cho Sin-hi 趙臣熙
Cho Yŏng-ha 趙寧夏
Ch'oe Che-u 崔濟愚
Ch'oe Ik-hyŏn 崔益鉉
Chŏlla 全羅
Chŏllyŏng-do 絶影島
Chŏn Pong-jun 全琫準

Ch'ŏndo Kyo 天道教
Chŏng Kyo 鄭喬
Chŏng Pyŏng-ha 鄭東夏
Chŏng Yŏng-t'aek 鄭永澤
Chŏngdong 貞洞
Chŏng'gyo Chaju 政教自主
Ch'ongni Taesin 總理大臣
Chŏnju 全州
Ch'onmin 賤民
Chōsen 朝鮮
Chōshū 長州
Chosŏn 朝鮮
Ch'ungch'ŏng 忠清
Chungch'uwŏn 中樞院
Chungin 中人
Chusa 主事

Daiichi 第一

Fukuzawa Yukichi 福澤諭吉

Hamgyŏng 咸鏡
Han Kyu-sŏl 韓圭卨

*The McCune-Reischauer System is used for the romanization of the Korean sounds.

Hanabusa Yoshitaka
花房義質
Hasegawa Yoshimichi
長谷川好道
Hayashi Gonsuke 林權助
Hayashi Tadasu 林董
Ho Ju-chang 何如璋
Hongju 洪州
Hong Yŏng-sik 洪英植
Hsü Shou-peng 徐壽朋
Humbuk Hŭnghak Hoe
咸北興學会
Hwajŏk 火賊
Hwalpin Tang 活貧黨
Hwanghae 黃海
Hwangje 皇帝
Hwangsŏng Sinmun 皇城新聞

Ihwa Haktang 梨花學堂
Ilchinhoe 一進會
Im-o 壬午
Inch'ŏn 仁川
Inoue Kakugorō 井上角五郎
Inoue Kaoru 井上馨
Itō Hirobumi 伊藤博文
Itō Miyoji 伊東巳代治
Iwakura Tomomi 岩倉具視

Kaehwa Tang 開化黨
Kajiyama Teisuke 梶山鼎介
Kanghwa 江華
Kang'wŏn 江原
Katsura Tarō 桂太郎
Kawakami Sōroku 川上操六
Keijō Nippō 京城日報
Kim Hong-jip 金弘集

Kim Ok-kyun 金玉均
Kim Yun-sik 金允植
Kōbe 神戶
Kobu 古阜
Kŏje-do 巨濟島
Kokuryūkai 黑龍會
Kŏmun-do 巨文島
Komura Jutarō 小村壽太郎
Kung (Prince) 恭(親王)
Kungmin Sinbo 國民新報
Kun'guk Kimuch'ŏ
軍國機務處
Kuroda Kiyotaka 黑田清隆
Kyŏnggi 京畿
Kyŏngsang 慶尚
Kyŏng'u Kung 慶祐宮
Kyŏng'un 慶雲
Kyorin 交隣

Li Hung-chang 李鴻章

Ma Chien-chung 馬建忠
Manmin Kongdonghoe
萬民公同會
Maruyama Jūshun
丸山重俊
Masan 馬山
Meiji 明治
Min 閔
Min Chong-muk 閔鍾默
Min Chong-sik 閔宗植
Min Yŏng-ch'an 閔泳鑽
Min Yŏng-gi 閔泳琦
Min Yŏng-hwan 閔泳煥
Min Yŏng-ik 閔泳翊
Min Yŏng-jun 閔泳駿

Miura 'Gorō 三浦梧樓
Montono Ichirō 本野一郎
Mutsu Munemitsu 陸奥宗光
Myŏn 面

Naegak 内閣
Nihon Yūsen Kaisha
日本郵船會社
Nishi Tokujirō 西德二郎

Ŏ Yun-jung 魚允中
Ōkuma Shigenobu 大隈重信
Ŏm Se-yŏng 嚴世永
Ōtori Keisuke 大鳥圭介

Paejae Haktang 培材學堂
Pak Che-sun 朴齊純
Pak Chŏng-yang 朴定陽
Pak Yŏng-hyo 朴泳孝
Paksa 博士
Paoting 保定
Poanhoe 保安會
Pusan 釜山
P'yŏng'an 平安
P'yŏng'yang 平壤

Sadae 事大
Saionji Kimmochi
西園寺公望
Sangmin 常民
Shibuzawa 澁澤
Shimamura Hisashi 島村久
Shimonoseki 下関
Sim Sun-t'aek 沈舜澤
Sin Hŏn 申櫶
Sin Ŭl-sok 申乭石

Shun (Prince) 醇 (親王)
Sŏ Chae-p'il 徐戴弼
Sŏ Kwang-bŏm 徐光範
Sŏ Sang-u 徐相雨
Sone Arasuke 曾彌荒助
Song Pyŏng-jun 宋秉畯
Sŏnggyun'gwan 成均館
Sōshi 壯士
Sŏwŏn 書院
Sugimura Fukashi 杉村濬
Sunch'ang 淳昌
Suwŏn 水原

Taehan Chekuk 大韓帝國
Taehan Hyŏp'hoe 大韓協會
Taehan Maeil Sinbo
大韓毎日申報
Taehan Sinmun 大韓新聞
Taewŏn'gun 大院君
Takezoe Shin'ichirō
竹添進一郎
Tao-t'ai 道台
Terauchi Masatake 寺内正毅
Ting Ju-ch'ang 丁汝昌
Tonghak 東學
T'ongni Amun 統理衙門
Tongnip Hyŏp'hoe 獨立協會
Tongnip Sinmun 獨立新聞
Tongnip Tang 獨立黨
Tōyama Mitsuru 頭山滿
Tsungli Yamen 總理衙門
Tsushima 對島

Uchida Ryōhei 内田良平
Uijŏng 議政
Uijŏngbu 議政府

Uiju 義州
Uibyŏng 義兵
Ullŭng-do 欝陵島
Unyō 雲楊

Wang 王
Wŏnju 原州
Wŏnsan 元山
Wu Ch'ang-ch'ing 吳長慶
Wu Ta-cheng 吳大澂

Yamagata Aritomo 山縣有朋
Yang Ki-t'aek 梁起鐸
Yangban 兩班
Yanghwajin 楊花津

Yi Ch'ae-ŭng 李最應
Yi Chun 李儁
Yi Chun-yong 李埈鎔
Yi Hyŏng 李㷆
Yi Ki-hyŏn 李起鉉
Yi Pŏm-jin 李範晋
Yi Sang-sŏl 李相卨
Yi Sŭng-man 李承晩
Yi Wan-yong 李完用
Yi Wi-jong 李瑋鍾
Yi Yong-gu 李容九
Yi Yu-wŏn 李裕元
Yong'amp'o 龍岩浦
Yüan Shih-k'ai 袁世凱
Yun Ch'i-ho 尹致昊

INDEX

Ajŏn, 8, 153. *See also* Yi dynasty: government structure
Amur Society, 141. *See also* Uchida Ryōhei
An Chung-gŭn, 210
Anglo-Japanese Alliance (1902), 97, 100–101, 127
Anglo-Japanese Alliance (1905), 126–127
Annexation of Korea: decision to annex, 164, 209, 213; advocates of, 207; and the *Ilchinhoe* memorial, 211–213; Korean reactions to, 211–213; treaty of, 213–215; foreign reactions to, 216
Aoki Shūzō, 70
Asahi Shimbun, 137
Asan, 78
"Association of Comrades on the Korean Question," 210

Banking system (in Korea), beginning of, 97–98, 115
"Bean controversy," 71–72
Bethell, E. T., 160, 181–182, 185, 188; trial of, 181–188; Korean reactions to, 187–188; death of, 188n
Bezobrazov, A. M., 98
Bourne (Judge in Shanghai), 185
Bryner, Jules, 93
Buddhism, Japanese encouragement of, 194

Cable, Rev. Elmer M., 191
Cheju, uprisings in, 117
Chemulpo (Korean–U.S.) Treaty, 176; negotiations at Tientsin, 21–24; signed, 24–25; accompanied by a letter from the Korean king, 25–27; ratification of, 28; Japanese views on, 29
Cheng Tsao-ju, 20
Chinese Merchant Marine Company, 68–69
Chinese troops in Korea: in 1882, 36–40; withdrawn in 1885, 58; sent to Asan, 78
Cho Pyŏng-se, 132
Cho Pyŏng-sik, 105, 113
Cho Sin-hi, 66
Cho Yŏng-ha, 30
Ch'oe Che-u, 75–76
Ch'oe Ik-hyŏn, 198
Chŏllyŏng-do (Deer Island), 95
Chŏn Pong-jun, 76–77
Chŏng Kyo, 114
Chŏng Pyŏng-ha, 89
Chŏngdong Club, 83
Ch'ongni taesin (prime minister), 82
Ch'ŏnmin, 8. *See also* Yi dynasty: social classes
Christianity in Korea: first converts to, 11–12; and the execution of French priests, 13; favoritism shown for converts, 117; and Protestant influence, 188–189, 191; growth of, 188–195; Japanese handling of, 191–192; and motives for conversion, 193–194. *See also* Missionaries
Chungin, 7. *See also* Yi dynasty: social classes
Civil Service Examinations: discontinued, 82; proposed restoration of, 116

DATE DUE

7-28-70			
JAN 18 1974			
AP 20 '82			
GAYLORD			PRINTED IN U.S.A.